KENNETH CALLAHAN

essays by
Thomas Orton
Patricia Grieve Watkinson

MUSEUM *of* NORTHWEST ART
LA CONNER, WASHINGTON
in association with
UNIVERSITY OF WASHINGTON PRESS
SEATTLE AND LONDON

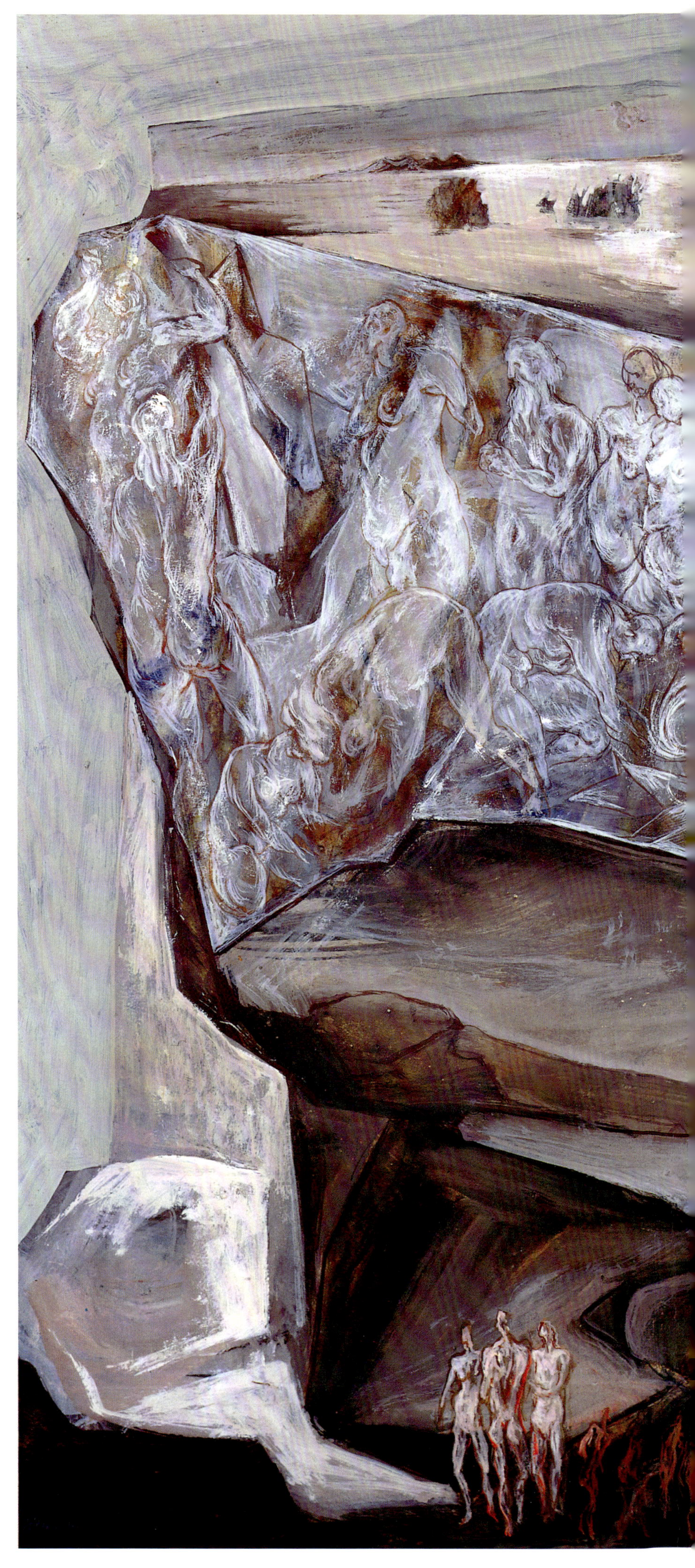

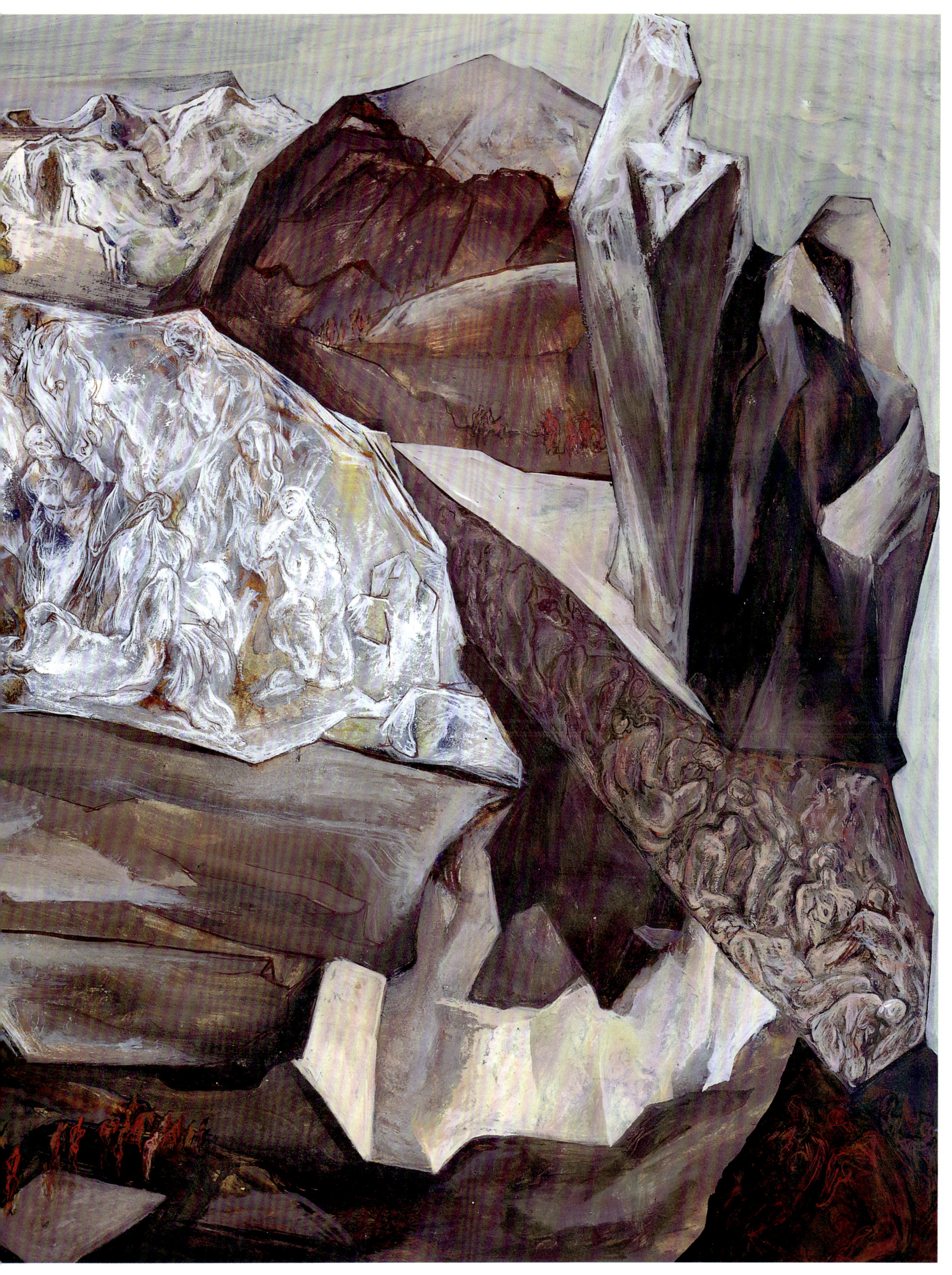

This book was Beth Callahan's final labor of love for her late husband, Kenneth Callahan. Beth passed away just days after approving the final galleys for this publication.

This publication accompanied an exhibition presented at the Museum *of* Northwest Art, July 14 through October 7, 2001.

Published by the Museum of Northwest Art, La Conner, Washington, and the University of Washington Press, Seattle.

Library of Congress Cataloging-in-Publication Data
Callahan, Kenneth, 1905–
Kenneth Callahan / essays by Thomas Orton, Patricia Grieve Watkinson.
p. cm.
Publication accompanying an exhibition presented at the Museum of Northwest Art, La Conner, Wash., July 14–Oct. 7, 2001.
Includes bibliographical references.
ISBN 0-295-98071-0 (hardcover)
1. Callahan, Kenneth, 1905– —Exhibitions. I. Orton, Thomas. II. Watkinson, Patricia Grieve. III. Museum of Northwest Art. IV. Title.
ND237.C19 A4 2000
759.13—dc21 00-45224

Front cover: *Red Figures*, n.d., acrylic on Masonite, 60 × 150 inches. Collection of Martin Selig.

Frontispiece: *Within the Rocks*, 1950, tempera on paper, 28½ × 22 inches. Collection of Mikell and Brian T. Callahan.

Page 6: *Space Fragment*, 1980, acrylic on rag board, 32 × 40 inches. Private collection.

Pages 12–13: *The Cove—Two Worlds*, 1952, tempera on paper, 20 × 24 inches. Collection of the Columbia Museum of Art, Columbia, South Carolina, gift of Emily Winthrop Miles, CMA 1964.15.

Pages 30–31: *Revolving World*, 1944, gouache on paper, 14⅛ × 18½ inches. Collection of the Metropolitan Museum of Art, gift of Francis Henry Taylor, 1949, 49.139.

Project coordinated by Beth Callahan with the assistance of Andrea Smith-Clarke and Marie Weiler
Edited by Jana Stone
Designed by John Hubbard
Produced by Marquand Books, Inc., Seattle
www.marquand.com
Printed and bound by C&C Offset Printing Co., Ltd., Hong Kong

CONTENTS

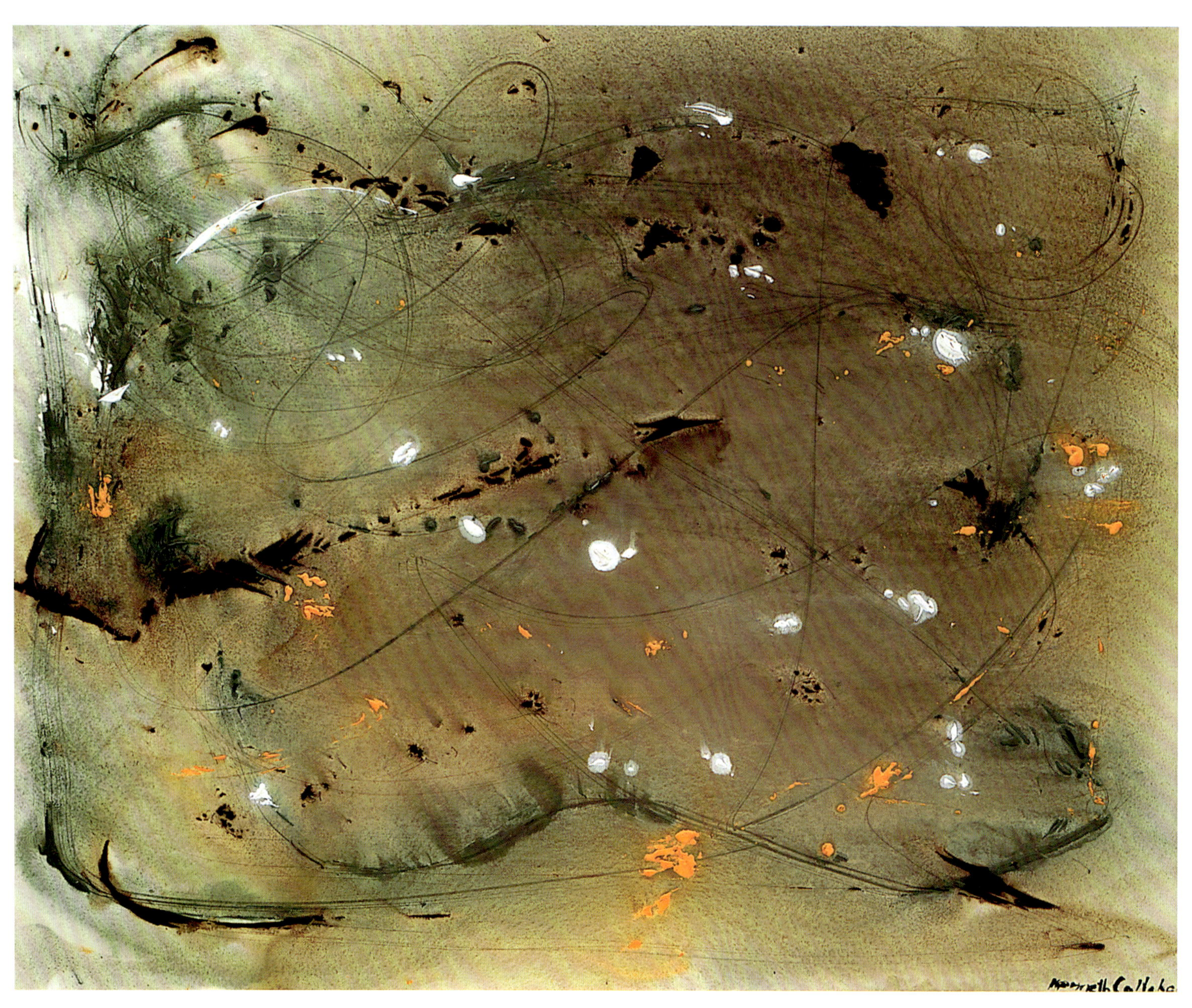

acknowledgments

For the publication of this most beautiful book in commemoration of my late husband's life and art, I first of all thank Patricia Watkinson for planting and encouraging the idea, for putting the groundwork in place, and for writing the introduction. Without her unflagging support the project would never have gotten off the ground. Second, I thank the collectors whose paintings appear in the book for allowing us access to their homes to collect their artwork for photographing and for trusting us with their treasures. Tom Blue showed the utmost patience and professionalism as he traveled around the Seattle area to collect those paintings and deliver them to the photographer's studio. I am indebted to Beverly Freeman, Peggy Gasper, and Lillian Zeigler for listening and offering moral and editorial support as I composed fund-raising letters. My thanks to Andrea Smith-Clarke for her help in contacting museums and collectors and compiling and organizing the data. I am grateful to Tom Orton for his sensitive essay documenting Kenneth's life. Finally, I am deeply grateful to the staff at Marquand Books for ushering the project through its various phases and for the production of the book. In particular, I thank Marta Vinnedge for her unfailing moral support, Ed Marquand for his publishing expertise and advice, John Hubbard for his handsome design, and Marie Weiler for her tenacity in hunting down the elusive editorial details.

For waiving the fees for reproduction costs and transparency rental, I thank Mikell and Brian T. Callahan, Seattle Art Museum, and Washington State University Museum of Art. For legal services, including filing for the book's copyright, I thank my attorney at Foster Pepper & Shefelman; for accounting services and keeping me within budget, my thanks go to Kristi Mathisen of Bader, Martin, Ross Smith. I thank the galleries: Foster/White Gallery, Seattle, Laura Russo Gallery, Portland, and Kraushaar Galleries, New York, for their encouragement and support; and the Museum of Northwest Art, La Conner, Washington, for holding an exhibition to coincide with this book.

Without the financial support of many, this book could not have been published. In addition to the galleries named above, my thanks go to Donna Benaroya, Ingolf Noto, Richard and Deanne Rubenstein, Lee and Barbara Yates, Ann and Peter Ormsby, Fountain Association, Carolyn and Guy Glenn, and Foster Pepper & Shefelman PLLC for their generous donations.

Thank you one and all.

Beth Callahan
Seattle, August 2000

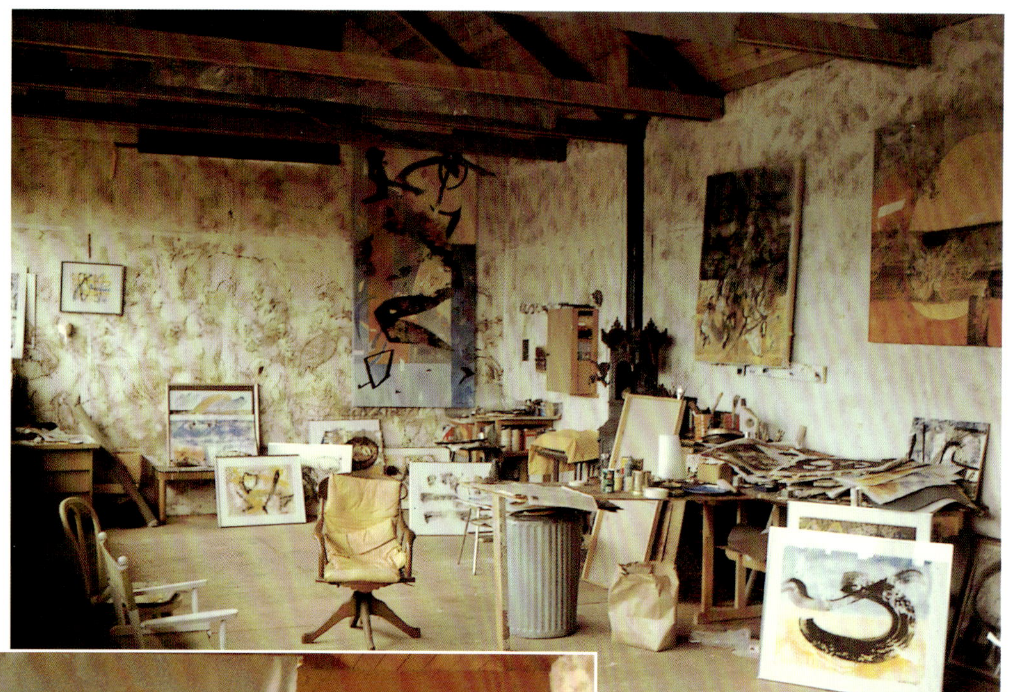

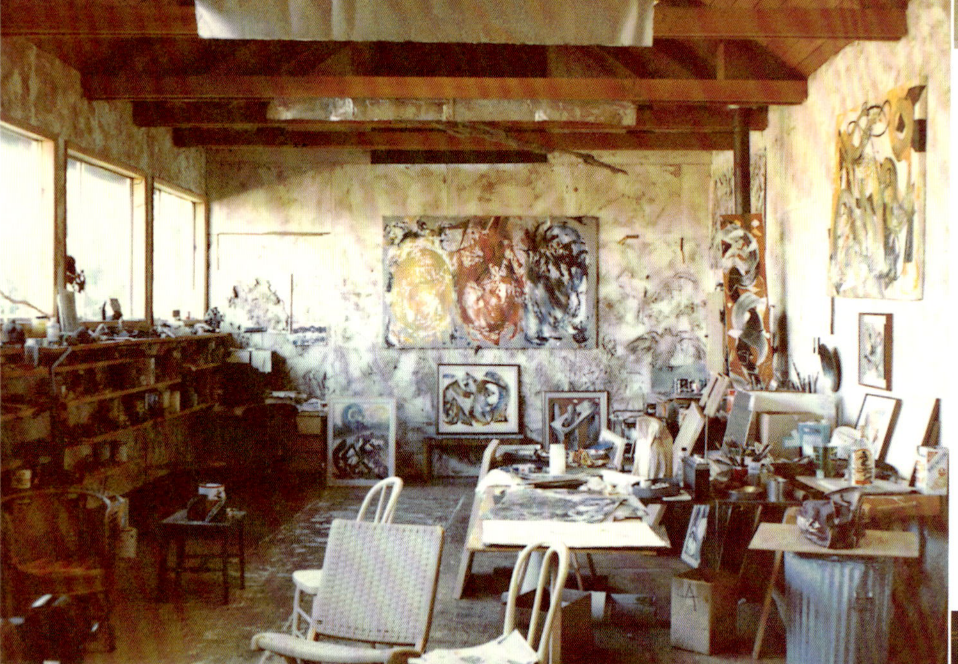

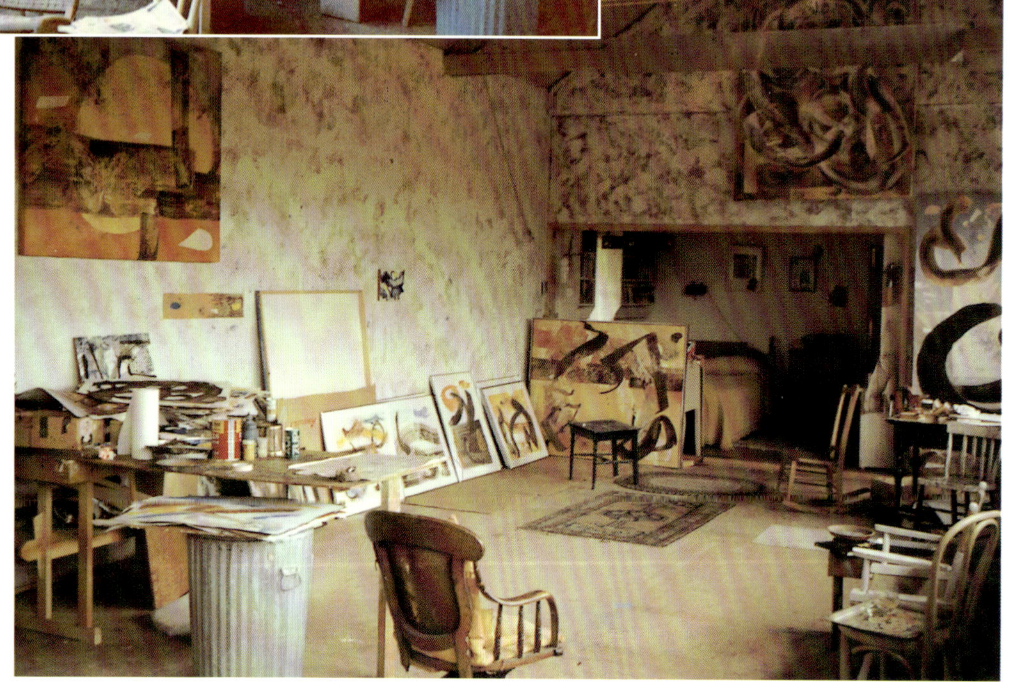

INTRODUCTION

For me there are two sources of art: nature and the art of the past. The past is all-inclusive, from cave paintings to the thing produced yesterday by the artist around the corner.

Nature is the most important, the initial source. Art based solely on other art, whether works of ancients or contemporaries, can become nothing beyond an echo, weak or strident, however clever, stylish or accomplished. It is nature, with its unlimited varied form, structure and color that constitutes the vital living source from which art must basically stem. Nature for me does not mean only men, mountain streams, animals and alpine meadows (important as these are to me personally). Nature does not mean just "subject matter." Nature is total phenomena experienced by human beings. Seeing is the thing, seeing with both inner eye and outer eye, not separately but interrelated, inevitably and irrevocably, as everything in the total of nature is interrelated.

—KENNETH CALLAHAN[1]

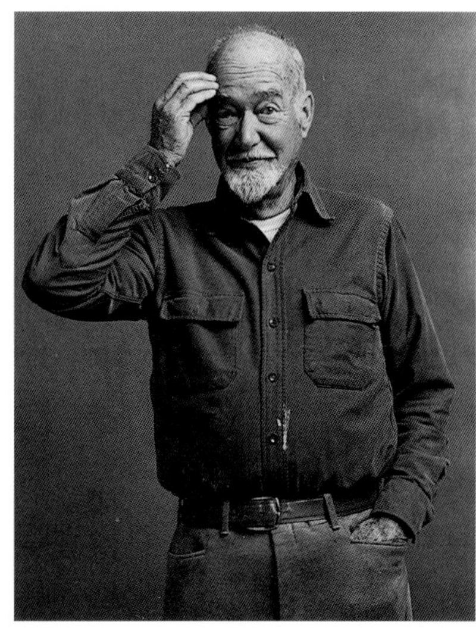

Kenneth Callahan, ca. 1983

by Patricia Grieve Watkinson

Written by Kenneth Callahan in 1959, these characteristically thoughtful words introduce us to the mind, writing, philosophy, and visual inspiration of an artist whose life spanned much of the twentieth century and whose art reaches further yet in its innate energy and holistic vision. Callahan's life began in Spokane, Washington, in 1906 and ended in Seattle, Washington, in 1986. These facts do not begin to reveal the magnitude of Callahan's oeuvre, his unstinting creativity, his courage to reinvent his artistic self, his long and active role in the national art scene, and the diversity of his contributions to art in the Pacific Northwest and the nation.

As an artist and a native of the Pacific Northwest, Callahan in his early years was associated with the three other most celebrated artists of the region: Guy Anderson, Morris Graves, and Mark Tobey. Indeed, the four were close friends in Seattle in the thirties and for a brief time were even labeled the "Northwest School," though eventually each was to follow a different path. Callahan's association with the Pacific Northwest was lifelong, however. Its landscapes of brooding mountains and shrouded seashores were at the heart of his work. Just as his paintings of these landscapes transcended geography to become cosmic in their intent, so, too, did Callahan's life and work extend beyond the boundaries of the region to encompass the nation and the globe. He traveled widely, spending time in Hawaii, Mexico, and Europe. His paintings were included in international exhibitions, from Brazil to New Zealand, from Italy to Japan. In this country, over 150 of his works were chosen for private and public art collections, among them some of the most prestigious in the nation. As a teacher, Callahan spent time at Penn State, Washington State, and Boston universities, as well

Kenneth Callahan's Long Beach studio in the 1970s.

as at the Skowhegan School of Painting and Sculpture in Maine. As a member of the International Association of Art Critics, Callahan was published regularly in Northwest and national journals and newspapers. But, of course, it was first and foremost as a painter that Callahan was known in an art world that extended from Seattle to Chicago to New York.

Kenneth Callahan was before all else a painter of nature. Nature for him, as his words above reveal, was more than "men, mountain streams, animals and alpine meadows." It was the life force that breathed spirit into each insect and each mountain peak. It was "the interrelationship of man, rock, and elements; the creating and disintegration, repeated over and over: man into rock, rock into man, both controlled by sun and elements."[2] It was an ineffable power, a seeming state of perpetual motion that created and consumed, that swirled and cycled and finally transcended the physical world. Callahan's was, in essence, a romantic vision of creation and creating.

The portrayal of nature's uniting energy, expressed through swirling line and dynamic composition, is a recurring characteristic in Callahan's art. In the thirties, in his paintings of the Cascade Mountains, he used expressive brushwork to convey energized mountain peaks and roiling clouds (see p. 39 bottom). Even scenes of laborers, such as those constructing a logging railroad (see p. 37), he choreographed so that the heroic bodies turbulently encircle a central figure.

In the forties and fifties, Callahan's prolific brush produced canvas after canvas where wraithlike humans, sometimes accompanied by equally ethereal horses, swirl and intertwine as if in some silent ballet or dream. These figures occupy mountainous, usually barren landscapes with rocky outcrops and crystalline structures and seem both to merge with and emerge from this matrix, in a constant state of flux. The overall effect is of humans seeking, striving upwards, reaching out, perhaps in joy, pain, or exultation, while the very landscapes they occupy echo their striving (see, for instance, pp. 55, 66, 74). The vertical composition of many of Callahan's paintings conveys the sense of an apocalyptic vision, and we are clearly reminded of the Last Judgments of artists such as Michelangelo and William Blake, both of whom Callahan greatly admired.

The biblical references in Callahan's work are many. Scenes familiar to us from the history of art—the Nativity, the Crucifixion, the Deposition, the Ascension—are recognizable in more than one of Callahan's paintings (see pp. 49, 53 bottom, 57). Callahan wrote, however, "I do not consider myself a religious man . . . as we understand the term. I have no specific religion. But there is an order, an inevitable relationship, a totality of the whole, that 'Godhead' as well as any other term describes for me."[3] Clearly Callahan was more than aware of the religious implications of his works and their effect on the viewer.

In the sixties, with increasing abstraction and the introduction of much brighter color, Callahan made one of many artistic changes in his long and varied career. The upward striving for some ineffable goal diminishes in favor of calmer, more earthbound works. Strongly vertical mountain landscapes give way to horizontal compositions of sky, sand, and shoreline, as Callahan himself moved his main residence from Seattle to the Washington coast. Instead of soaring heights and deep distances, Callahan created large, singular, calligraphic brushstrokes on a flatter, shallower field, as if presenting us with a much magnified detail of earlier works. Hard, shardlike geometric shapes float against the textures of sea and sky. Spaces have become airy and filled with bright light. These paintings are distinctly different from those that went before, and Callahan seemed confident in the new departures.

Kenneth Callahan died in 1986, at eighty years of age, after six full decades of a prolific and active career. He was drawing up until two days before his death. Those decades saw a range of painting styles and artistic concerns, a long list of national and international exhibitions, and a large and loyal circle of private art collectors as well as many international ones.

However, one thing was missing: the decades had never produced a significant publication to commemorate Callahan's life and achievements. It was this oversight of history that haunted Callahan's widow, Beth, when she and I talked in Seattle some ten years after her husband's death. During that conversation Beth Callahan decided to rectify matters. As keeper of Callahan's archives, she knew the location of his works and had most of the materials that should be recorded for historical purposes. A book would not only be an important complement to Callahan's paintings but would capture forever a significant and as yet undocumented chapter of the art history of the Pacific Northwest. Through her unfailing and courageous determination, such a book has come about. *Kenneth Callahan* is a tribute to her husband and companion of more than twenty years and to a great Northwest artist whose paintings continue to delight and move us.

notes

1. J. H. Reese, "Conversation with an Artist: Kenneth Callahan" (Tully, New York, n.d.).

2. Michael R. Johnson, ed., *Kenneth Callahan: Universal Voyage*, exh. cat. (Seattle: University of Washington Press in association with the Henry Art Gallery, 1973), 26.

3. Reese, "Conversation with an Artist."

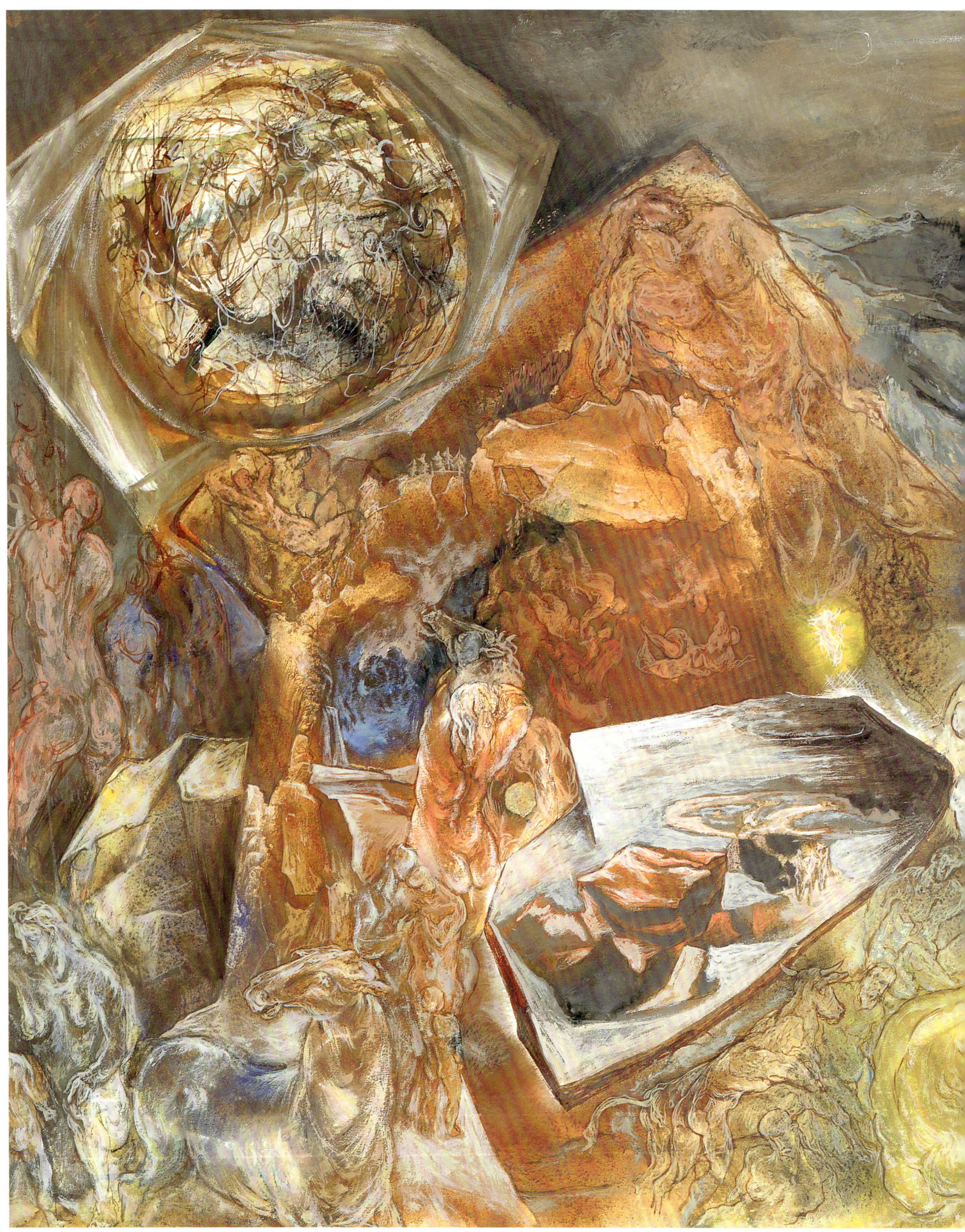

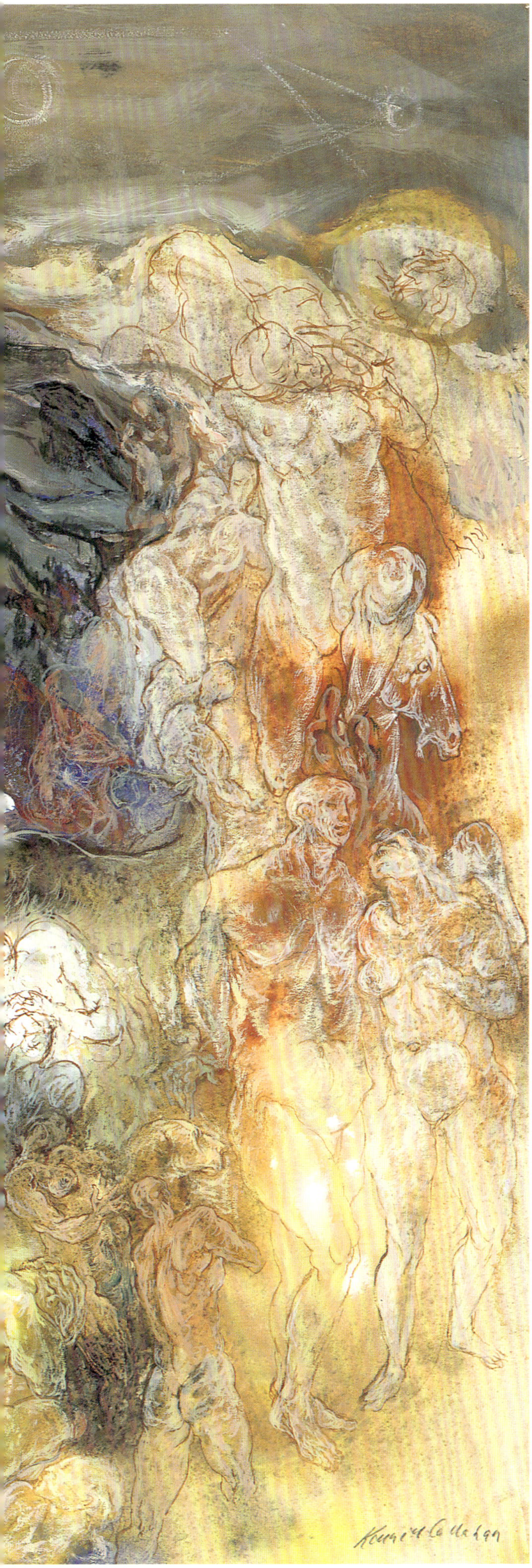

KENNETH CALLAHAN

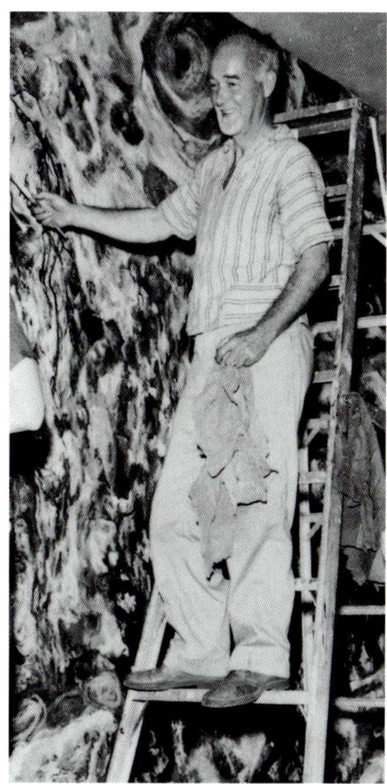

by Thomas Orton

In 1963 Kenneth Callahan was visiting a village outside Mainz, Germany, when his son Tobey, named for his old friend, painter Mark Tobey, cabled him with terrible news: the family's beloved retreat, the cabin and studio they had built in the mountains outside Granite Falls, Washington, had burned to the ground.

The fire was transforming: the intense heat had melted the silverware, turning it into puddles that cooled into unrecognizable lumps. Typically, Callahan downplayed the loss of the cabin by seizing on this less significant detail. In recent days he had been through worse. A little over a year earlier his wife, Margaret Bundy Callahan, had become ill with cancer and died in a matter of months. Callahan and Margaret had built the cabin themselves. They'd virtually raised their son there. The studio at Granite Falls contained many of Callahan's own paintings as well as works by other artists including Tobey and Morris Graves. For two decades this cabin had been the place where Callahan connected with nature, the major source of all his art. The cabin was also where his art merged with his life. Now that life was gone.[1]

Callahan was fifty-eight years old but his accomplishments could have filled several careers. For three decades he had produced paintings and drawings at a prodigious rate. He had been curator of painting at the Seattle Art Museum and written criticism for national art journals. As a New York art outsider he had won over the skeptical East Coast critics.

Along with Tobey and Graves, he had been named a leading figure of what the art world knew as the "Northwest School," and his paintings had long been part of the permanent collections of many major museums in America. He'd won awards and traveled widely. He'd been an art ambassador for the United States Information Agency, and he was in great demand as a visiting professor at universities all over the United States. His career was still on the rise.

Over these last months he had experienced the sort of loss that would make anyone question the importance of such things. He had lost a way of life when Margaret died, and now the hub of that life was gone. Nothing was what it had been.

But Callahan understood that even such a compounding of loss was part of a larger order. Embracing the inevitability of such natural cycles was as necessary to his life and art as breathing. "There's a basic rhythm going through everything," he often said. "It's identical in every form of life."[2] The world contained millions of smaller worlds, but this rhythm transcended all the rational categories we imposed on life. Dichotomies were resolved simply because our experience could contain them. Callahan himself was living proof. A shy, modest man, he was also well known for his hospitality and love of laughter. He sought out companionship with the thirst of someone who understood that the solitude he craved in equal measure was key to creation. Slender and urbane-looking with his neat Vandyke, he was equally at ease at a New York opening of his paintings or splitting cedar shakes in the woods. Despite his fame he was eminently approachable, both genuinely intellectual and egalitarian, possessed of what his friend and Seattle art dealer, Don Foster, called "a remarkably common touch."[3] He was a painter with a pragmatic, clear-headed sense about the world and earthbound beliefs about art that didn't always fit with later descriptions of him and other Northwest painters as "mystics." His quiet vitality and positive outlook belied the brooding intensity at the core of his most enduring work.

Born in Spokane, Washington, on October 30, 1905, Callahan moved to Glasgow, Montana, with his parents and six brothers and sisters when he was still very young. His mother, Martha Anna Cross Callahan, liked to draw and encouraged her son, often

Two Horses and Rider, n.d.
Ink and Conté on paper
24 x 30 inches
Collection of Mr. and Mrs. Michael D. Alhadeff

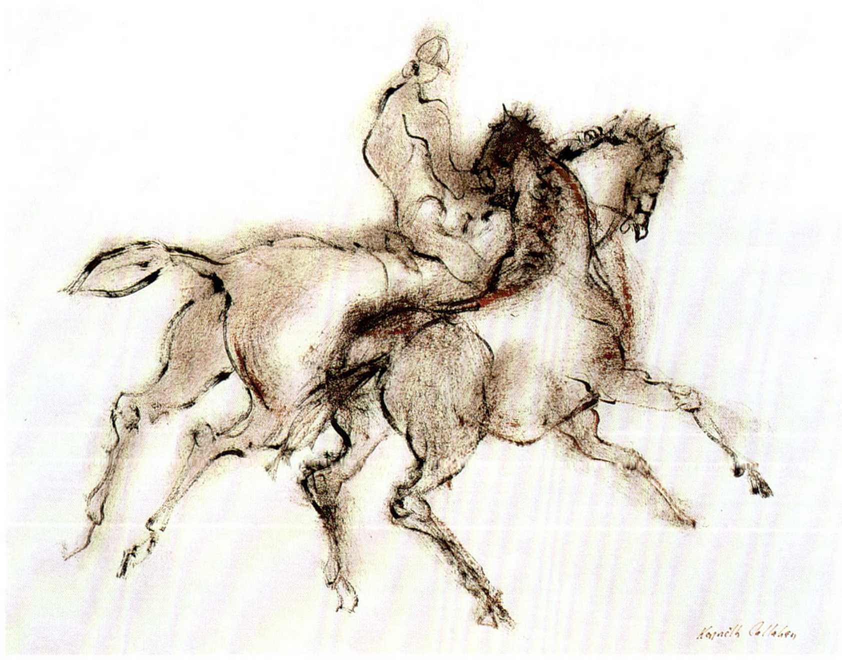

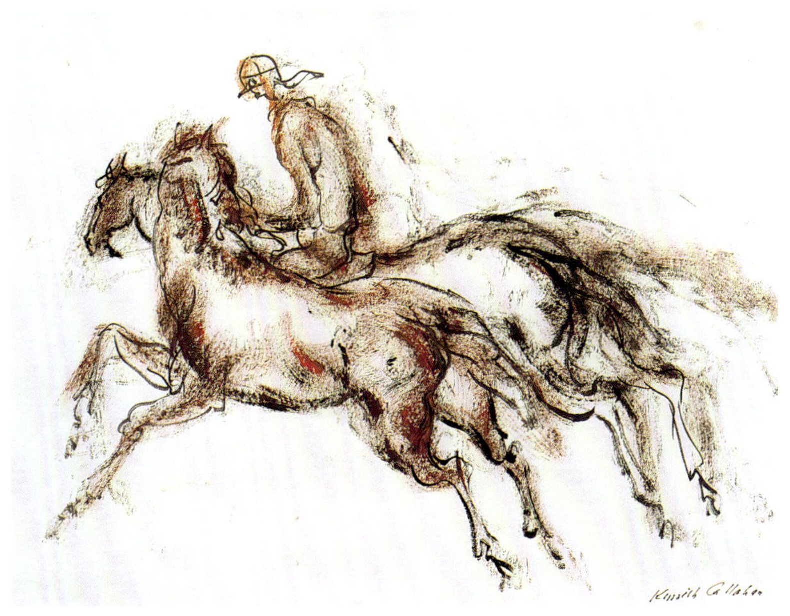

Two Horses and Rider, n.d.
Ink and Conté on paper
24 × 30 inches
Collection of Mr. and Mrs. Michael D. Alhadeff

helping him with school art projects. The great Western painter Charles Russell was a friend of the family, and when he passed through town he often slept in the Callahan's attic. Russell painted on paper with a cheesecloth backing and carried his pictures rolled up in his saddlebags. When he showed up in Glasgow to sell a piece or two, Callahan's mother would dampen the cheesecloth backs and iron out the wrinkles.[4] Ralph Breckenridge, a less peripatetic neighbor, was part Blackfoot Indian and ran a livery in Glasgow. Breckenridge was a local bronc-riding champion. Coincidentally, he was also a painter and portrayed scenes from Western life in the style of Russell. He had fixed up part of the livery's harness room as a studio and invited young Kenneth to watch. Not many in Glasgow would dare suggest to a rodeo champion that painting was an unmanly pursuit, and if someone challenged Callahan's growing interest in art, he had only to point to Breckenridge as a role model.

Martha Callahan died when Callahan was in his middle teens, after which the family moved briefly to Raymond, Washington, then to Seattle. Callahan finished high school at Broadway High on Seattle's Capitol Hill, where he drew cartoons for the school newspaper. After graduation he took classes at the University of Washington, worked as a busboy at the Chanticleer Cafeteria, and painted in the evenings. "How well I painted, I question," he later wrote, "—but with a great deal of enthusiasm."[5] A piece of his was accepted and won second place in a local competition, the prestigious Northwest Annual, but it was nearly as important for Callahan that his work was being considered alongside that of professional artists.[6] Following that success, one of his watercolors was accepted for an even larger juried exhibition in California.

> *I became unbearable, I am sure. I was right in there, elbow to elbow with Rembrandt and Sargent. . . . Actually what I was doing, through ignorance, were clever naturalistic renderings of what I saw in the world around me—superficial, attractive color, skillful technique at best, but no more.*[7]

Already driven to make art but not yet old enough to understand the bounds of his ambition, Callahan knew that a classroom would not cultivate that ambition as thoroughly as firsthand experience of the world. So, he left the university in 1925 and together with two friends paid $40 for a Model T and drove to San Francisco.

Soon after arriving, Callahan landed a job working the late shift as an orderly at a county hospital and later found part-time work as an illustrator for a children's magazine called *The Treasure Chest.* Eventually he moved downtown to a studio in the old Montgomery Building. The Montgomery—known to its colorful residents as the Montgomery Block or "Monky Block"—was a ramshackle office building predating the 1906 quake and fire. The Monky Block was home to many other artists, writers, and musicians, and Callahan found that he fit right in.[8] San Francisco itself was synonymous with romance. Callahan was enthralled by the ethnic mix, the "exaggerated realism" of Italian fishermen and the Chinese residents in traditional dress.[9] He spent all his free time drawing in North Beach and Chinatown, occasionally selling a piece to a tourist. In 1926 he mounted his first one-man show at the Schwabacher-Frey Stationery Store and Gallery.

One afternoon a friend brought Madame Guilka Sheier to Callahan's studio. Madame Sheier had recently arrived from Germany to promote several contemporary European artists and had brought with her a number of original works by Paul Klee, Wassily Kandinsky, Lyonel Feininger, and Alexei von Jawlensky. Known as the "Blue Four," these painters were renowned in Europe. Callahan had never before heard of them, but he would never forget them. "There were no mats or mountings," he recalled. "We spread them all over the room on the floor, table, chairs. I did not know what to think."[10] To this point in his life, much of the original artwork Callahan had seen in museums struck him as safe or indifferent. But at first sight it seemed these four painters had gone too far in the opposite direction. They not only risked displeasing, but seemed to court outright failure. Callahan thought von Jawlensky "crude and

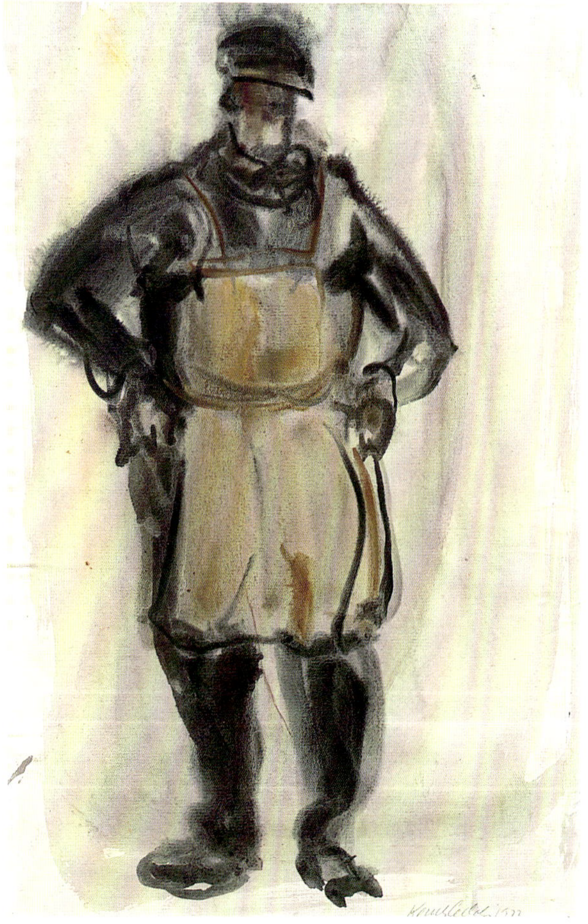

Market Figure, 1922
Watercolor on paper
15 × 10 inches
Private collection

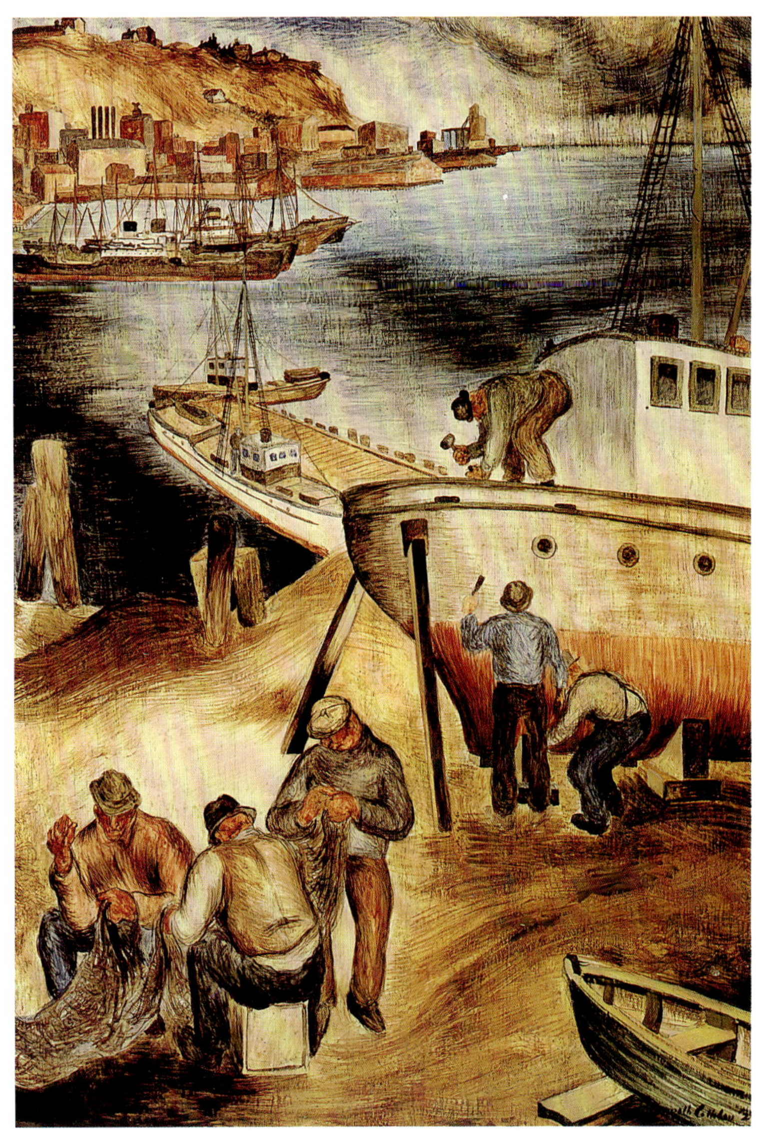

Fishermen, Lake Union, 1929
Tempera on paper on board
34 × 26 inches
Law Offices of Morse & Bratt, Vancouver, Washington

insensitive," and his assessment of the other three was not much better.[11] But now, as at other crucial moments in his life, Callahan would allow change to envelop and direct him, embracing and even welcoming unsettling events as inevitable and necessary springboards for change.

For days afterward he walked the streets, unable to think about anything else. Unsettling as these works were, their impact was undeniable. The art of these four was intensely personal; it acted not only upon the consciousness but upon the world. For better or worse, their work mattered.

> *I had to recognize that each in his different way had created a world of his own . . . a world that existed in these works positively and emphatically . . . they existed as real art with a definite life of their own.*[12]

This, Callahan realized, was what he wanted for himself: to produce works of art that would bear his identity into the world, that could not be mistaken for the work of others—a vision set apart by terms based not on pleasure or even survival but on a fastidious honesty.

Seeing the work of the Blue Four may have influenced Callahan's decision to leave San Francisco—in fact, to leave the country altogether. He had come to San Francisco to gain experience. Now it was time to test his developing vision by taking a bigger step. He decided to go to sea.

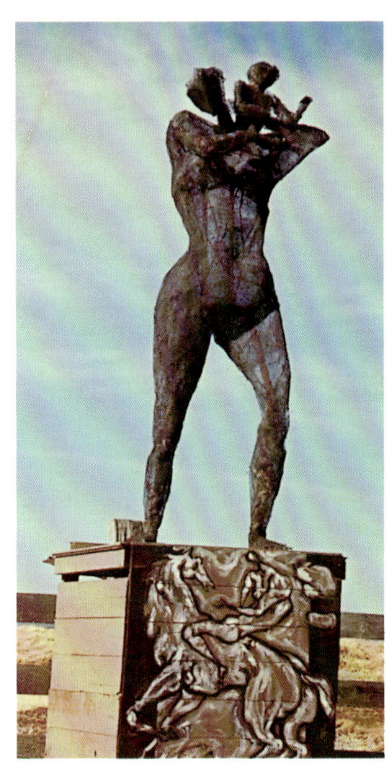

Woman and Child, 1965
Chicken wire, rocks, plaster of Paris
destroyed

Callahan left San Francisco in 1927, and for the next four years, working aboard freighters as a ship's steward, he made trips across both the Atlantic and Pacific oceans. His first passage took him to Europe. In London, Paris, and Florence he saw the original works by artists he would claim as lifelong influences—Michelangelo and Masaccio, Turner, El Greco, and Blake. "In William Blake I found what I felt might be called a direct distinguished ancestor of mine."[13] Seeing the lifelike sculptures of the Pantheon, Callahan was convinced that "the plaster casts of Greek sculptures I had seen previously here and there in museums and schools were as dead and ugly as I had thought them."[14]

After a fistfight with another crew member on a trip to the Orient, Callahan was put ashore without pay in Waikiki. During his time aboard ships, he managed to keep drawing and painting. Marooned in Hawaii, Callahan slept on the beach and sold drawings to tourists by the docks, often taking less than his asking price so that he could buy a meal. Eventually he found working passage back to the United States and returned to Seattle.

The city was growing rapidly, and Callahan would have found it changed. But big as it was, Seattle seemed dwarfed by the surrounding landscape, hemmed in by mountains and forests, by brooding weather and pristine bodies of salt and fresh water. It was further isolated by perceptions of it as a wilderness city which, in the 1920s, were not all that far-fetched. In her essay in *Northwest Traditions*, Martha Kingsbury points out that in the early part of the twentieth century Seattle hung in the balance between its pioneer beginnings just decades earlier and an "urban future that would include participation in the higher forms of culture."[15] During his travels Callahan had certainly seen more sophisticated places, but he may already have understood that only in the Northwest could he create a body of work that was indelibly his.

Callahan moved into an old stable and converted it into a studio, and in 1929 he held his first Seattle one-man show at the Art Institute. In 1930 he put down more roots when he married Margaret Bundy, the editor of a small newspaper called the *Town Crier*, and moved with her into the tiny, top-floor apartment of a three-story house.[16]

"It was around this time," Callahan remembered, "that Dr. F[uller] called to say that he and his mother would like to come to look at paintings."[17] Dr. Richard E. Fuller was a respected geologist and, along with his mother, also named Margaret, an avid art collector and patron. Several years earlier the Fullers had endowed the Seattle Art Museum, which Dr. Fuller now ran. The Fullers were passionate about Japanese art; they had amassed one of the country's premier collections and had made it the centerpiece of the museum's new art deco building in Volunteer Park. A tall, quiet man, Richard Fuller complemented his extrovert mother, who radiated the energy of someone much younger.[18] The entrance to the Callahan's apartment was a trap door in the kitchen floor, but the dignified mother and son nevertheless made their way in gracefully. As Callahan would come to learn during his long association with the Seattle Art Museum, Dr. Fuller could be both extremely generous and intensely single-minded. The Fullers selected a number of Callahan's paintings and, much to the Callahans' surprise, paid five hundred dollars for them.[19]

The Mexican Shrine, 1932
Gouache on cardboard
12¼ x 15¾ inches
Seattle Art Museum, Eugene Fuller Memorial Collection

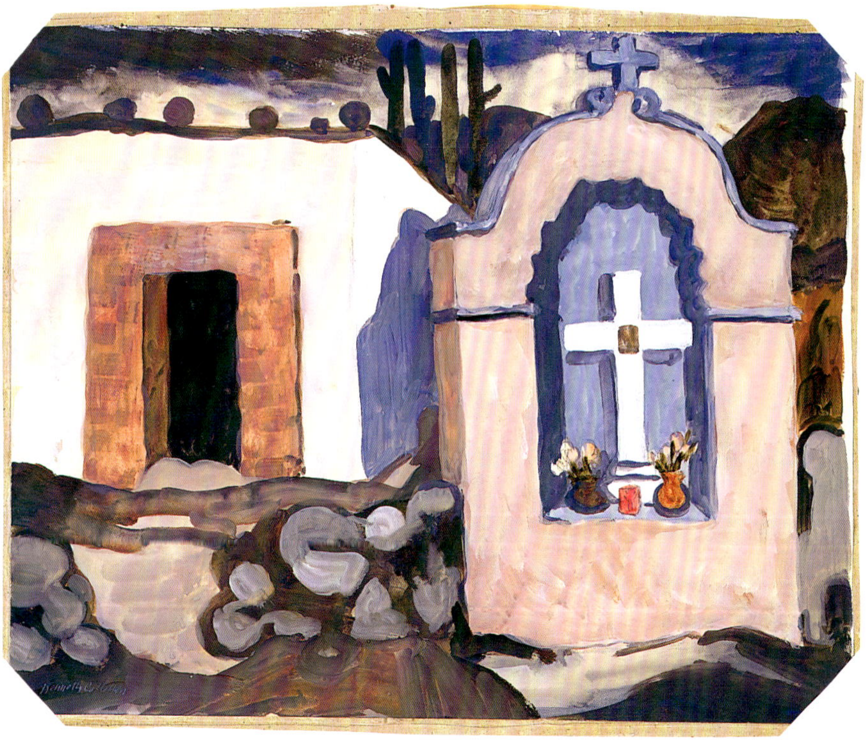

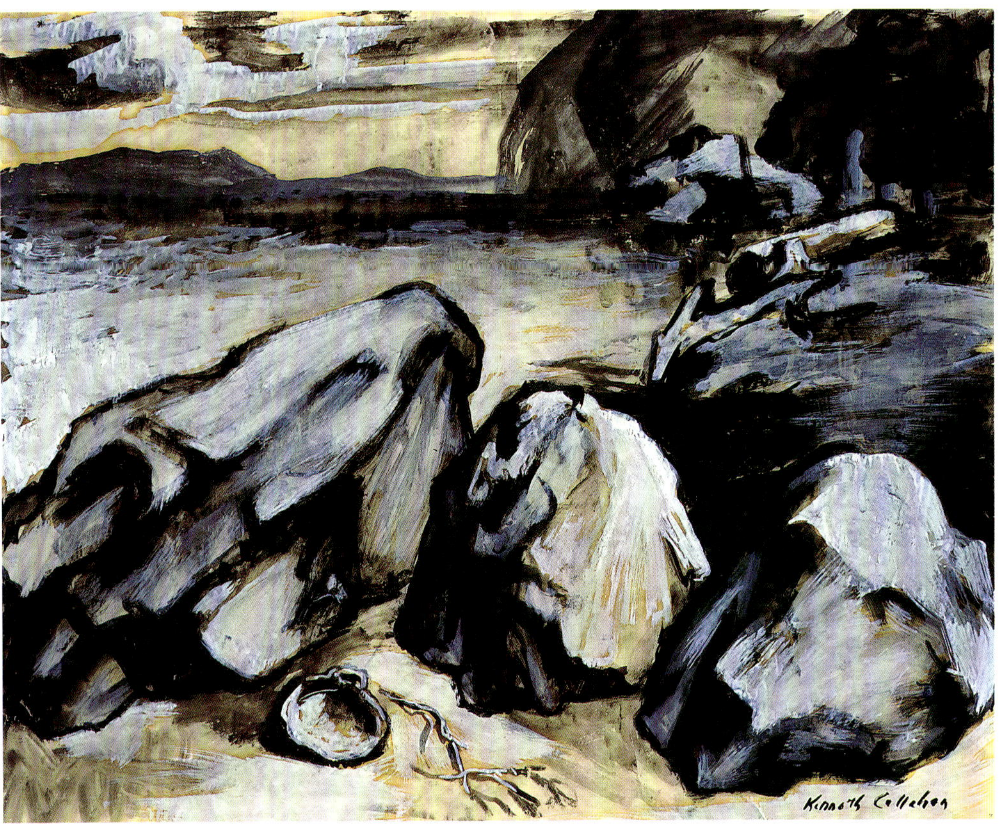

Rocks and Shore, ca. 1930s
Ink and white pigments on paper
18½ x 23 inches
Collection of Patricia M. Baillargeon

Delighted with the sale of the paintings, Callahan and Margaret decided to use the money for a trip to Mexico. Callahan had become interested in mural painting and had found no better practitioners of the art than two noted Mexicans, Diego Rivera and José Clemente Orozco. With the money from the Fuller sale, plus the extra Margaret could make sending articles back to the *Town Crier*, the Callahans planned a six-month stay.

In Mexico City the Callahans became acquainted with the painter Ruffino Tamayo, who introduced them to Frances Tour, known as the Gertrude Stein of Mexico City.[20] At Tour's large apartment the Callahans met both Orozco and Rivera as well as Rivera's wife, the painter Frida Kahlo. Callahan and Margaret spent most of their time "wandering around in mountain and valley villages drawing, painting, and looking." His first month's work, he decided, was too "picturesque," and he threw it all out.[21] Meeting and mingling with "real" artists boosted Callahan's self-assurance, but his pursuit of absolute honesty in his painting would also mean maintaining a rigorous level of self-assessment.

Returning to Seattle, his confidence high after his trip, Callahan began producing work at a staggering pace. He also continued exhibiting in regional shows and, in 1933, in the *First Biennial Exhibition of Contemporary American Sculpture, Watercolors, and Prints* at the Whitney Museum of American Art in New York.[22] But Callahan was not yet making a living from his art, and so that same year he approached the Fullers about a job at the Seattle Art Museum, and Richard Fuller happily obliged. Callahan worked there mornings, unpacking crates and hanging exhibitions. In those early years, Dr. Fuller often pitched in with the physical work. Callahan regularly got him to hire Morris Graves and other artists struggling to make ends meet during the Depression, and Fuller was glad to help. Callahan would be associated with the museum for twenty-two years—including many years as curator of painting—until the summer of 1954, when his relationship with Fuller would come to a bitter end.

But for now Callahan and Dr. Fuller held one another in high regard. Callahan's first mural, the fruit of his meetings with Orozco and Rivera, was exhibited at the Seattle Art Museum in 1935 and was followed by a commission from the Weyerhaeuser Logging Company in Tacoma, after which he won competitions for mural installations for post offices in Centralia and Anacortes, Washington. His desire to paint matched his prodigious output. He became restless, almost nervous, anxious to fill every blank surface[23] including the walls of his studios, which he covered with a filigree of human and animal figures. Restlessness, channeled by discipline, became initiative. Art, Callahan had discovered, was reacting; it was not thinking but doing.[24]

In the late thirties, an association of Seattle artists known as the "Group of Twelve," of which Callahan was a part, began to change character.[25] Guy Anderson moved to Seattle from Spokane. In 1938 Mark Tobey returned to the Northwest after seven years in England. In Seattle he and Morris Graves became close friends and both set about establishing studios. Graves was known for his reclusiveness, which no doubt went a great way toward giving Northwest painters the reputation as mystics. Mark Tobey, who by coincidence Callahan had run into earlier in Mexico, was by this time an established painter fifteen years older than either Callahan or Graves. While Callahan was no doubt impressed by the durability of Tobey's commitment to his art, which still had not made him much money, he did not, as some have thought, view Tobey as a mentor. The bonds among these three were intense and the level of mutual respect high. Such an unexampled uniting of talent was likely to result in friendships that would run extraordinarily deep and, in time, be sorely tested.

Among their friends the Callahans were one of the few married couples and, with the birth of their son Brian Tobey Callahan in 1938, they became even more singular as a family. Their home was a gathering place for weekly dinners of local and visiting artists alike. Actors and dancers from traveling shows were also welcomed at the Callahan's table. Writers Thomas Wolfe and Sinclair Lewis visited the Callahans on trips west. Callahan's warmth and integrity probably surprised many visitors who did not expect to find these two things combined with a high level of sophistication. If a certain dinner guest was a celebrity in New York he or she soon found it didn't matter much in Seattle.[26] As gracious and easy-going as Callahan could be, he also had a temper—fools were never tolerated.[27] Conversation was rich and varied. Mark Tobey could speak at length about how the pattern of the universe repeated itself in a simple flower.[28] William Cumming, an occasional guest and a leading figure of the Northwest School, was also well versed in classical music.[29] Cumming also read a great deal and lent books to Callahan.

In the early forties, the war was a frequent topic of discussion at the Callahans' gatherings. Callahan, Tobey, and Graves were all united in their opposition. As an exercise each tried to create an image that symbolized the horror of worldwide violence, an experiment that Callahan later admitted failed.[30] "Nothing meaningful ever came from a collective effort,"[31] he said. Analysis, he had found, was the enemy of painting; too much of it produced disappointing "illustrations."[32] "There's an immediacy about living," Callahan said. "And if you try to pin it down, by the time you get it pinned down, the whole . . . thing is shifted."[33]

For Callahan, art did not derive from a single source but only from the totality of nature. His growing certainty about the relationship between what he called "the inner eye and the outer eye" almost certainly found voice and richer definition during these evening discussions.

> *My inner eye deals with the relationship of things; the flux and flow of the way things are interrelated. The flow of the ocean and its waves, the winds, the mountains, insects—they're all interrelated. I think that's what most artists are trying to get at; to tap the essence.*[34]

The outer eye represented all of the artist's visual experience and the inner eye the totality of all previous experience. This expression of the dialogue between mind and nature was a kind of creed, which Callahan repeated throughout his life. It was as close as he ever came to the mystical pronouncements of his more poetic counterparts. The relationship between the inner eye and the outer eye had a very pragmatic application to his painting life. It was simple cause and effect, embodying the everyday mechanics of the spiritual journey.

In the late thirties and early forties the Group of Twelve broadened to include artists of more varied styles and backgrounds and there was now talk of the existence of a "Northwest School."[35] Though Callahan was recognized as one of its figureheads, he denied the existence of such a school from the very beginning. "It must be recognized," he wrote, ". . . that no standardized formulas set our painting apart in a fixed 'regional school.'"[36] Still, he recognized traits shared by many Northwest painters: "A consistent use of broken forms and greyed color; preference for tempera . . . leanings toward Symbolism and Expressionism; and the influence of Oriental art."[37] School or not, the cohesiveness of Northwest art in the forties and fifties was remarkable for a region that had seen few cultural movements of any kind and was so recently removed from its pioneer beginnings. In *Northwest Traditions* Martha Kingsbury writes that it was the East Coast artists instead who "sometimes seemed like frontiersmen without, any longer, a frontier. . . . The Northwest group seemed to embody a humility and a tenuous optimism seldom present in New York."[38]

"Humility and optimism" were also elements of religious faith, and another shared characteristic of Northwest artists was an interest in formal spiritual thought. Guy Anderson was attracted by the American transcendentalists. Tobey was a longtime follower of the Bahai faith and Graves was seriously devoted to Zen. Callahan found useful elements in all of these.[39] But he was drawn less to formal ideologies than to the notion of a spiritual quest. Painting itself was his religion. Like Tobey, Callahan believed in the oneness of the world, "a holistic vision of cosmic unity."[40] His "inner eye and outer eye" had less to do with religions or cultures than with total immersion in the cycles of birth, life, and death. This immersion was no casual intellectual concept but, for Callahan, an absolute necessity.

From the mid-thirties to the mid-forties the Callahans spent all their free time in a rented cabin on the Robe Ranch, a remote, wooded valley near Granite Falls, Washington. Callahan set up a studio for himself there. In better weather he worked outside, laying his paper on the ground and weighting the corners with stones. He often dampened the paper with a rag first before sitting down to sketch, leaning on one arm, sometimes almost reclining as he worked.[41] In 1946 the Callahans bought 145 acres and built their own cabin from second-hand materials, splitting shakes from cedar trees on the property. Local loggers donated an old bakery truck, which the Callahans used as a storage shed and whose broad, blank sides Callahan could not resist covering with rearing, cantering, writhing horses.

In the early forties Callahan continued to exhibit nationally, and in 1942 won a commission for a mural at the post office in Rugby, North Dakota.[42] But something momentous was on the horizon. In that same year Callahan began working for the U.S. Forest Service at a one-man lookout station in the Cascade Mountains, a job he returned to each summer and fall throughout the war years. When he spoke about this experience much later he was circumspect, typically focusing on the less important details—the rich light of his kerosene lantern, the precautions against electrocution during lightning storms.[43] But there was clearly something more going on during these vigils. In the preface to an article Callahan later wrote for *Northwest Art News and Views*, the magazine's editor quoted from a letter Callahan had written during one of these fire-watch seasons:

> *This is a rugged country. Great jagged cliffs, tortured and distorted, piled on one another—innumerable waterfalls twist and scatter out of clouds and mist and fog, which swirl and alternately blanket, then disclose, the peaks.*[44]

Callahan's work was undergoing a transformation, perhaps less unsettling or as sudden as his experience with the Blue Four in San Francisco, but no less profound. In the paintings of this period "mists creep over the landscapes." Figures are often on horseback, unclothed and grouped "in purgatorial clusters" or trapped inside the rock itself.[45] Callahan explained it as the "interrelationship of man, rock and the elements; the creating and disintegration, repeated over and over."[46] The dark landscapes of the thirties now took on a symbolism that had risen out of the earth itself.

In 1946, Callahan had a one-man show of paintings he created out of the experience of these seasons in the wilderness. The show took place at the American British Art Center in New York and critical response was terrific. Howard Devree wrote in the *New York Times:*

> *A newcomer to local galleries, Kenneth Callahan of Seattle provided one of the outstanding events at the American British Art Center. . . . From . . . landscape statements made with compelling power he has turned to an intensely personal and deeply religious interpretation of nature . . . the manner in which he peoples his landscapes with myriad figures is individual and deeply moving. Behind the paintings one senses a sensitive spirit brooding over the chaotic state of the world.*[47]

As other rave notices came in, friends, critics, and associates tried to convince Callahan that his moment had come: he must seize this rare opportunity, move to New York City and pursue his career.[48] Callahan had always loved New York. But he was wary that its fad-driven art market would force him to produce only more of what it, and not he, wanted.

That same year, Callahan submitted a proposal for an article to *Art News* in New York. The editor, Aline B. Louchheim, asked that the piece deal not so much with the leading figures of the Northwest School as with other artists and art forms.[49] Though Tobey and Graves were represented in the piece, the article angered them both, though it is not completely clear why. The two confronted Callahan, angrily accusing him of not caring for other artists as much as for himself.[50] Perhaps they saw Callahan's already powerful position at the museum unfairly redoubled by this even more powerful and far-reaching venue for his opinions.

Trouble was developing on another front as well. Among the newer staff at the Seattle Art Museum there was dissatisfaction with Callahan—his curatorial position at SAM, his status as a nationally known art critic, and his growing success as a painter. In 1947 Callahan had a celebrated one-man show in New York at the Maynard Walker Gallery. (He would continue to regularly exhibit there for the next eighteen years.) And in 1948 his first one-man show in Europe opened at Galerie Georges Giroux in Brussels.[51] His reputation was growing. But some believed his position at the Seattle Art Museum represented a conflict of interest, and by the spring of 1953 these murmurings had reached a head.[52] That summer the Callahans had no sooner left for the country than he received a letter from Dr. Fuller with two month's salary and a letter telling him not to come back.

Callahan was less shocked than enraged. Only a few years earlier he had written that Fuller was "an individual who has, to as great a degree as any I have ever known, absolute standards of integrity, honesty and generosity."[53] In his letter Dr. Fuller argued that Callahan had no real expertise as a curator of painting, but what incensed Callahan most was that Dr. Fuller would choose to fire him by mail.[54] Ironically, a now famous *Life* magazine article on Northwest art appeared that same year with photographs of Callahan, Tobey, Graves, and Anderson and described the sovereignty of the "Northwest School" when in fact some of its principals were hardly speaking to one another. The article also stated that Callahan had "retired" from the Seattle Art Museum.[55]

Interviewed on these painful subjects much later in his life, Callahan surprisingly seemed to harbor no ill will, even admitting that Dr. Fuller and Graves and Tobey had all been right in their assertions and accusations.[56] During this period Callahan had read a brief profile of himself as a noted curator, art critic, and painter. He later admitted that this description made him feel like a dilettante.[57] "I believe in freeing oneself," Callahan said, "toward the end of functioning as fully as possible. . . . The lesser enemy in achieving this is people and things and the world exerting their pressures on you. The essential enemy is one's own greed, pride, fear and inhibitions."[58]

It is possible Callahan realized that he had begun to function less fully as an artist. Relieved of his other responsibilities, he now began to paint more.[59] The next year, 1954, he was awarded a Guggenheim Fellowship and took his family to Europe. That same year, true to his habit of taking part-time work, Callahan began supplementing his art income with temporary teaching jobs, and in the summer accepted a position as a visiting artist at the University of Southern California. Also in 1954 he was represented in the exhibition *Younger American Painters* at the Solomon R. Guggenheim Museum in New York, and the following year his work appeared at the Musee de Arte Moderna in São Paulo, Brazil. In 1957–58 he was in Europe once again, traveling to Denmark, Germany, Great Britain, and elsewhere, this time on the first leg of a tour sponsored by the United States Information Agency.[60] In the summer of 1959 (and again in 1963 and 1966) he was artist in residence at the Skowhegan School of Painting and Sculpture, where he

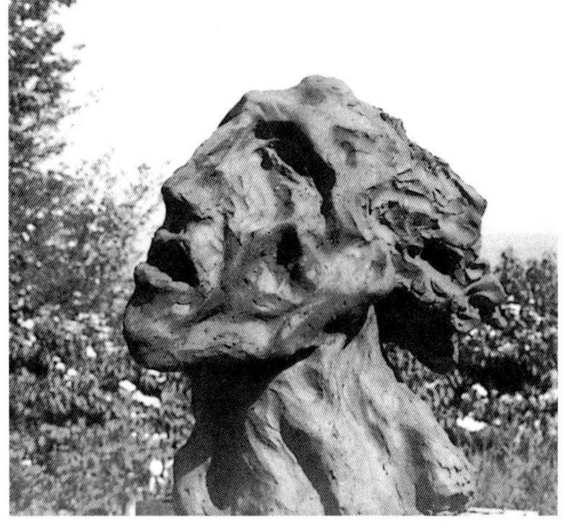

Job, 1956–57
Fired clay
14 × 13 inches
Collection of Mikell and Brian T. Callahan

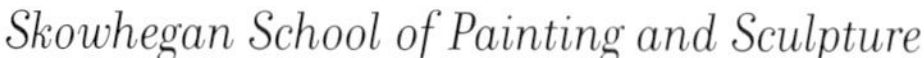

Skowhegan School of Painting and Sculpture

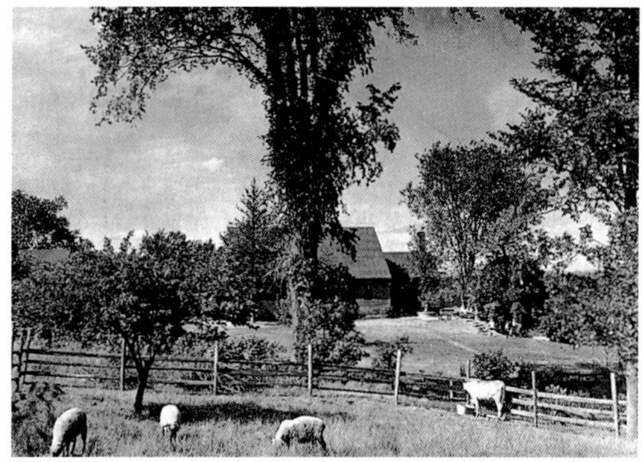

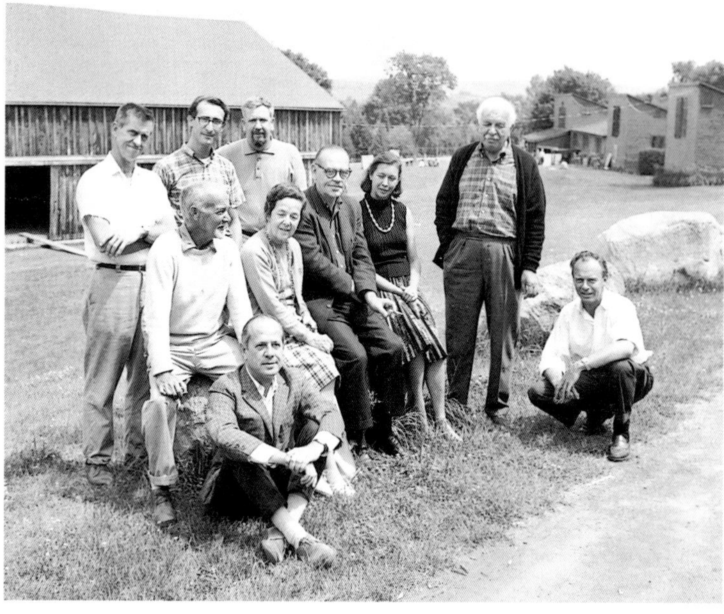

Front: John Eastman, director.
Second row, l–r: Kenneth Callahan, Bernarda Shahn, Walter Murch, "Johnny" Franzen.
Standing, l–r: Ambrose Patterson, Sidney Hurwitz, Robert Broderson, Ben Shahn, (kneeling) Bill Cummings, ca. 1965

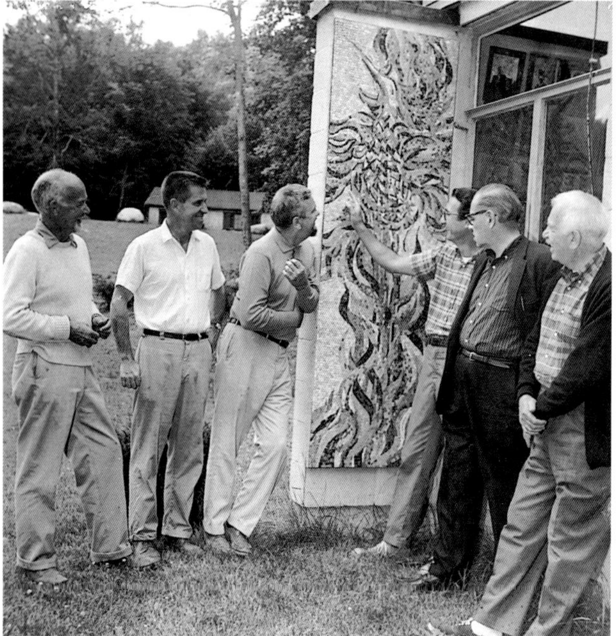

l–r: Kenneth Callhan, Ambrose Patterson, Robert Broderson, Sidney Hurwitz, Walter Murch, Ben Shahn, ca. 1965

befriended the artist Walter Murch. Also in 1959 Margaret Callahan's father, Ed Bundy, who had been living with them, died. The following year Callahan and Margaret spent a great deal of time at their beloved Granite Falls cabin almost as if they knew what was coming.

Margaret died in the early autumn of 1961. Their son, now known simply as Tobey, had married and was attending Yale, and at Christmas that year Callahan went back to New Haven, grief-stricken, numb, and inconsolable. Ironically, all the time Margaret lay ill, Callahan's career continued its steady climb, his work represented continuously in shows both nationally and abroad. But it all must have seemed to be happening without him. The following year he took a job as visiting professor of art at Washington State University, another temporary position, and when that job was finished he left for Germany, staying there nearly a year until word came from his son that the Granite Falls cabin and studio had been destroyed.

The news was as difficult for Callahan to hear as it was for Tobey to impart.[61] A photograph taken just days afterward shows only the chimney left standing, a scorched, precarious column of stones, less an emblem of a lovingly built life than of an absolute nightmare. But surprisingly, Callahan "took the loss in stride."[62] Perhaps being physically so far away softened the blow, helping him realize that this catastrophe meant that a part of his life had come to an end.

In 1964 Callahan married Beth Gotfredsen, the nurse who had cared for Margaret's father and for Margaret Callahan herself in her last months. Immediately following the wedding, Callahan and Beth left for Syracuse, New York, where Callahan had a mural commission. From Syracuse they moved on to Rochester, New York, where Callahan took a visiting artist post at the Rochester Memorial Art Gallery, at the University of Rochester. That same year, the Callahans bought a home and built a studio on a stretch of wild coast in Long Beach, Washington. Though they kept an apartment in Seattle, Long Beach would be their permanent home for the next twenty years.

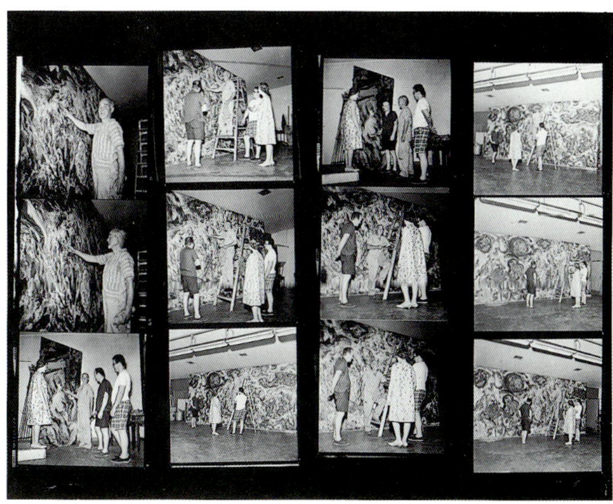

Kenneth Callahan at Syracuse University with his painting *The Cycle*, 1950s

By the mid- and late-sixties, Callahan's life had begun to assume the settled character of one who has reached the height of his powers. At Long Beach, he began his habit of walking the beach each morning, wearing his trademark watch cap. Callahan always dressed unpretentiously, not wishing to stand out but also wanting to watch others without being noticed. On these beach walks he quite often found a starting point for each day's work—a bird skeleton or a piece of kelp or patterns the wind left in the sand. Just after lunch each day, he went into the studio and worked steadily through the afternoon, occasionally taking a brief nap. Callahan claimed to paint only when he wanted to, but his desire never seemed to ebb. Often he set aside a painting and started another, coming back to the first and finishing it later. Paintings needed their own time. The move to Long Beach changed Callahan's palette, which became lighter and more open, and though more abstract, the paintings now contained bright planes of primary colors.[63] His work took on a playful aspect. In the woods near his studio he constructed a giant woman entirely of rope found on the beach, and in among the tree trunks and branches he strung wire that resembled giant spider webs.

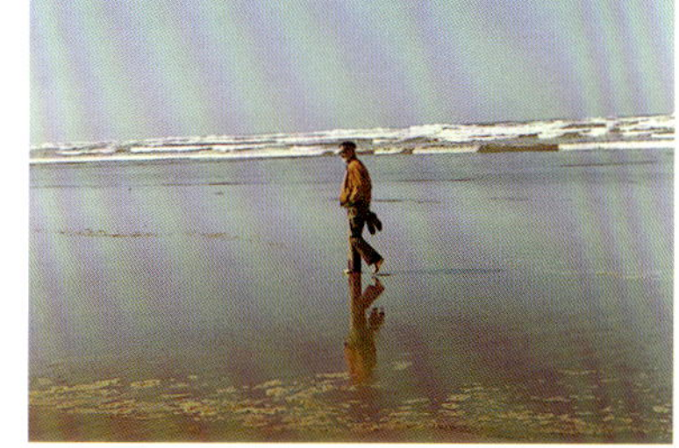

Kenneth Callahan on the beach at Long Beach, 1971

In the late afternoon when the day's work was done, Callahan enjoyed a gin and water and the occasional ribbing from his family for favoring such a flavorless drink. Callahan read widely—everything from Shakespeare to Agatha Christie—and often passed the evenings with a book except on autumn Mondays, when he watched Monday

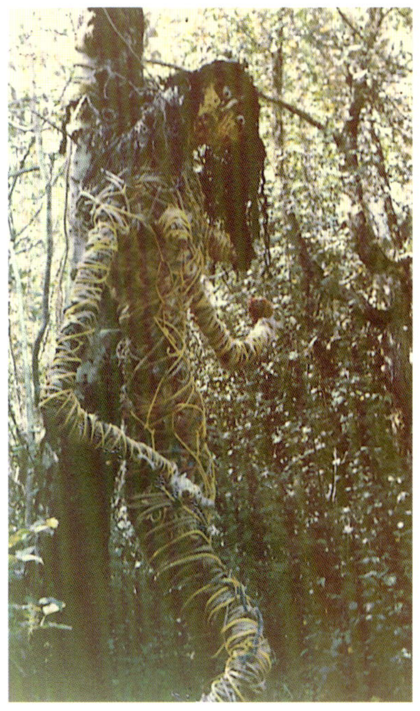

Rope Woman, 1971
Mixed media
Collection of Ann S. and John W. Ormsby

Farm sculpture, 1970s
Found rope

Night Football. He later befriended the former Detroit Lions football great Alex Karras, who was married to the actress Susan Clark. The Callahans had met her when Callahan was invited to design sets and costumes for a Seattle Repertory Theater production of *Macbeth*. Clark wrote the Callahans long letters, as did Martha Gellhorn (Ernest Hemingway's ex-wife) and jazz legend Benny Goodman, who was a friend for many years. Even the briefest acquaintance prompted spontaneous expressions of warmth and affection from the Callahans. Grateful notes also came from local business and civic leaders thanking Callahan for participation in benefits, fund raisers, and special events. True to Callahan's egalitarianism, friends from every walk of life were welcomed at Long Beach, including Karras and Clark and old Seattle friends like John Uitti, a picture framer, and painter Tom Blue. On Labor Day each year, the Callahans hosted a croquet match, after which everyone pitched tents for the night on the sand dunes.

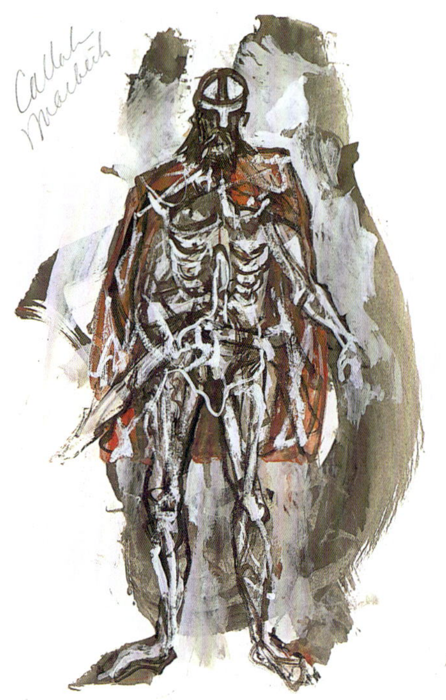

"Macbeth" Sketch, 1972
Ink and water-soluble paint on paper
10 × 7¼ inches
Collection of Mrs. William Wesselhoeft

Some days Callahan and Beth drove to a different part of the coast, taking along a picnic basket with paper, pens, and India ink. The paper itself was a rare extravagance and came from a dealer in New York's Chinatown. Whenever the big packages arrived Callahan loved to open them slowly and touch the paper, relishing the rich texture, the bright blank expanse. Out on the beach or hiking in the mountains, or on a favorite drive up the Columbia River, he would fasten a sheet of paper to a piece of cardboard with clothes pins. Sometimes he used a ballpoint pen. On trips out of town he packed an extra sketchbook and sometimes taped drawings up on his hotel room walls.[64] Periodically he and Beth crated up his canvasses and sent them off to Callahan's New York gallery, the Kraushaar Galleries, which began representing him in the sixties and still represents his work today.

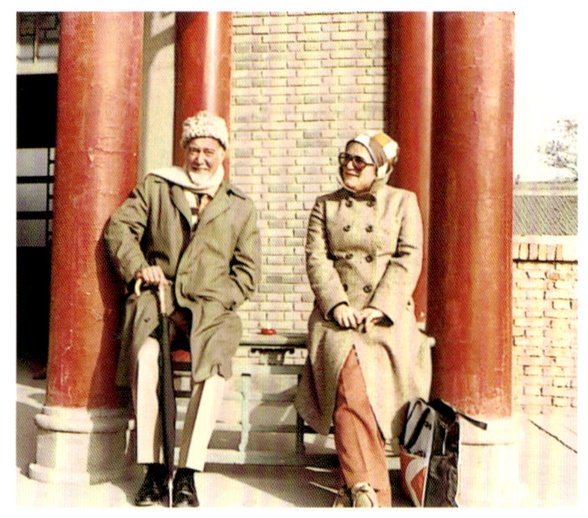

Kenneth with his wife Beth outside of the Forbidden City, Beijing, 1980

In 1965 Callahan was honored by the inclusion of ten of his paintings in the *Inaugural Exhibit of the Manfred Selig Collection of Art* at the State Capitol Museum in Olympia, Washington. The section in which his work hung came to be called "Callahan's Corner."[65] In the late sixties and early seventies the Callahans traveled widely, visiting Australia, Fiji, Hong Kong, New Zealand, and the Philippines and taking each of their grandchildren to Europe. Callahan also maintained a regular schedule of visiting professorships, though in time he would cut back on his teaching. In 1972 he was approached by W. Duncan Ross of the Seattle Repertory Theatre. Ross was mounting a production of *Macbeth* and wanted Callahan to design the set and costumes. Callahan was very excited about working for the theater. He considered it an honor to be asked, and his brooding designs contributed in great part to the production's critical success.[66]

It was also in the early 1970s that the Callahans were invited to Longacres, the horse racing track owned by Morris Alhadeff. Alhadeff was an inveterate art collector, and he arranged for Callahan to come and go as he pleased at the track. Callahan would show up in the early mornings to watch and sketch the workouts. When he finally showed Alhadeff the tall stack of sketches he'd done, Alhadeff was so impressed he bought much of what he saw and later built a special gallery at the track called the "Callahan Room" to house these works.[67] In drawing and painting horses there was a pleasing symmetry. The horse was a universe of motion unto itself and a timeless image rooted deeply in Callahan's past and in the art of those—Ralph Breckenridge and Charles Russell—who had first put the idea in his mind that he might make a life from painting.

In the late 1970s Callahan's work was exhibited in the Washington, D.C., home of Vice President Walter Mondale. But Callahan's painting career may well have culmi-

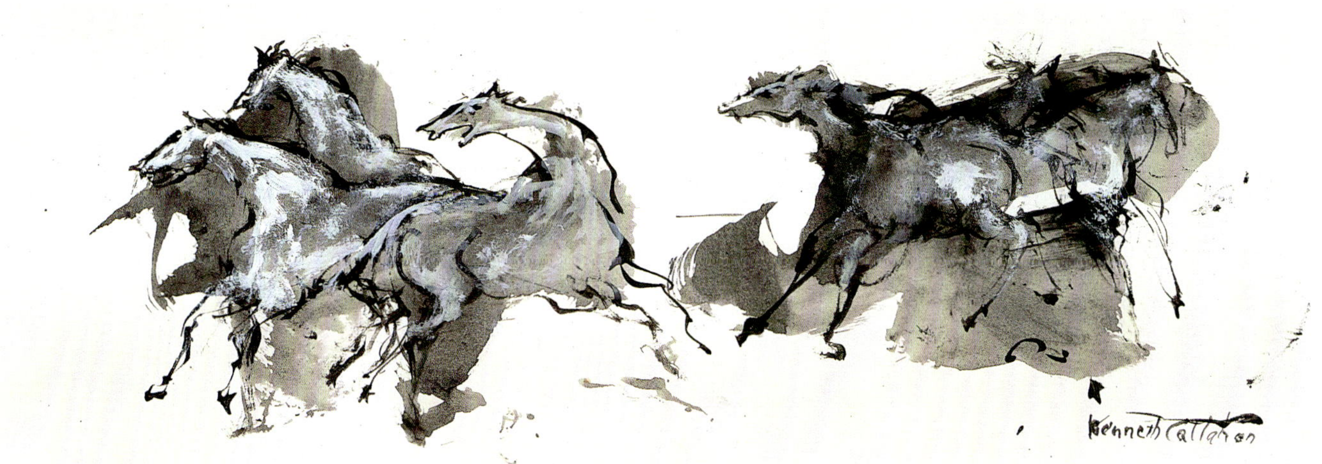

Horses, ca. 1970s
Sumi ink on paper
6½ × 19 inches
Collection of Dr. and Mrs. Nicholas Berman

nated in 1976 when he had a one-man show in Seattle at the Foster/White Gallery. At the opening the gallery was filled to capacity all night. Every painting sold. Later Callahan called it "the best show I ever had."[68] In 1973 the Henry Art Gallery mounted a retrospective, *Kenneth Callahan: Universal Voyage*, which *Seattle Times* art critic Deloris Tarzan called "quite simply the finest exhibition I have ever seen."[69]

Given the success of these two shows, it was almost inevitable that the Seattle Art Museum's 1979 retrospective would be anticlimactic. The show opened in December. For some reason no catalogue was printed and just after the opening the museum dropped the term "retrospective," calling it instead a "major exhibition."[70] Moreover, the choice of work that appeared was uneven and inconsistent. The museum did not extend its search for paintings beyond a handful of other museums and collectors. Callahan paintings were not solicited from the Museum of Modern Art, the Whitney Museum of American Art, or the Metropolitan Museum of Art, nor from prominent private collections outside Seattle. Often, the most emblematic pieces from each period in the painter's life were missing, and not all the periods of his work were represented.[71] Callahan's Seattle gallery, Foster/White, supplied the Seattle Art Museum with a list of local collectors, few of whom were actually contacted.[72] Critics and art patrons alike were outraged that so beloved a figure should receive less than he deserved from the city's most prestigious museum.

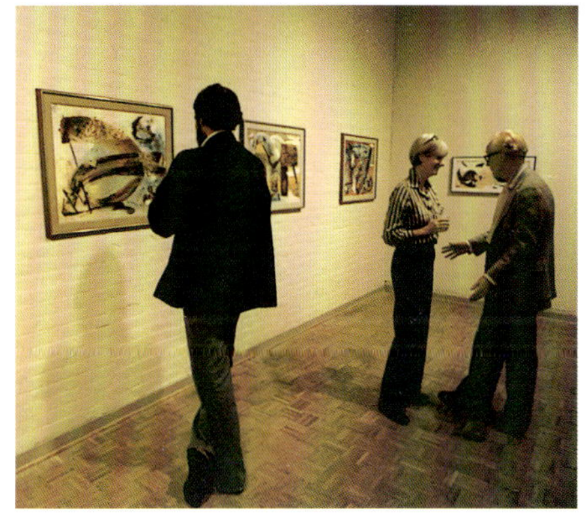

Kenneth Callahan exhibition at Foster/White Gallery, 1970s

Callahan himself thought the show good but he told one reporter, "I feel it could be better."[73] His attitude was not conciliatory but, typically, neither was his disappointment deep. Heart trouble in 1976 had slowed Callahan down to the extent that he traveled and taught less than he had, but increasingly his Long Beach home and studio were visited by artists, admirers, critics, journalists, and film and video crews. Though clearly uneasy before the camera, Callahan relaxed most when talking off the subject of himself and his art. Shy as he was, and protective of his privacy, his success and longevity were inevitably making an icon of him. Callahan appeared with then–Seattle Supersonics basketball coach Bill Russell in a full-page newspaper ad supporting a Seattle mayoral candidate. His regular shows at Foster/White had become media events. But the biggest consolation was still the work: there was always more to be done. Callahan often said life wouldn't be worth living if he couldn't paint.[74] Work was the one constant. It leveled out the highs and lows. It embraced the totality of life and made the worst seem bearable, even the thought of death.

In 1985 the Tacoma Art Museum mounted a show celebrating Callahan's eightieth

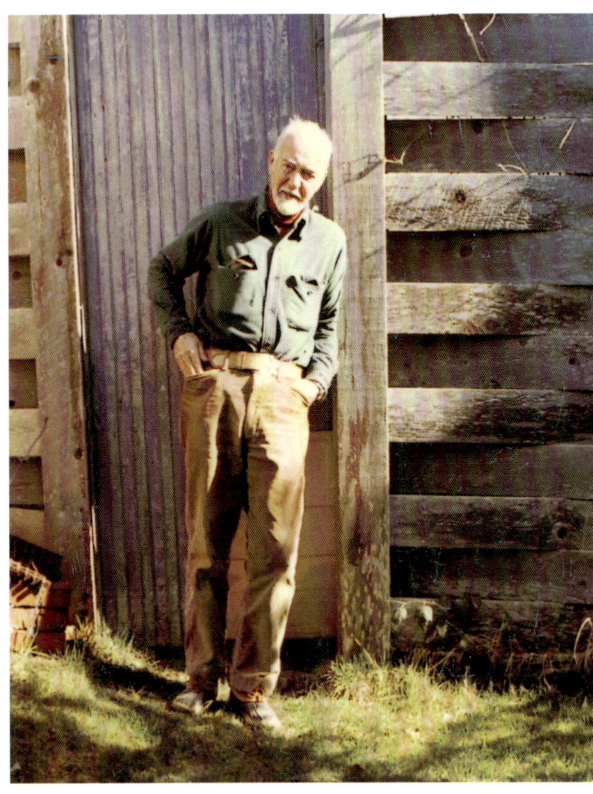

Kenneth Callahan, ca. 1960s

birthday. At Thanksgiving of that year Callahan caught a bad cold. Over the following weeks his health did not improve, and by the time he and Beth drove back to their Seattle apartment the cold had turned into pneumonia. The move proved to be a permanent one.

Being away from the beach was difficult, but over the following months Callahan continued to work, painting and drawing every day. On an afternoon in May in 1986, he and Beth took a short walk in Leschi Park on Lake Washington. Across the lake, silhouetted against the sky, were the Cascade Mountains where Callahan had lived and hiked and painted, where he'd conceived many of the images that had given him what he had always wanted—an art that was singular and unmistakably his own. Two days later, months short of his eighty-first birthday celebration, Kenneth Callahan died. Only during the last two weeks of his life was he unable to work.

Seattle mourned the loss of one of its cultural progenitors. In tribute, the Seattle Art Museum put up a selection of his paintings from its permanent collection. Don Foster, Callahan's Seattle dealer and friend, praised his restless search for new themes and directions. "Kenneth was always experimenting, setting up new problems for himself."[75] His friend Morris Alhadeff could barely contain his emotion when interviewed. "He was an intensely vital man, a beautiful man. He never ceased to think and dream about his work."[76] Even at the height of his notoriety, the habits of modesty and curiosity had left Callahan unspoiled in some essential way, willing, through his art, to surrender to the present moment and to the inevitable, to re-imagine the sources of significance that inform all the elements of our experience, the ordinary and the exalted, the dark sweep of the landscape and the smallest gestures of the heart.

notes

1. Brian T. Callahan, interview by author, November 1998.

2. Kenneth Callahan, "Interview with Kenneth Callahan," interviewed by Sue Ann Kendall et al., videocassette, 4 vols., Seattle Public Library, 1984.

3. John Hessburg, "Painter Kenneth Callahan Is Dead," *Seattle Post-Intelligencer*, 10 May 1986, A1.

4. Sue Ann Kendall, "Northwest Oral History Project: Kenneth Callahan, NWOHP No. 3," Archives of American Art, Smithsonian Institution, 27 October, 21 November, 19 December 1982, 1.

5. Kenneth Callahan, "Ruminations," *Puget Soundings*, May 1965, 19.

6. Kendall, "Northwest Oral History Project."

7. Callahan, "Ruminations," 19.

8. Ibid., 24.

9. Ibid., 19.

10. Ibid., 27.

11. Ibid.

12. Ibid.

13. Ibid., 19.

14. Kenneth Callahan, "Some Reminiscences from Kenneth Callahan When Asked About His Career," notes to an exhibition at Foster/White Gallery, August 1977.

15. Martha Kingsbury, in Charles Cowles and Sarah Clark, *Northwest Traditions*, exh. cat. (Seattle: Seattle Art Museum, 1978), 9.

16. Callahan, "Ruminations," 30.

17. Ibid.

18. Brian T. Callahan, interview.

19. Callahan, "Ruminations," 30.

20. Kendall, "Northwest Oral History Project," 17.

21. Callahan, "Ruminations," 31.

22. Michael R. Johnson, ed., *Kenneth Callahan: Universal Voyage*, exh. cat. (Seattle: University of Washington Press in association with the Henry Art Gallery, 1973), 77.

23. Brian T. Callahan, interview.

24. Beth Callahan, interview by author, 10 October 1998.

25. Kingsbury, *Northwest Traditions*, 11.

26. Callahan, "Interview."

27. Brian T. Callahan, interview.

28. Kingsbury, *Northwest Traditions*, 18.

29. Kendall, "Northwest Oral History Project," 24.

30. Callahan, "Interview."

31. Jim Faber, "Callahan's Island in Time," *Seattle Post-Intelligencer*, 29 October 1967, 12.

32. Callahan, "Interview."

33. Kendall, "Northwest Oral History Project," 41.

34. Kenneth Callahan, in *A Tribute to Kenneth Callahan on the Occasion of His Eightieth Birthday*, exh. cat. (Tacoma: Tacoma Art Museum, 1985).

35. Kingsbury, *Northwest Traditions*, 13.

36. Kenneth Callahan, "Pacific Northwest," *Art News*, July 1946, 22.

37. Ibid., 24.

38. Kingsbury, *Northwest Traditions*, 49.

39. Callahan, "Interview."

40. Kingsbury, *Northwest Traditions*, 41.

41. Brian T. Callahan, interview.

42. Kenneth Callahan, letter to the Postmaster, Rugby, North Dakota, 2 March 1942, collection of Beth Callahan.

43. Callahan, "Interview."

44. Kenneth Callahan, "Kenneth Callahan," *Northwest Art News and Views*, March/April 1970, 36.

45. Deloris Tarzan, "Callahan's 'Universal Voyage' at Henry Gallery," *Seattle Times*, 1 April 1973, H1.

46. Emily Winthrop Miles, *An Exhibition of Paintings and Drawings by Kenneth Callahan* (New York: Ram Press, 1960).

47. Howard Devree, "Exhibition Tide Rises to a Flood," *New York Times*, 10 February 1946, sec. 2, 6.

48. Callahan, "Interview."

49. Aline B. Louchheim, letter to Kenneth Callahan, 7 December 1945, collection of Beth Callahan.

50. Callahan, "Interview."

51. Johnson, *Kenneth Callahan: Universal Voyage*, 78.

52. Brian T. Callahan, interview.

53. Kenneth Callahan, letter to editor, *The New World*, collection of Beth Callahan.

54. Brian T. Callahan, interview.

55. "Mystic Painters of the Northwest," *Life*, 28 September 1953, 87.

56. Callahan, "Interview."

57. Ibid.

58. Johnson, *Kenneth Callahan: Universal Voyage*, 58.

59. Brian T. Callahan, interview.

60. Beth Callahan, interview.

61. Brian T. Callahan, interview.

62. Ibid.

63. Beth Callahan, interview.

64. Ibid.

65. "Callahan's Corner," *Seattle Times*, 17 January 1965, S2.

66. Beth Callahan, interview.

67. Deloris Tarzan, "Art Is Good Bet at Longacres," *Seattle Times*, 27 July 1976, A11.

68. Deloris Tarzan, "Callahan: Our Greatest Painter?" *Seattle Times*, 25 January 1976, A8.

69. Tarzan, "Callahan's 'Universal Voyage' at Henry Gallery."

70. Eric Scigliano, "Callahan Show a Rich—If Incomplete—Panorama," *Argus*, 4 January 1980, 6.

71. Mayumi Tsutakawa, "Callahan's Paintings Impressive in a Major Exhibition at S.A.M.," *Seattle Times: Tempo*, 14 December 1979, 3.

72. Scigliano, "Callahan Show," 6.

73. Ibid.

74. Beth Callahan, interview.

75. Hessburg, "Painter Kenneth Callahan Is Dead."

76. Ibid.

CATALOGUE

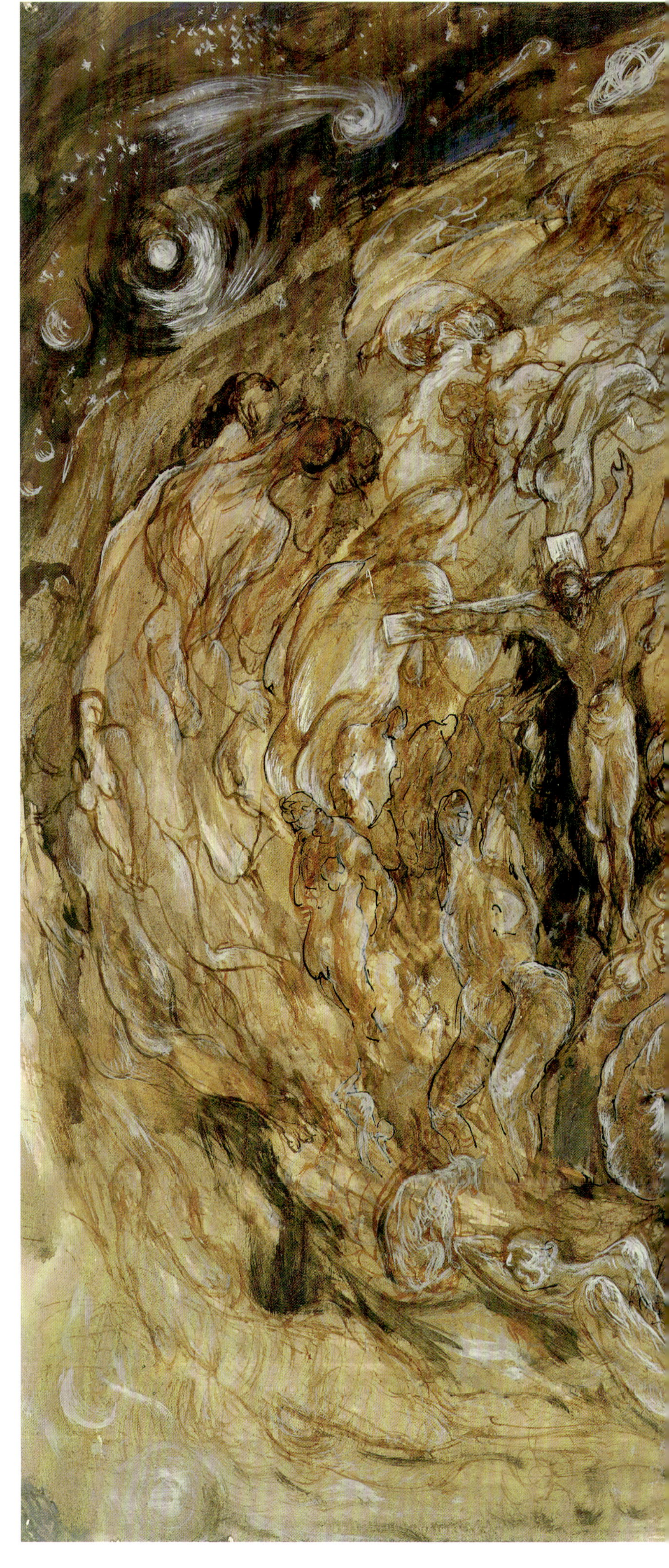

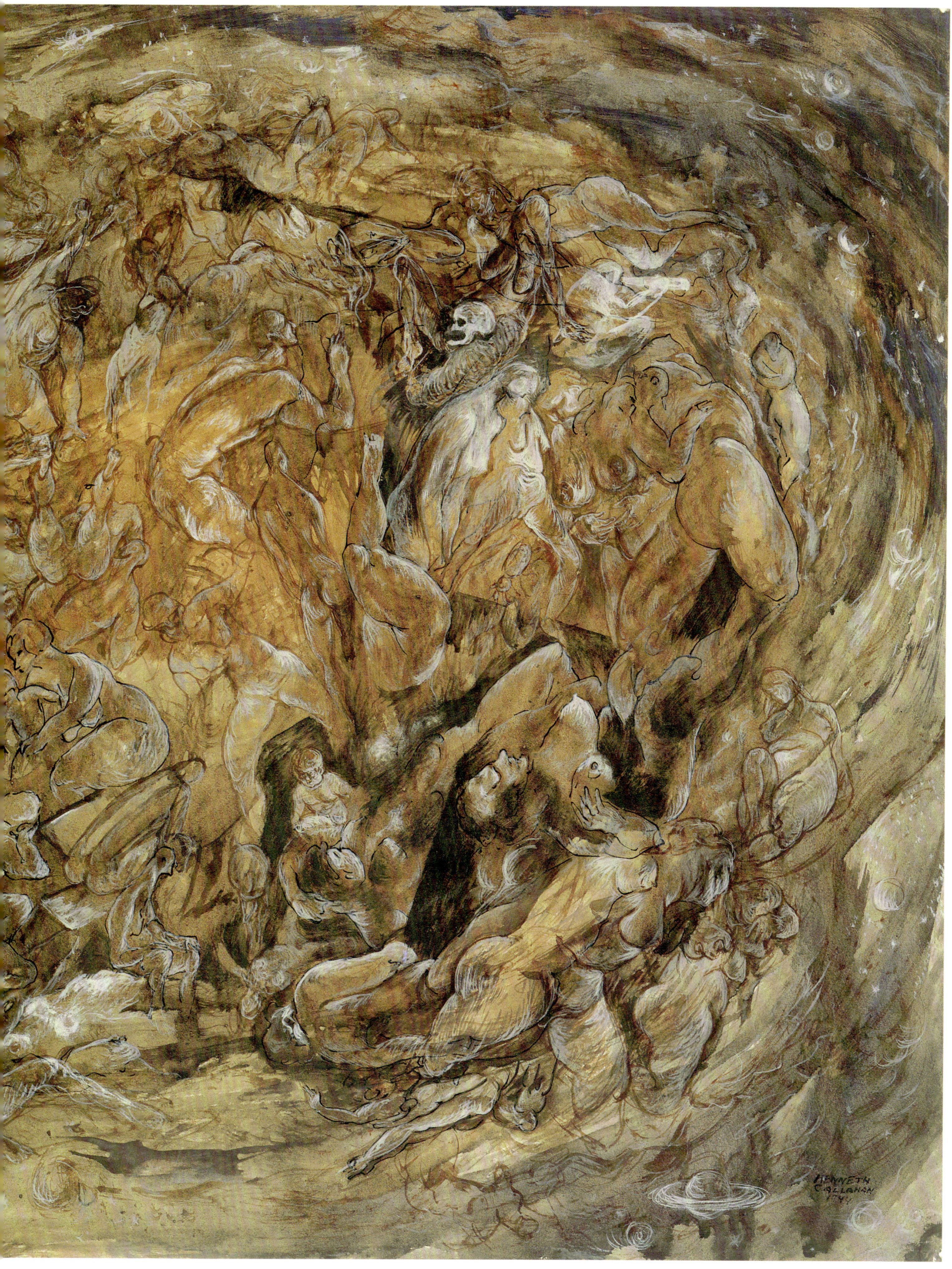
KENNETH
CALLAHAN
1941

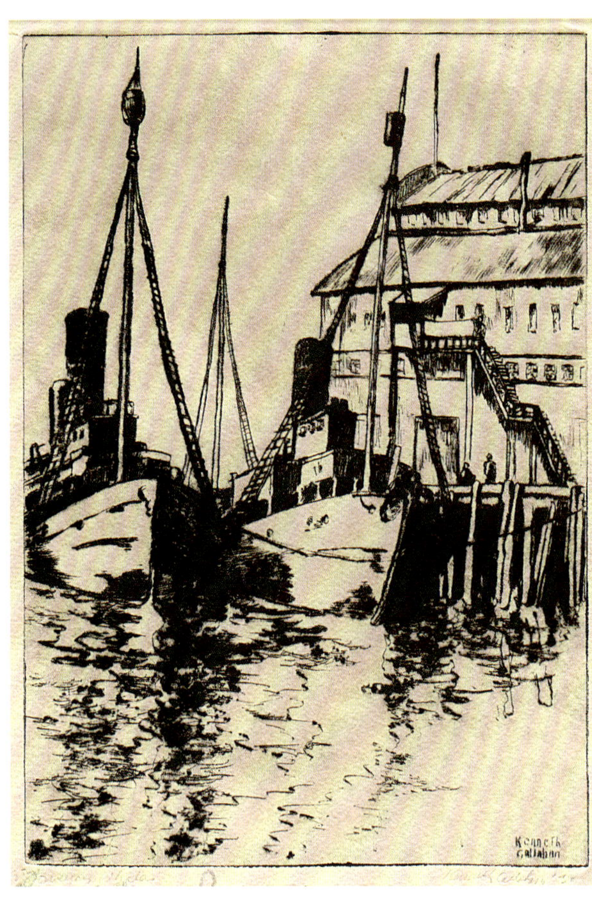

Pier with Boats, 1930
Drypoint
$7\frac{1}{2} \times 5\frac{1}{2}$ inches
Collection of Mr. & Mrs. Steven L. Sherman

Skid Row Fight, 1931
Drypoint
$6\frac{7}{8} \times 7\frac{3}{4}$ inches
Portland Art Museum, Oregon,
Gift of Gordon W. Gilkey

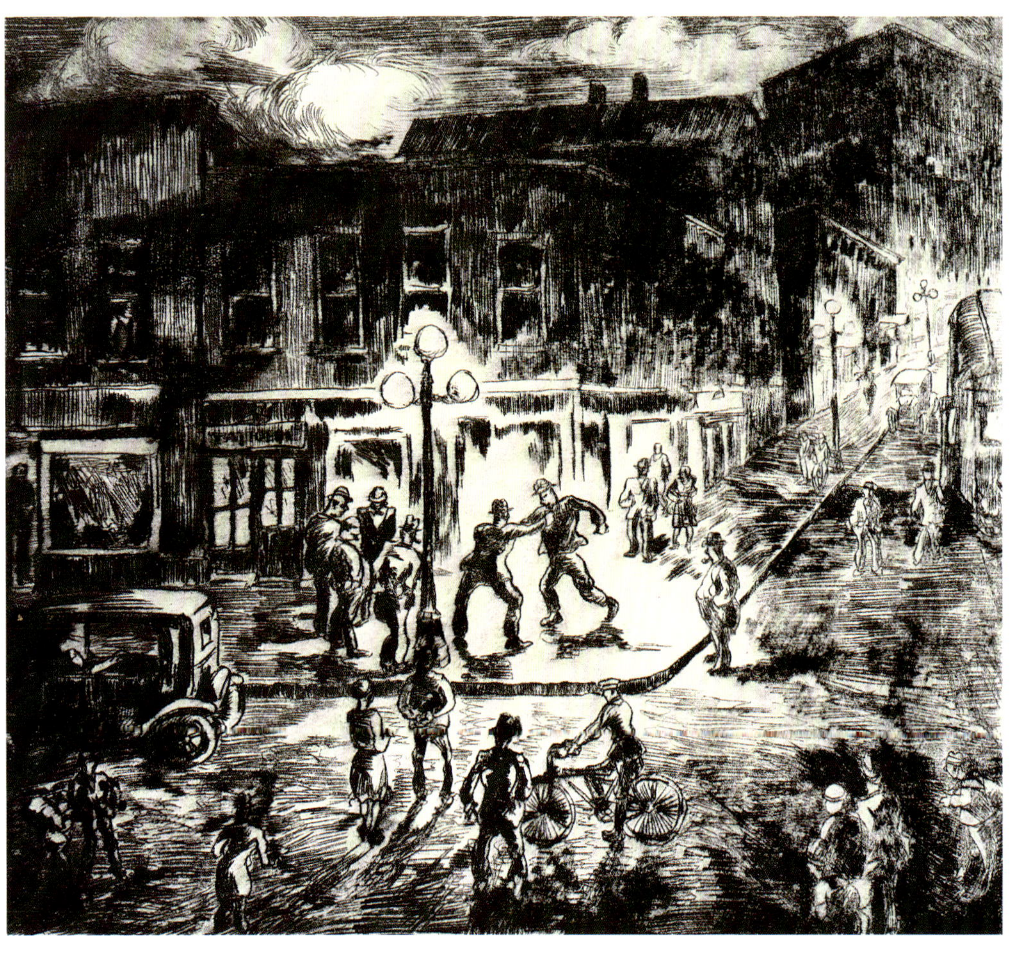

Untitled [Ilwaco Waterfront], ca. 1930s
Tempera on wood
$7^{3}/_{8} \times 17^{1}/_{2}$ inches
Museum of Art, Washington State University. Gift of the WSU College of Business and Economics in honor of Ivar Haglund

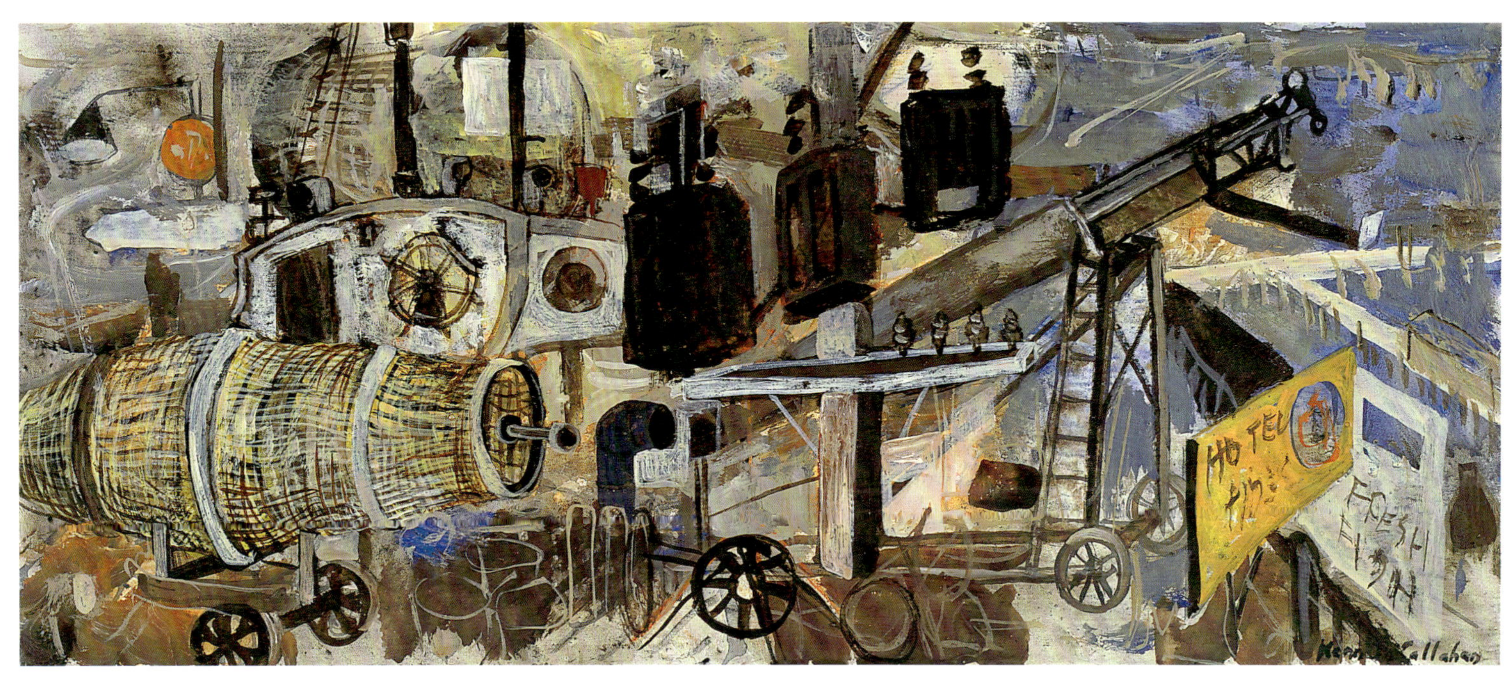

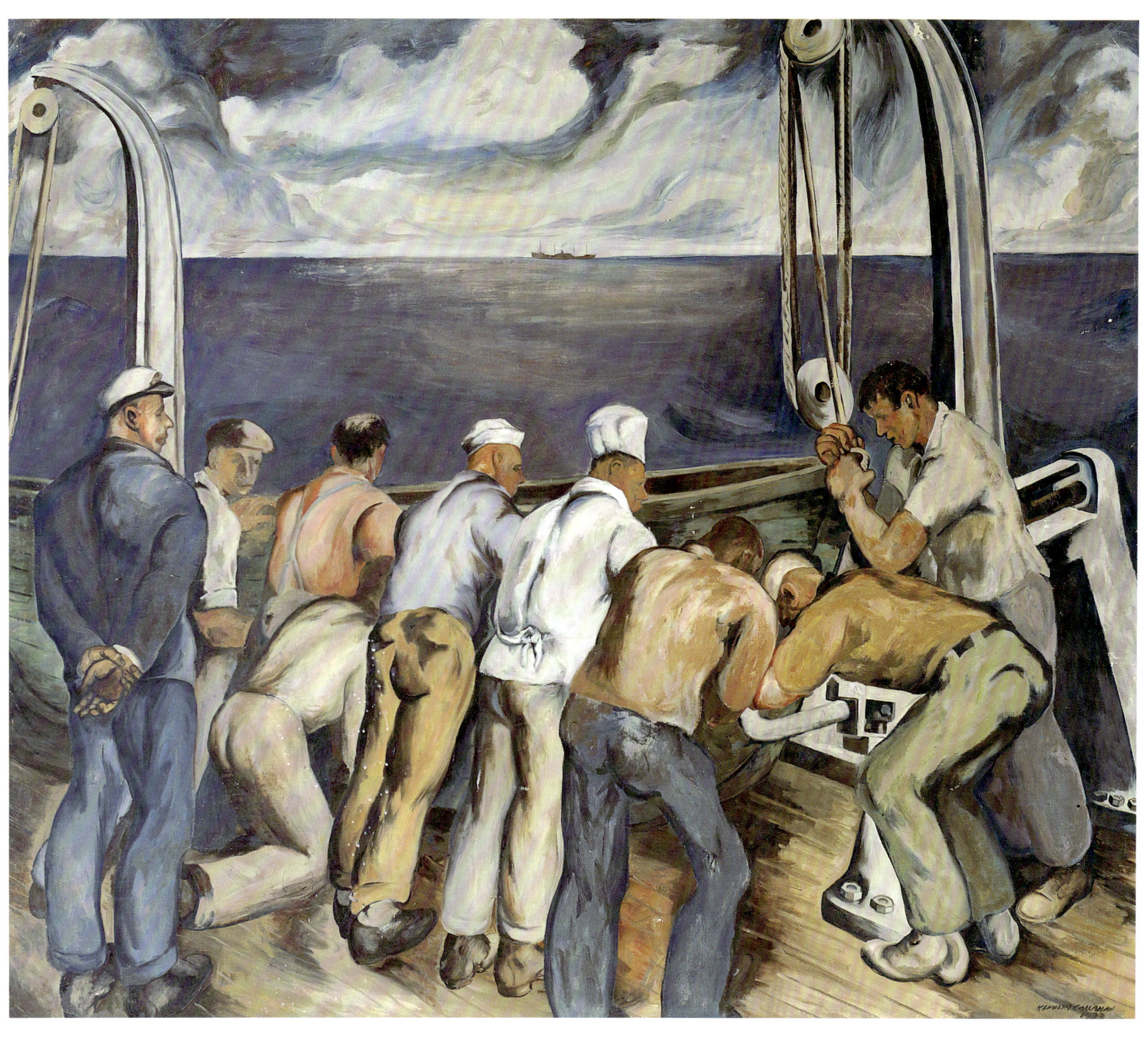

Men Who Work the Ships: Lifeboat Drill,
ca. 1933
Oil on canvas mounted on Masonite
Panel 5 of an 11-panel mural
110 × 94 inches
Museum of History and Industry, Seattle

Men Who Work the Ships: Scraping and Painting,
ca. 1933
Oil on canvas mounted on Masonite
Panel 7 of an 11-panel mural
88 × 94 inches
Museum of History and Industry, Seattle

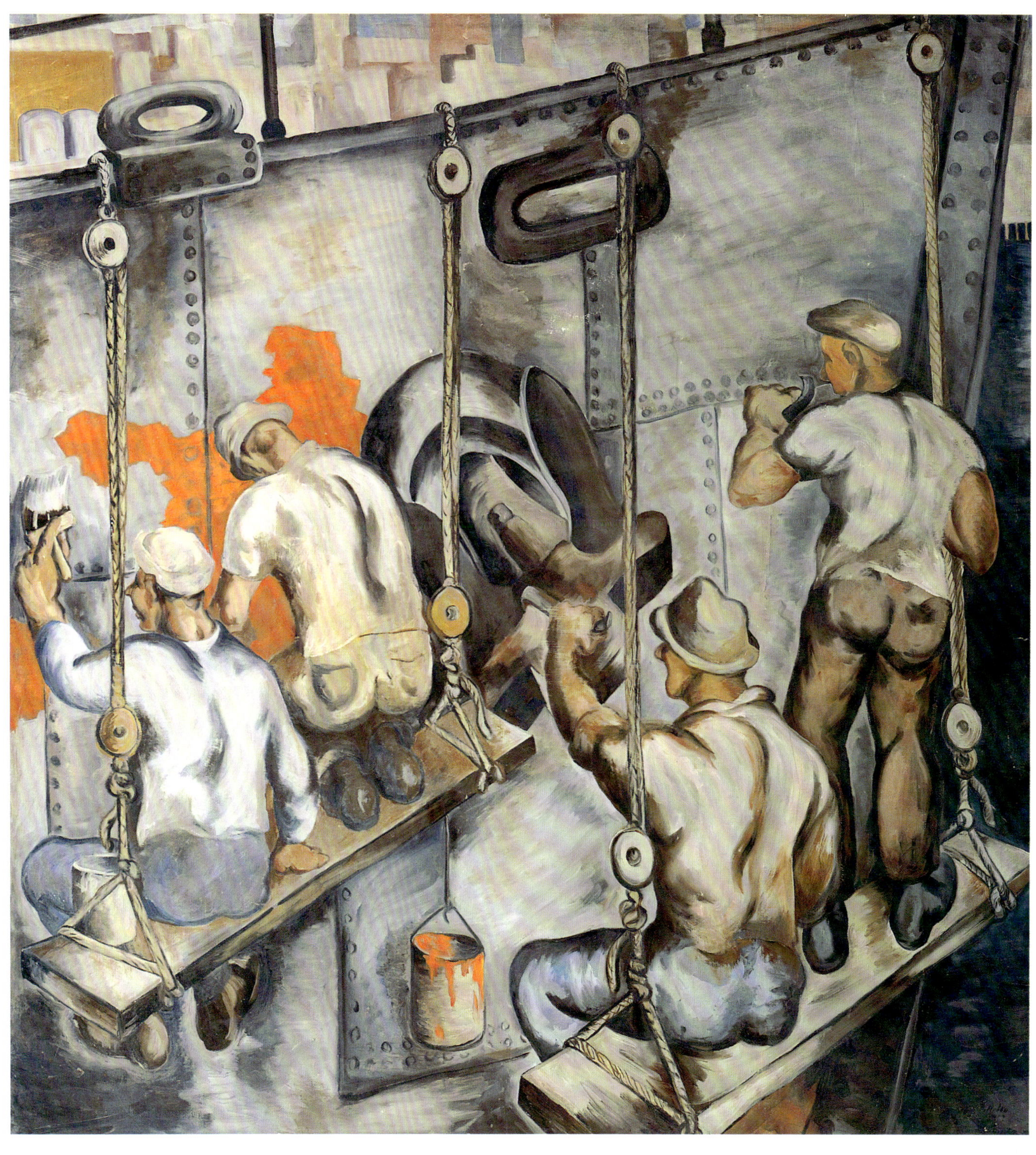

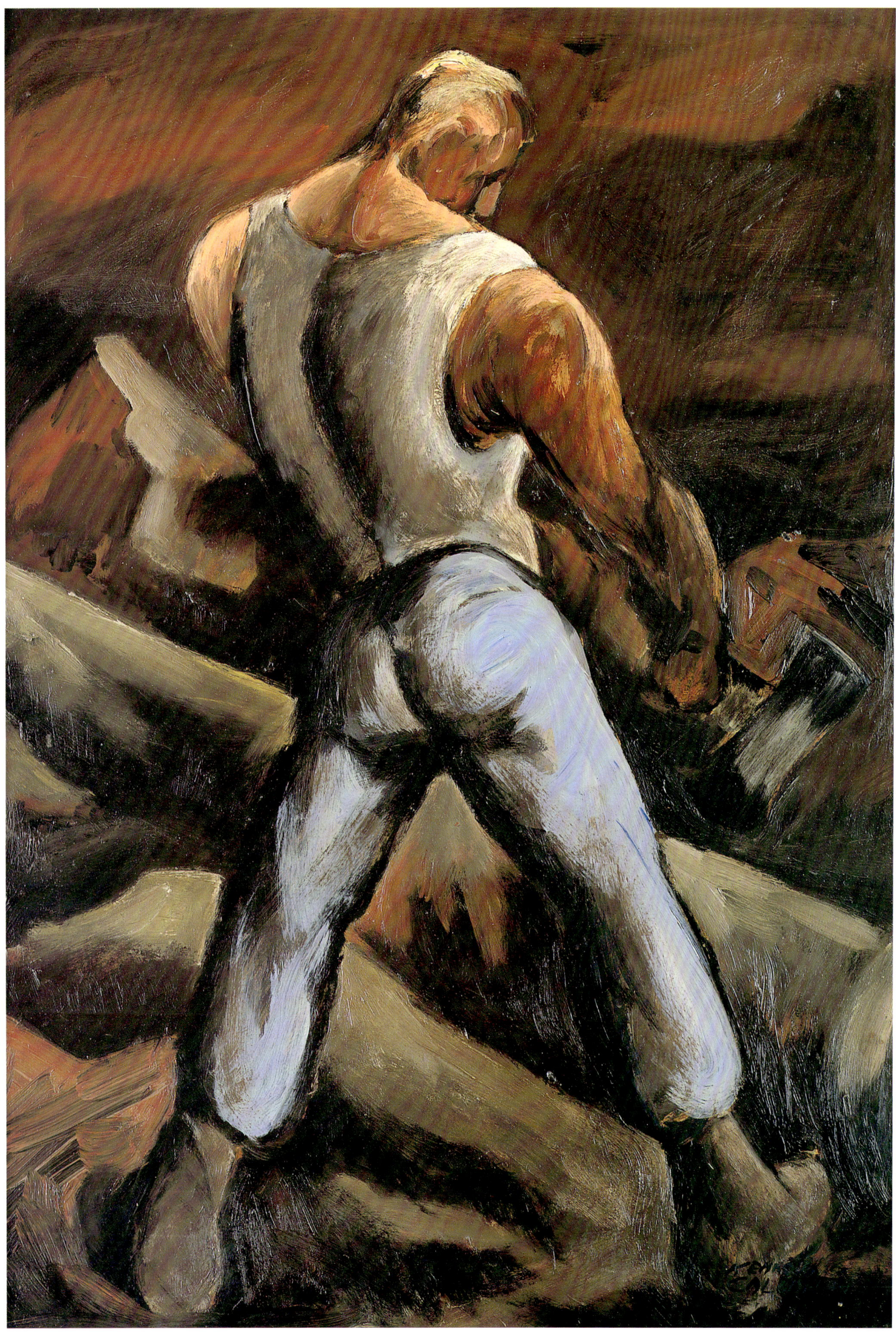

OPPOSITE:
Feller, 1934
Oil on canvas
31 1/8 × 22 inches
Seattle Art Museum, Eugene Fuller Memorial Collection

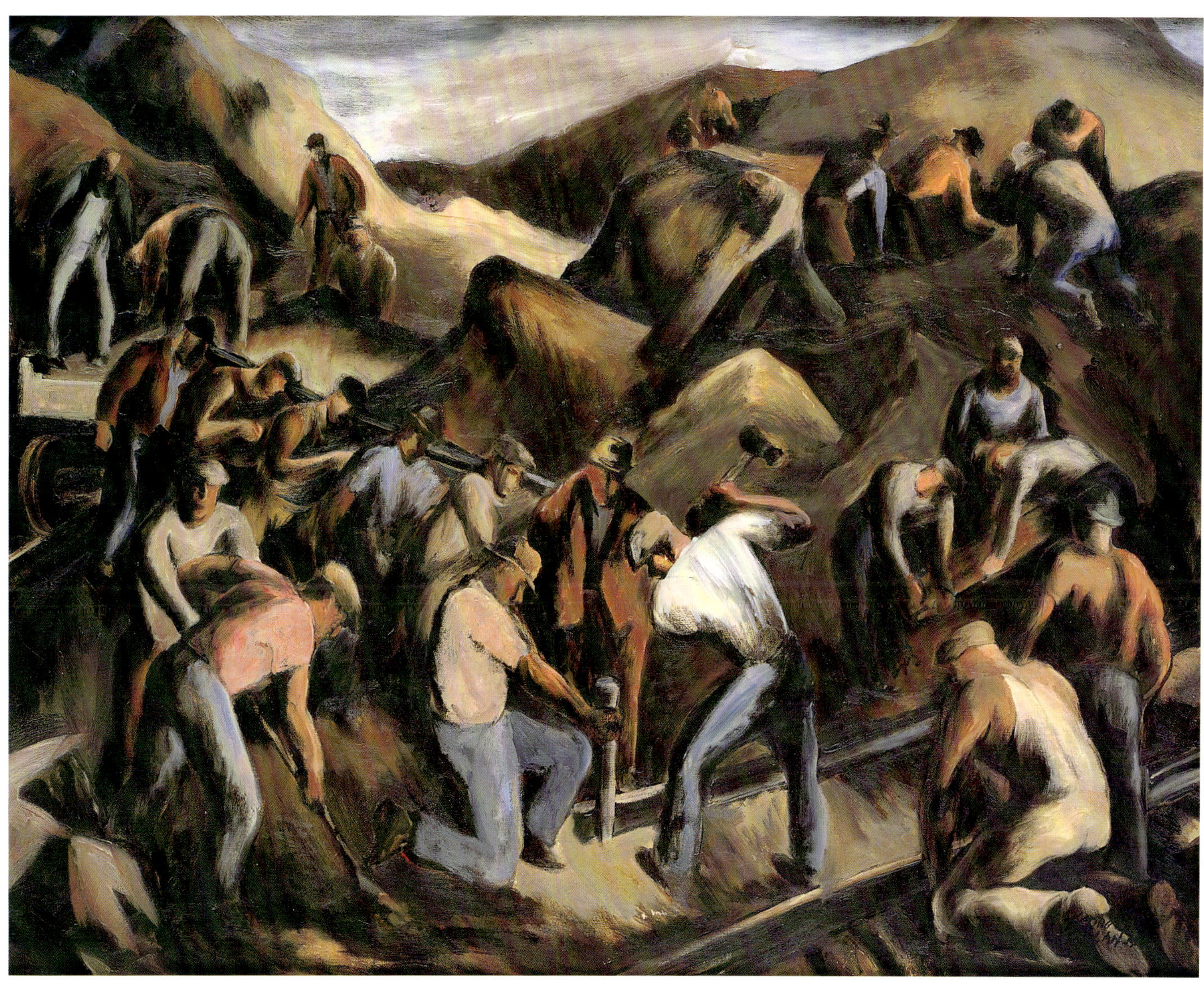

Logging Rail Road Construction, 1937
Oil on canvas
34 1/2 × 44 1/2 inches
Seattle Art Museum, Eugene Fuller Memorial Collection

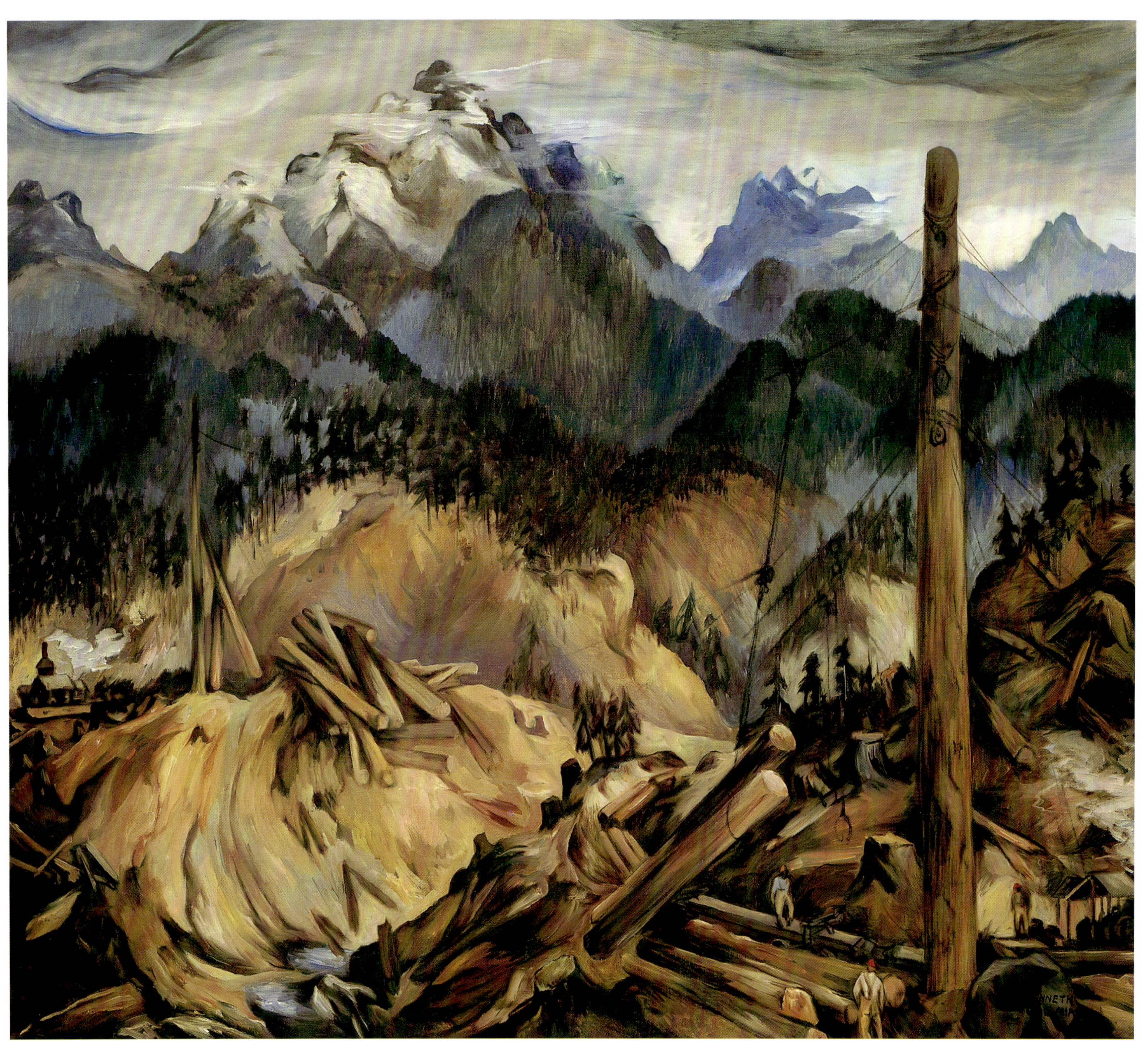

Northwest Logging, ca. 1930s
Oil on canvas
64 × 74 inches
Rainier Club, Seattle

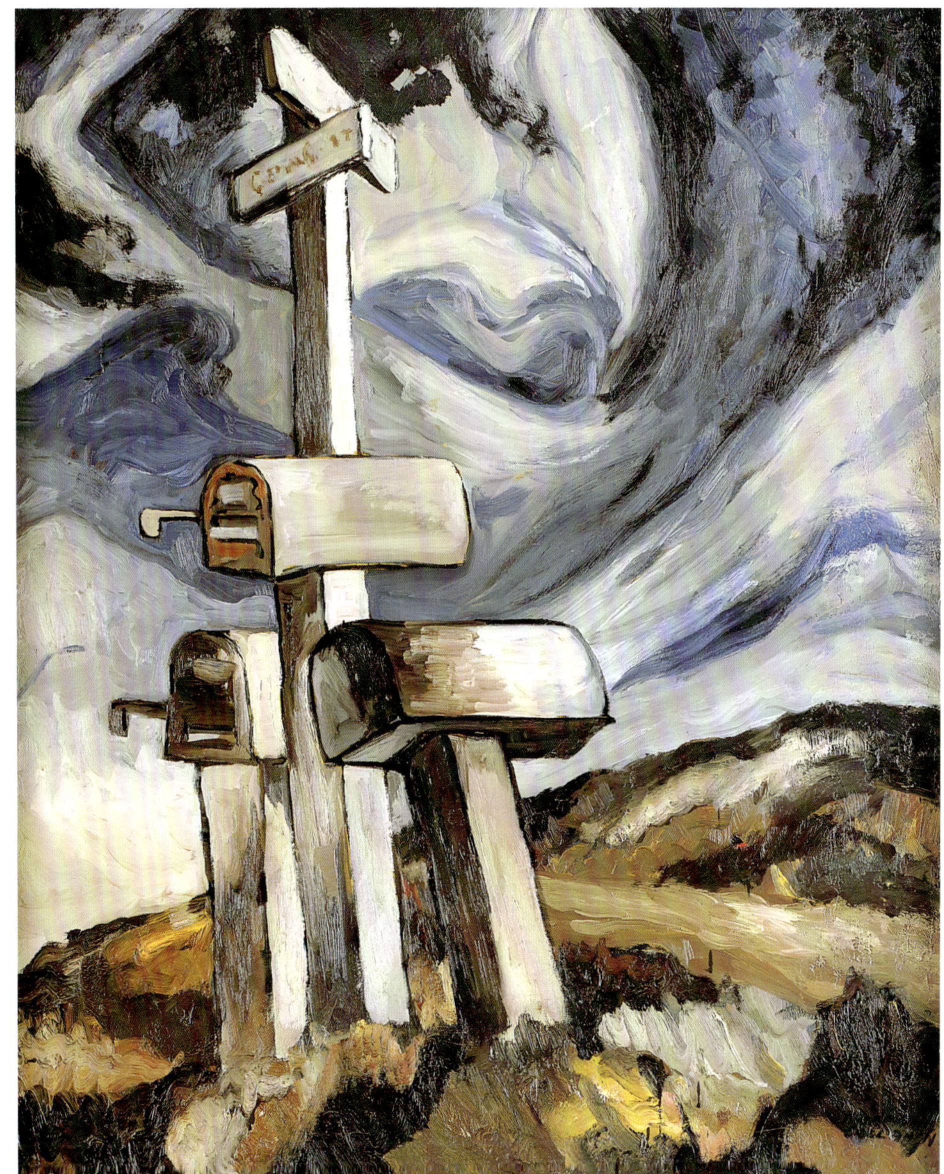

Mail Boxes, 1935
Oil on canvas
32¾ × 26¾ inches
Seattle Art Museum, Eugene Fuller Memorial Collection

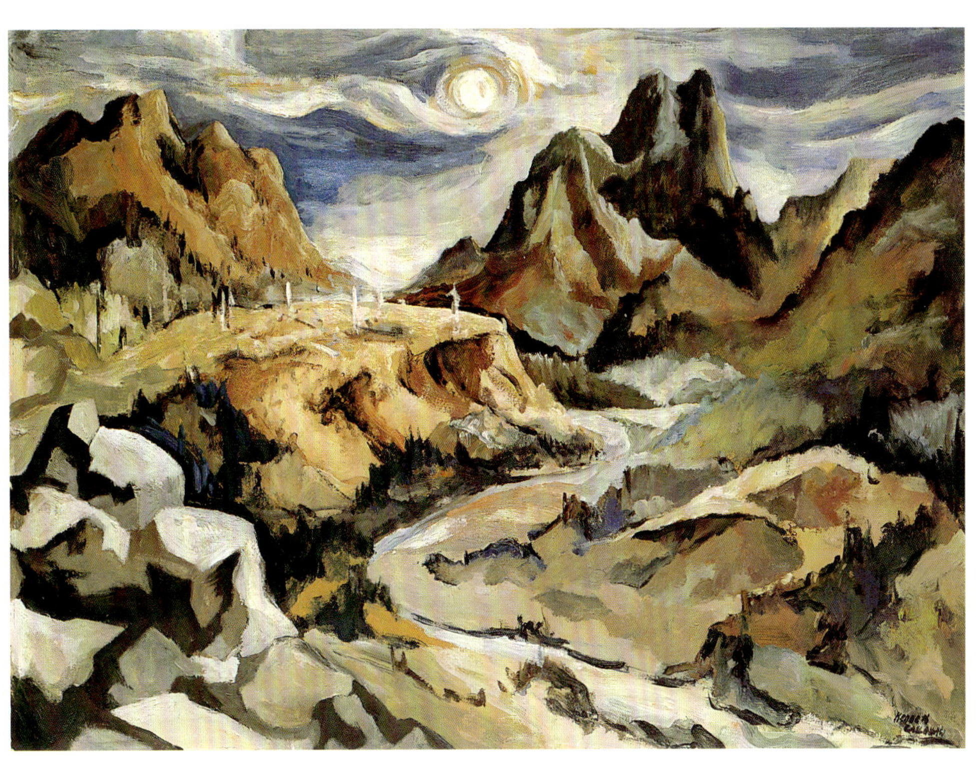

Northwest Landscape, 1934
Oil on board
34 × 47 inches
Seattle Art Museum, Eugene Fuller Memorial Collection

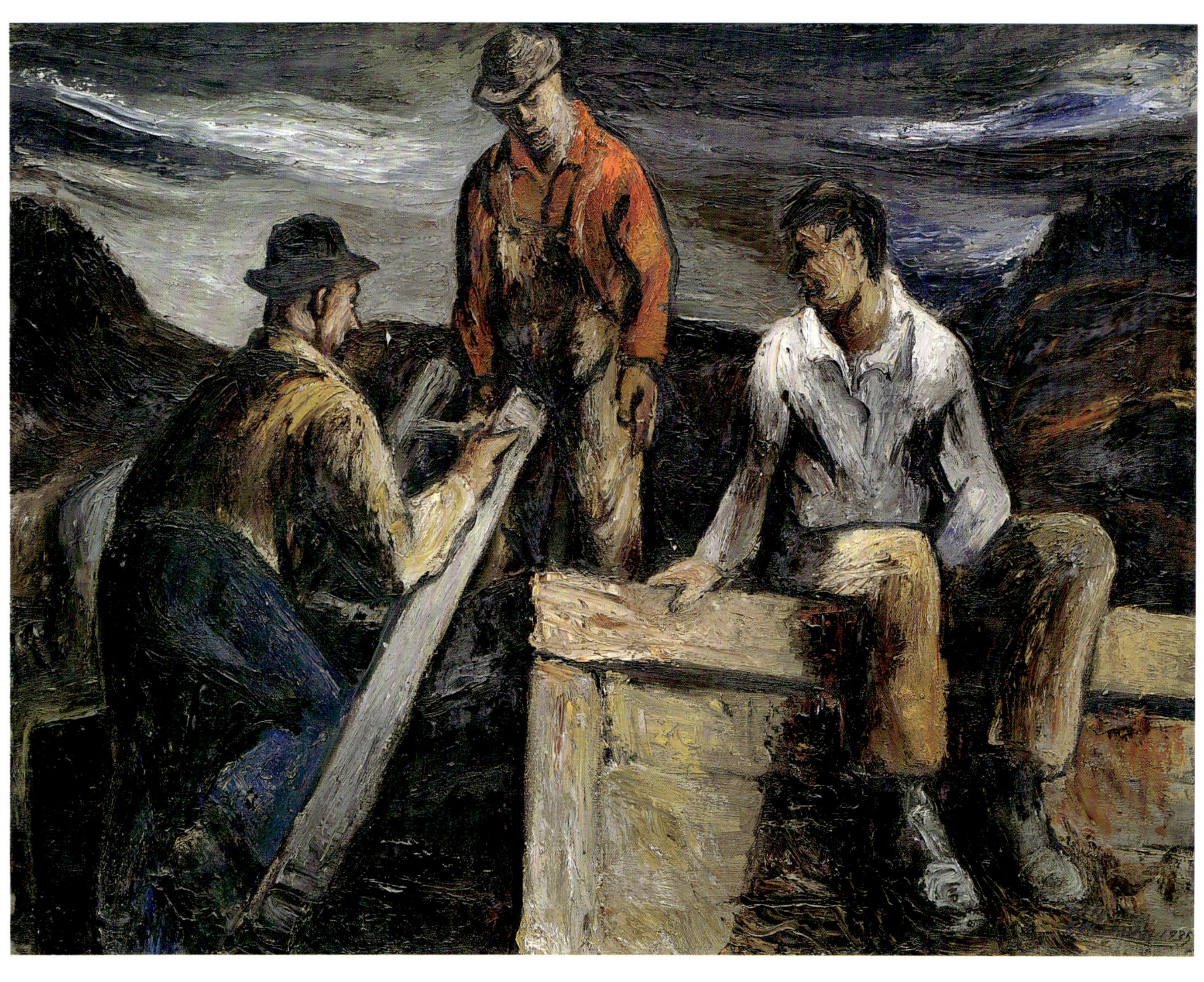

Untitled, 1935
Oil on canvas
34 × 45 inches
Collection of Kathryn L. Sherman

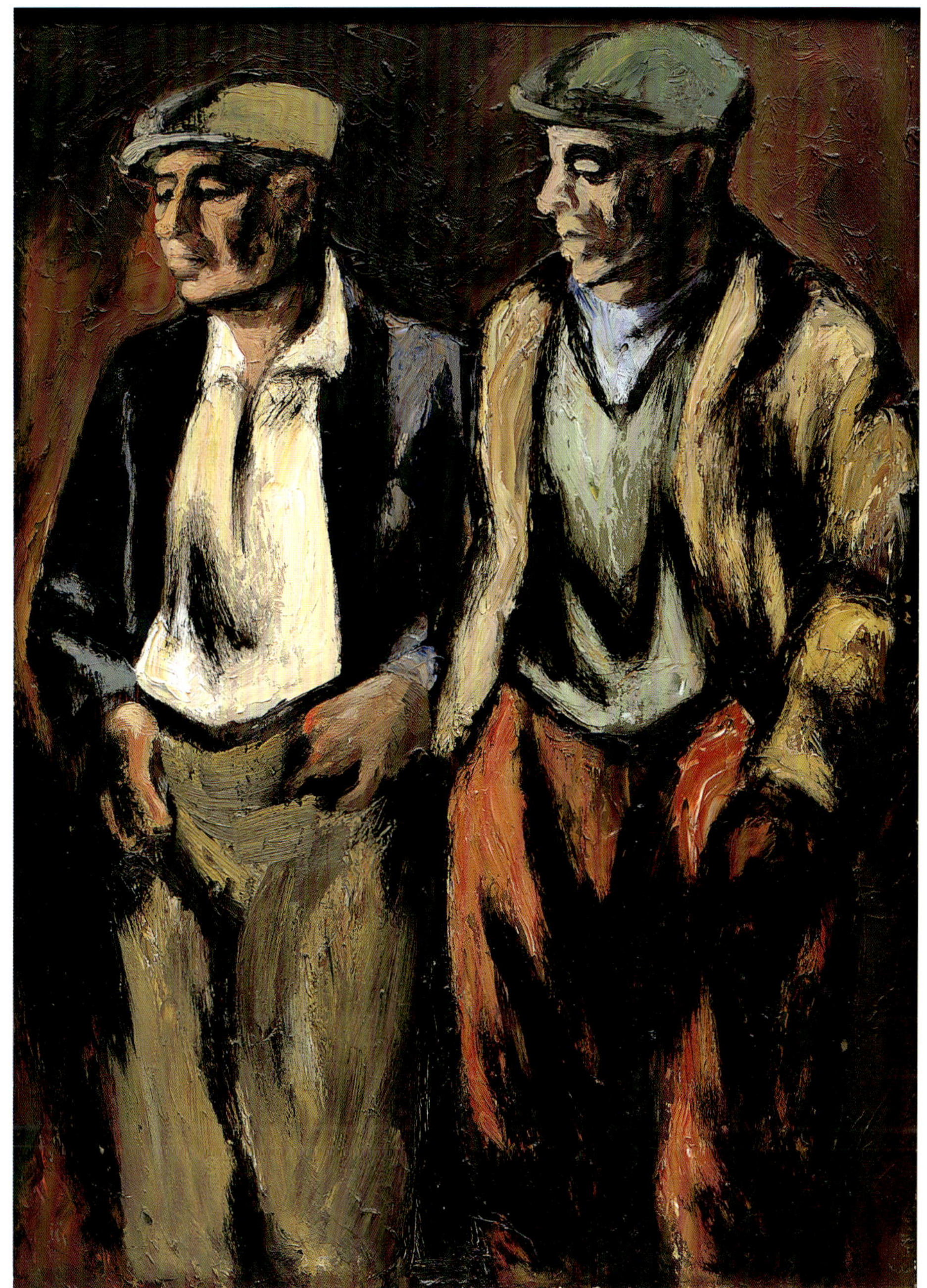

Two Men, 1935
Oil on board
27½ × 20 inches
Collection of John and Heidi Rabel

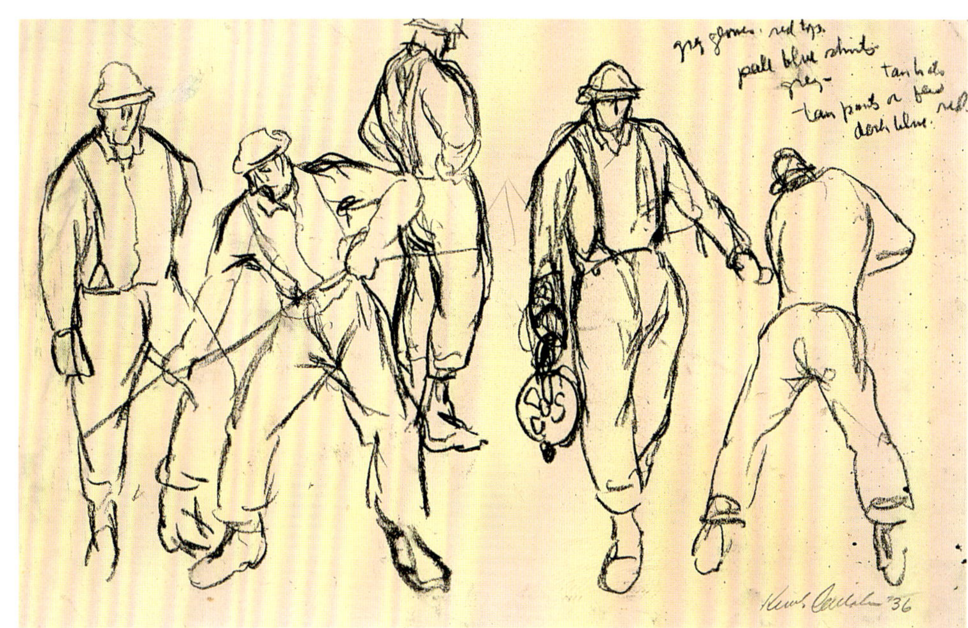

Sketch for Mural, 1936
Conté on paper
15¾ × 23¼ inches
Collection of Neil Goldschmidt and Ms. Diana Snowden

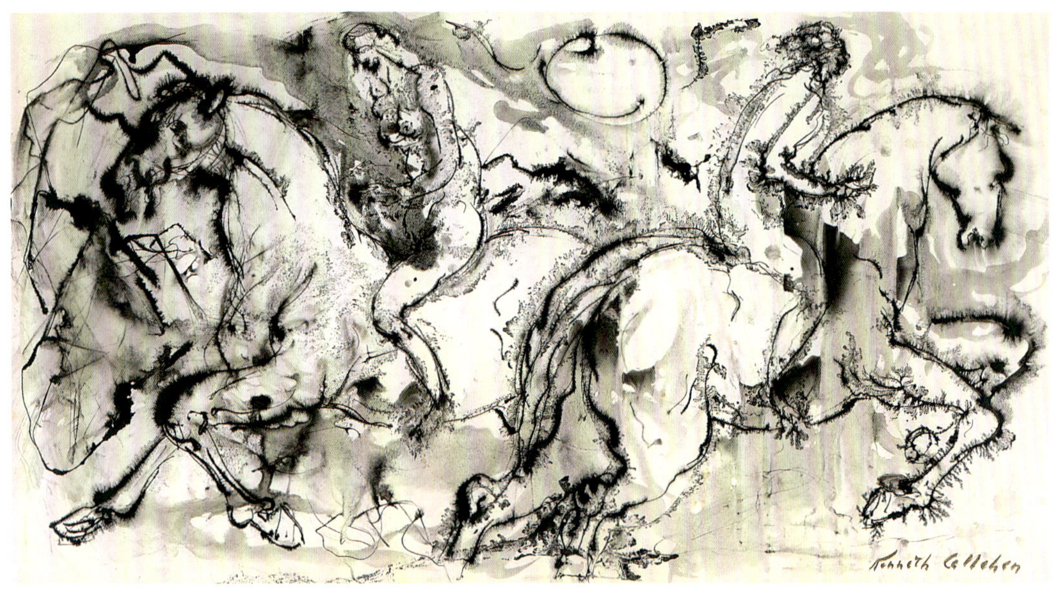

Horses and Riders, 1939
Drawing on paper
17 × 30 inches
Collection of Arlene and Harold Schnitzer

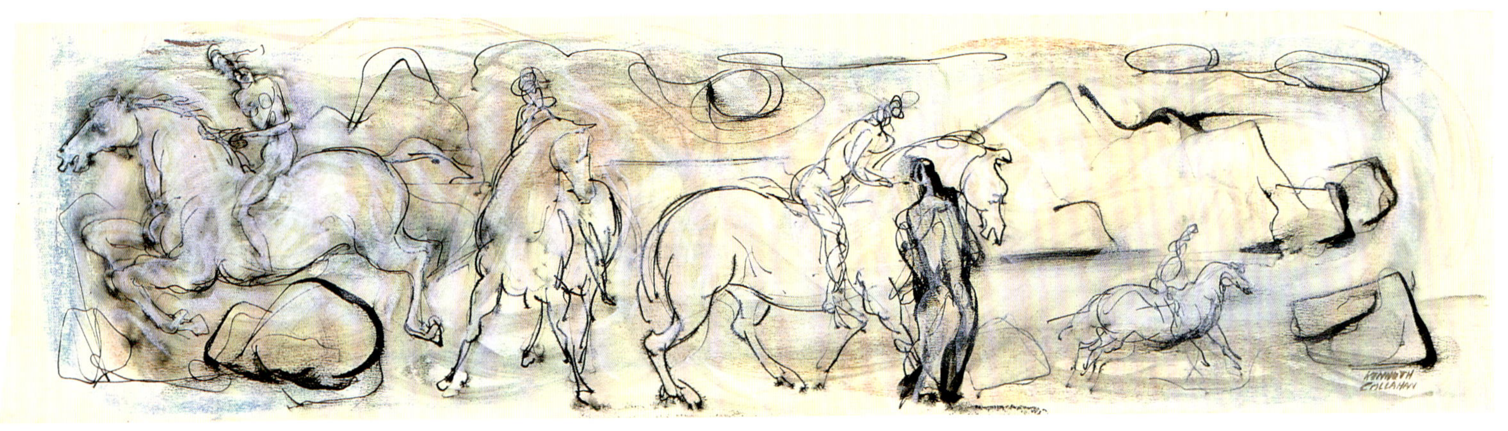

Horses and Riders, n.d.
Ink and wash on paper
6 3/8 × 24 inches
The Saint Louis Art Museum,
Eliza Macmillan Fund

OPPOSITE:
Four Horses and Riders, n.d.
Pastel on paper
40 1/2 × 13 1/2 inches
Collection of Lee and Barbara Yates

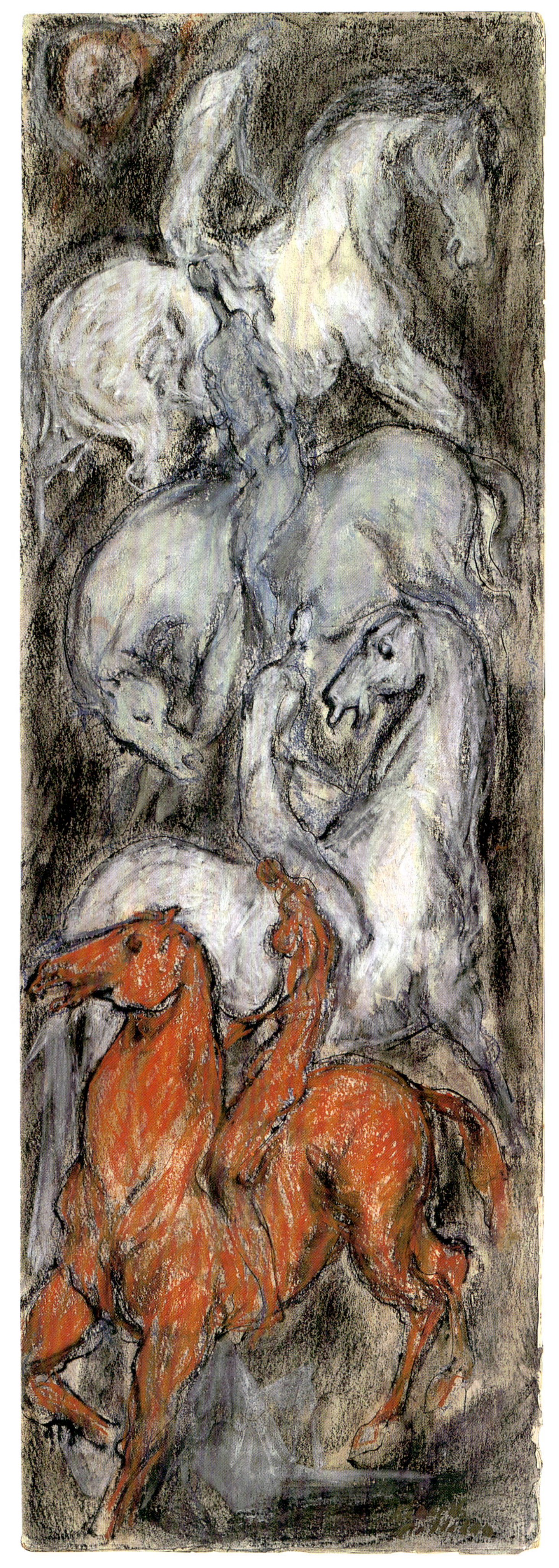

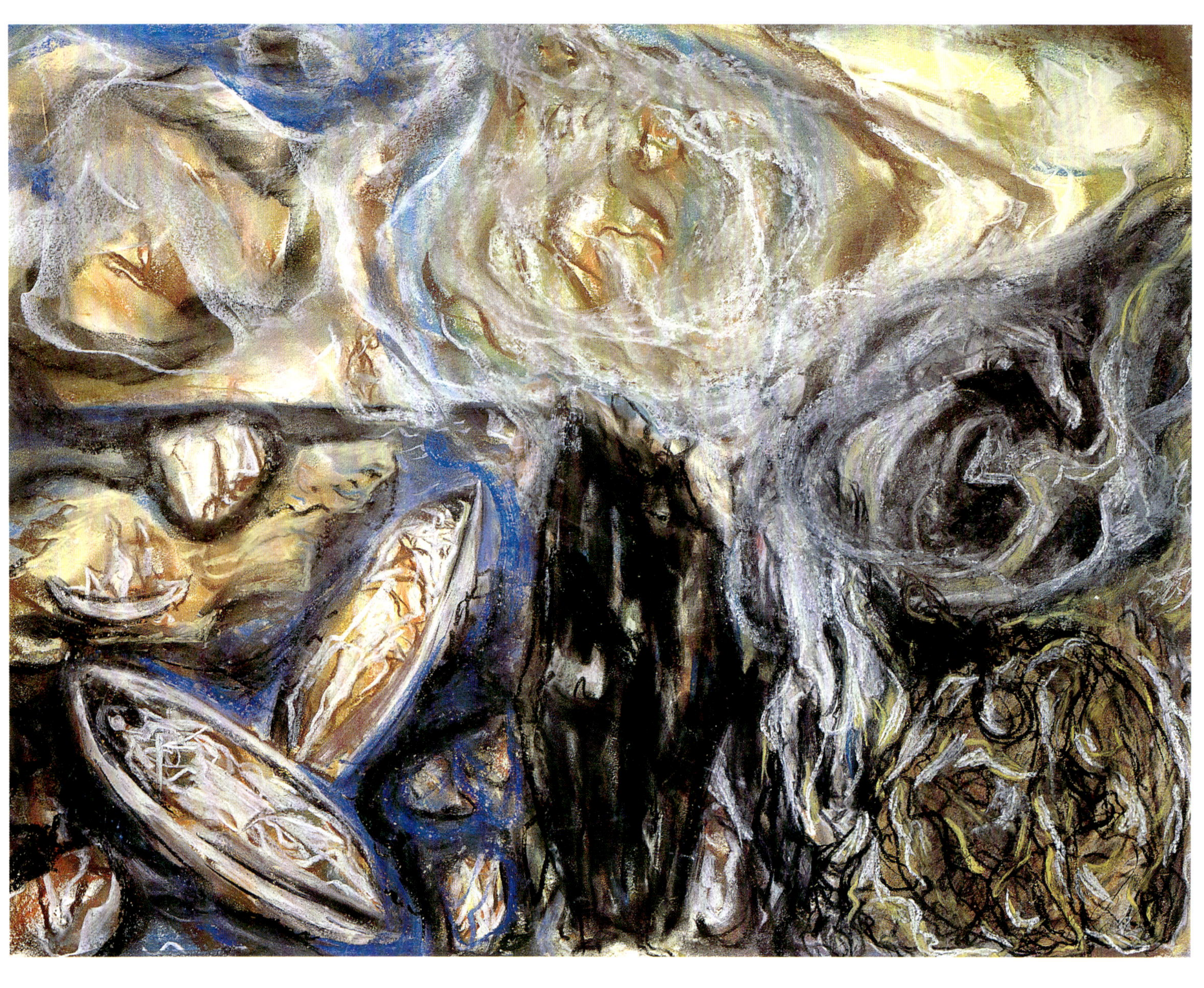

Figures and Boat (B.C.), 1940
Pastel on paper
$17^1/_2 \times 23$ inches
Collection of the Jordan and Mina Schnitzer Foundation

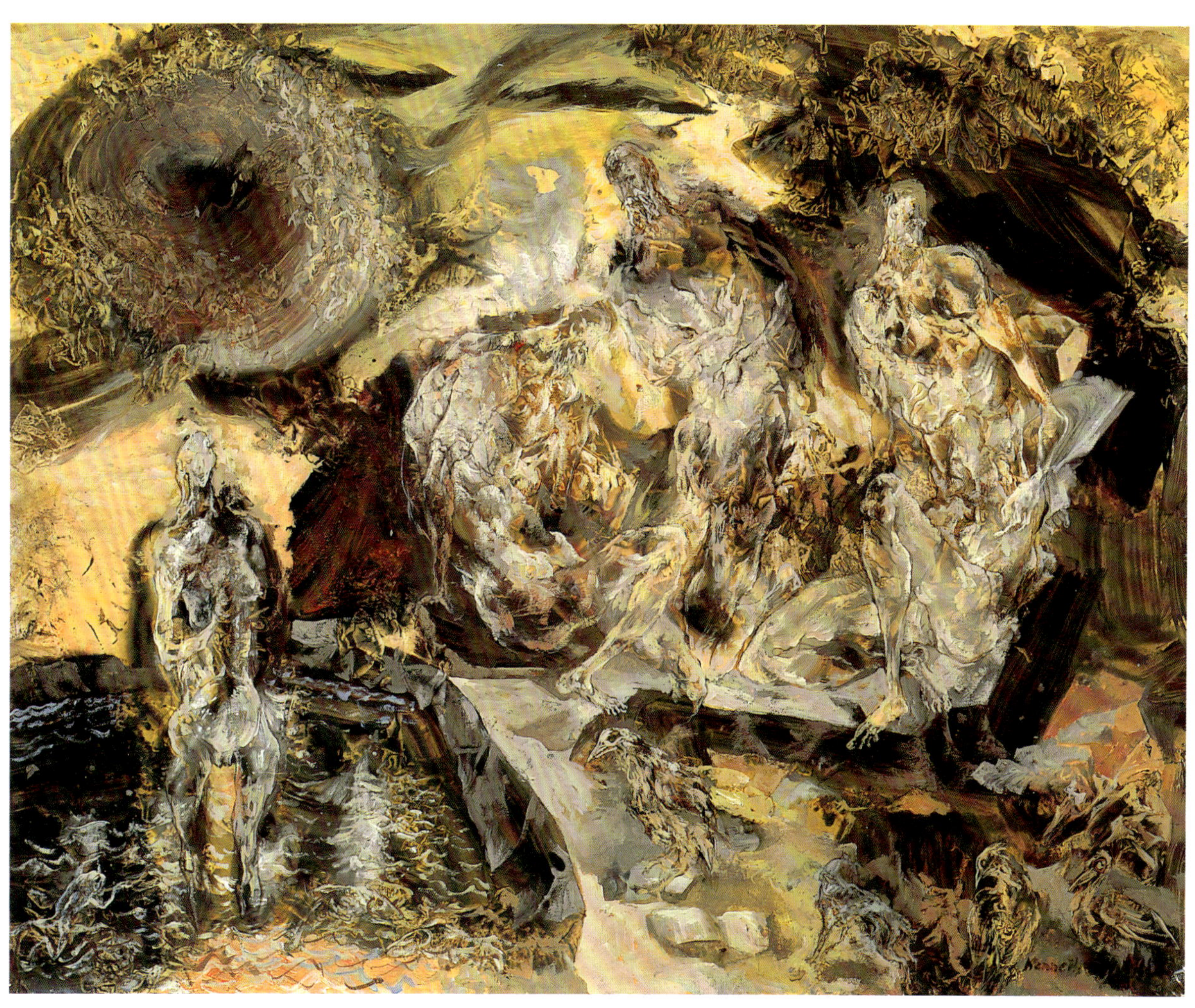

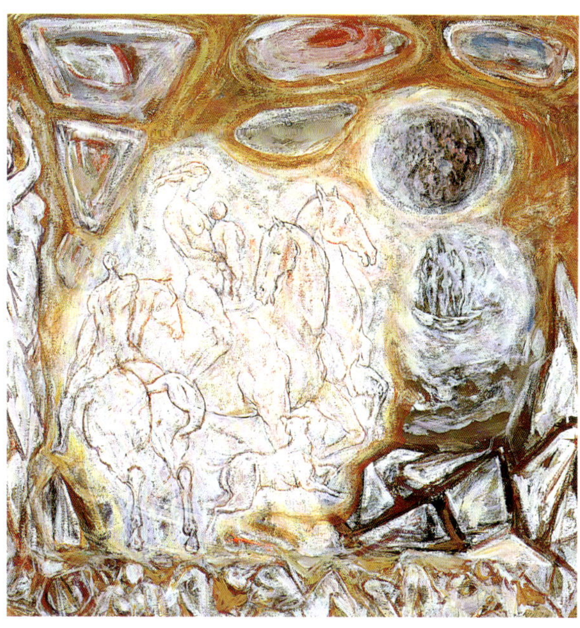

TOP:

Untitled, ca. 1940s
Tempera and oil on canvas
23 × 29 inches
Collection of Donna Benaroya

BOTTOM:

The Family, ca. 1940s
Tempera on board
15 × 15 inches
Collection of Hal and Ruth Saltzman

Houseboat and Horse, 1940
Oil on canvasboard
19 × 30 inches
Collection of Margaret and Ingolf Noto

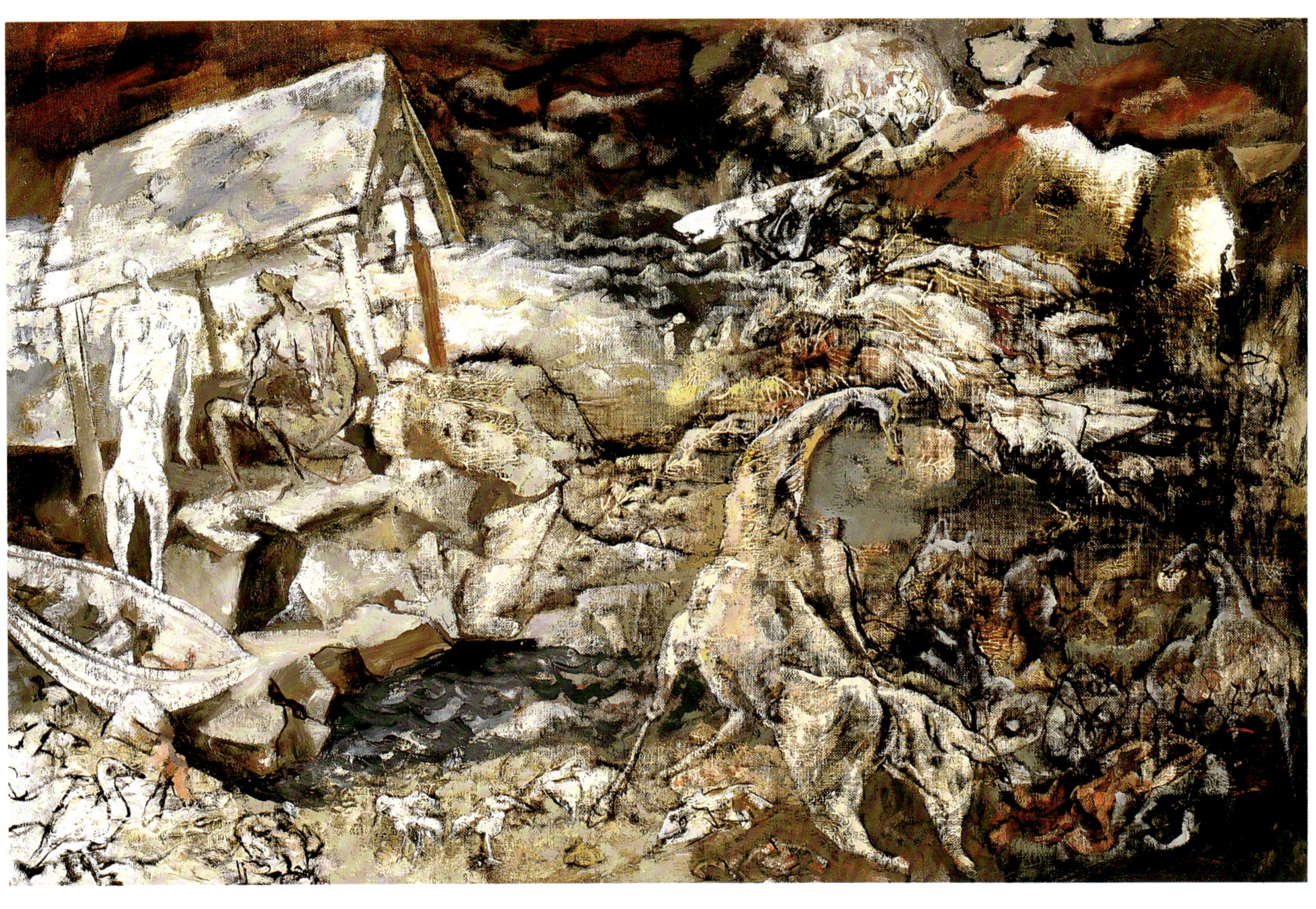

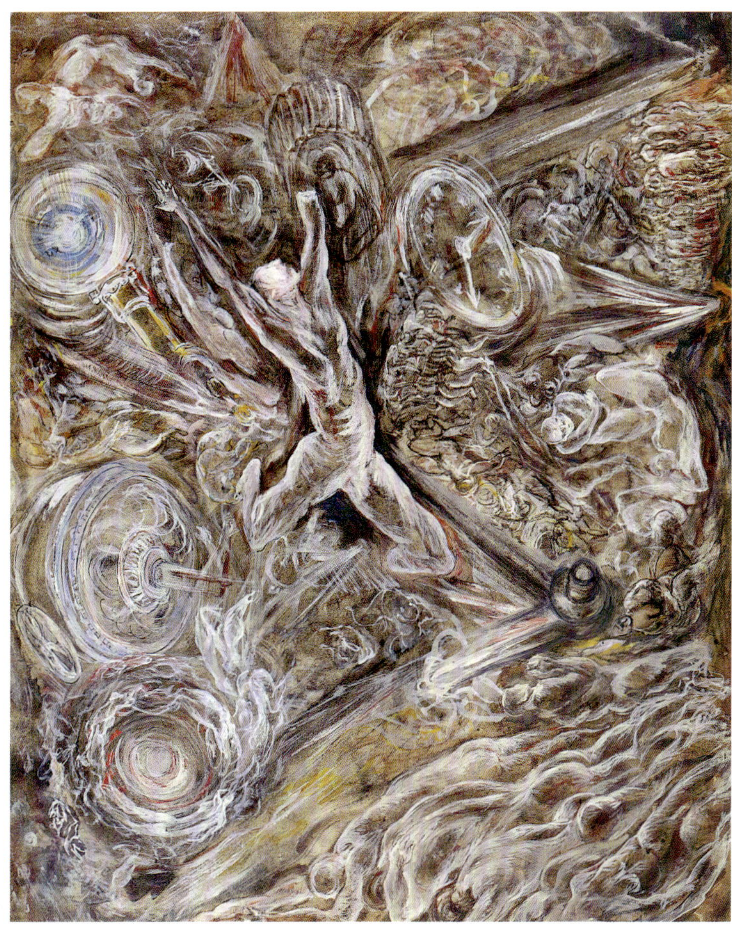

Man, Time, and the Machine, 1944
Tempera on paper
$17^{3}/_{4} \times 14^{3}/_{4}$ inches
Collection of Mikell and Brian T. Callahan

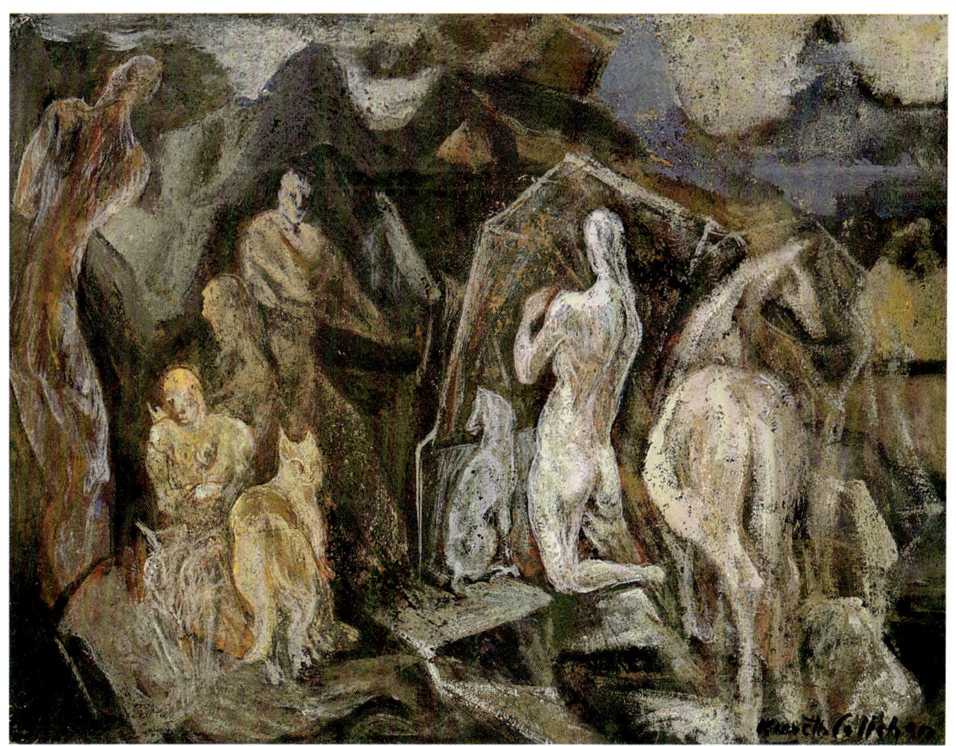

Group, 1944
Tempera on board
9 × 12 inches
Collection of Mr. and Mrs. Robert M. Sarkis

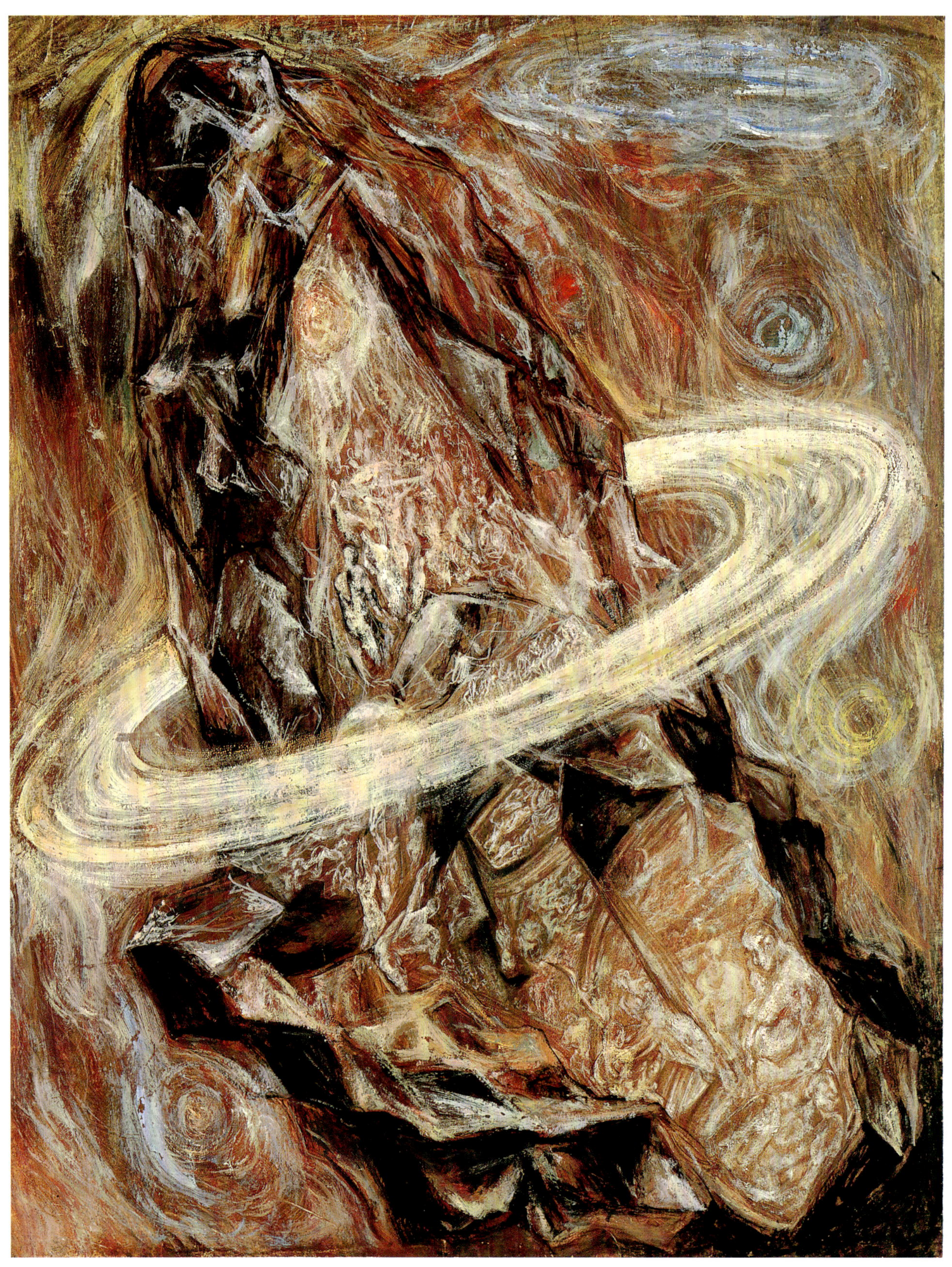

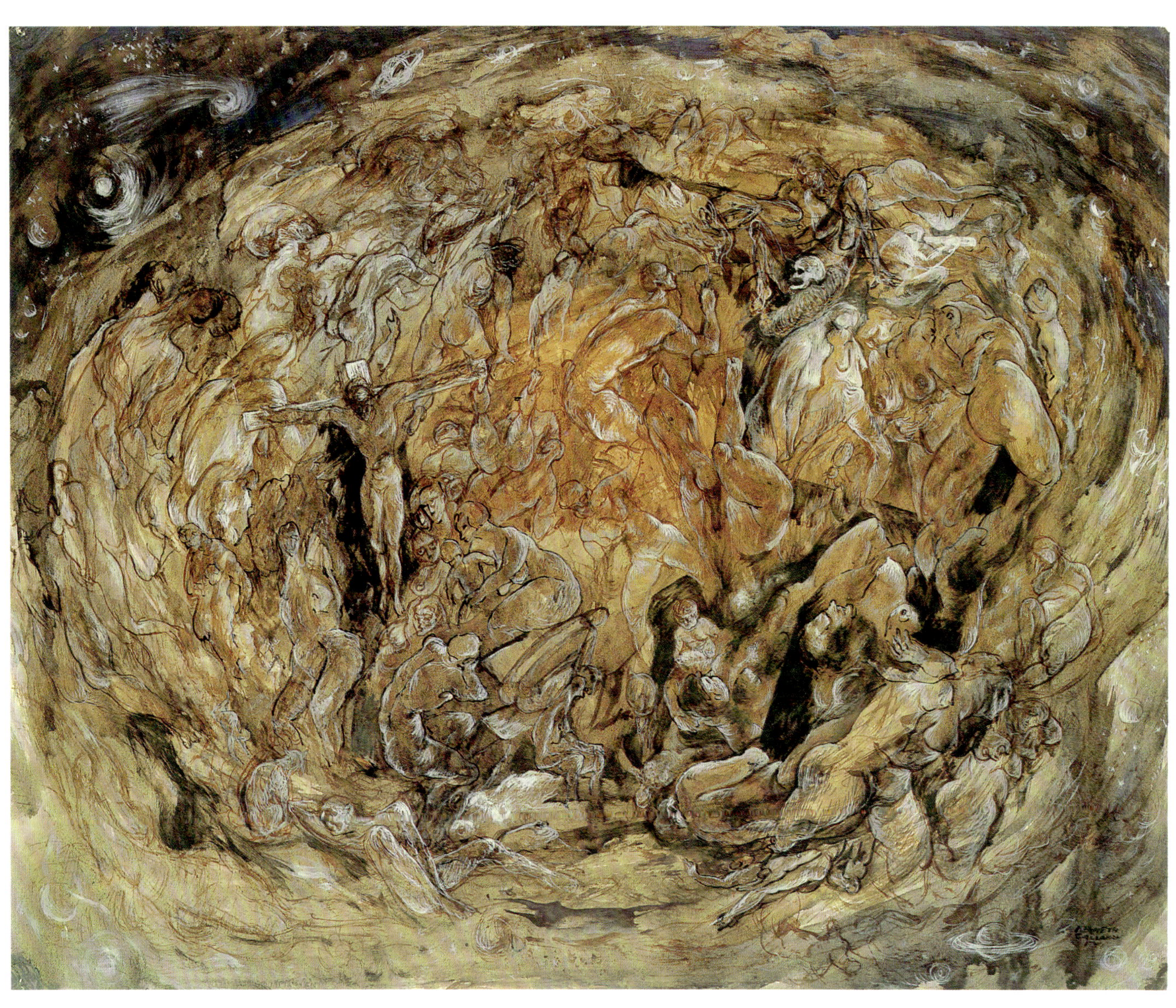

OPPOSITE:

The Ring #2, 1944
Tempera on paper
28 × 23 inches
Collection of John E. and Mary Jo Morse, Vancouver, Washington

Revolving World, 1944
Gouache on paper
14 1/8 × 18 1/2 inches
The Metropolitan Museum of Art, Gift of Francis Henry Taylor, 1949, 49.139

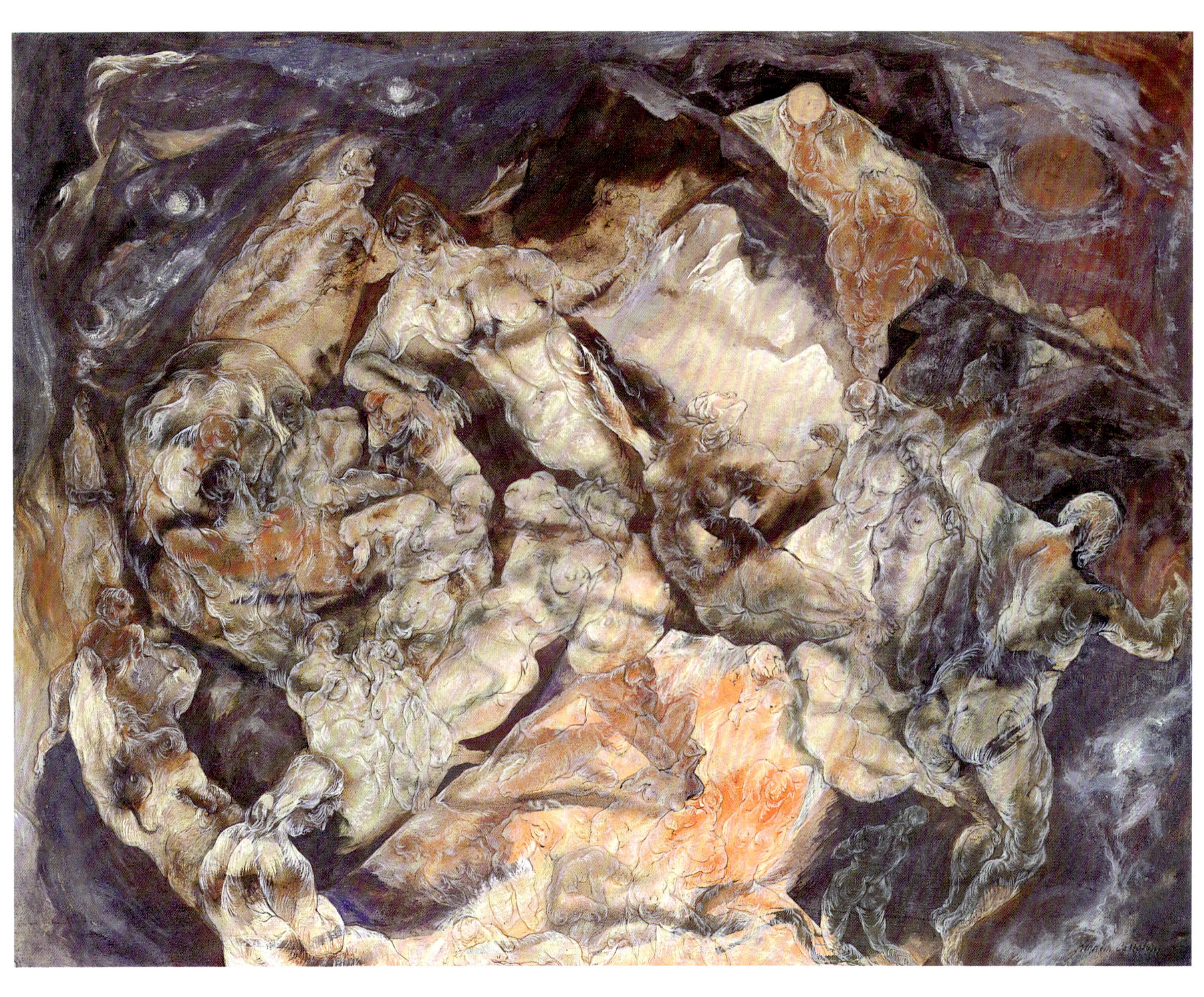

Conversation, ca. 1944–45
Watercolor and gouache heightened with white on paperboard
$17^{3}/_{8} \times 20^{1}/_{4}$ inches
Brooklyn Museum of Art, Museum Collection Fund

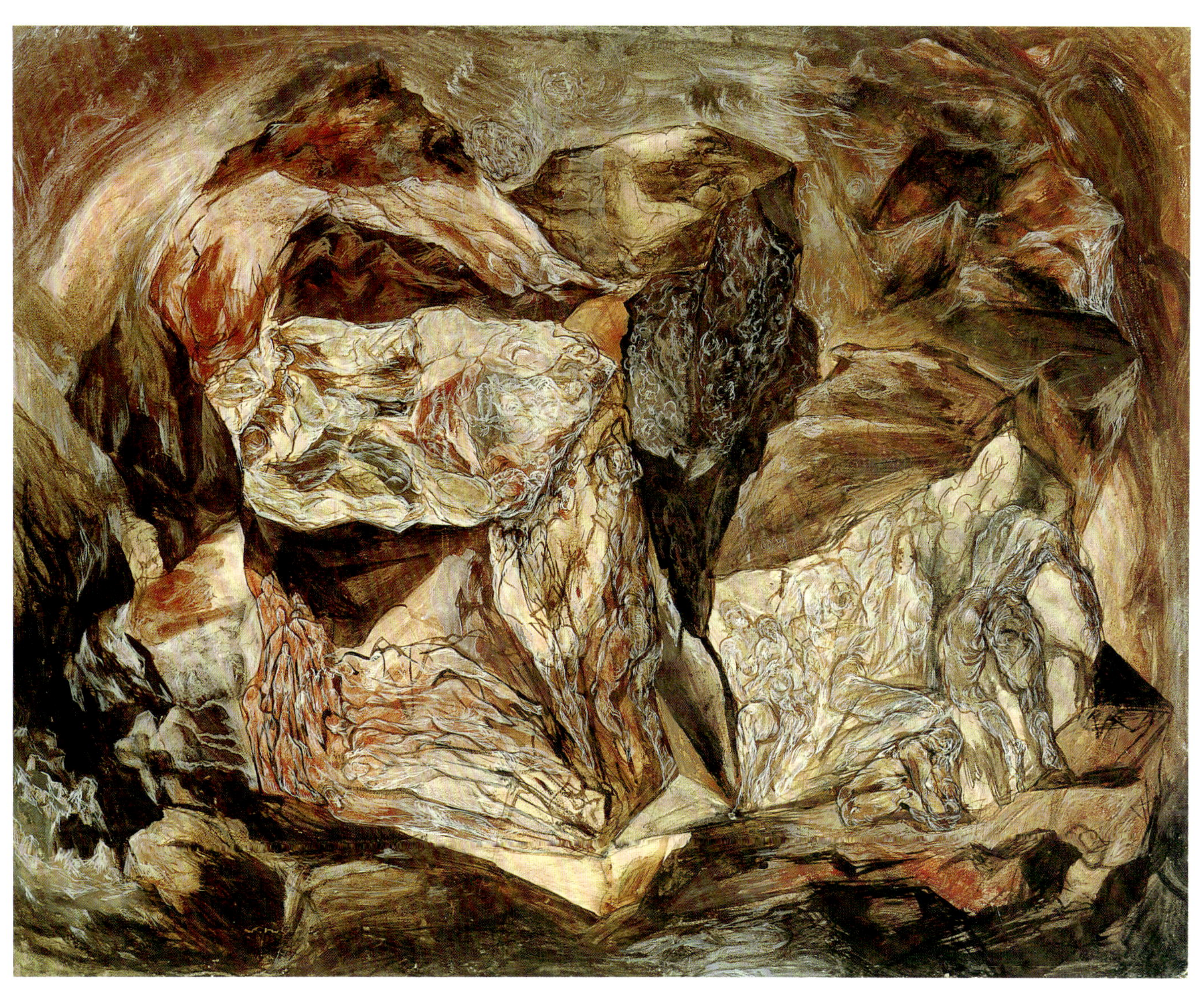

Dwellers in the Cliffs, ca. 1946
Tempera on canvasboard
17 1/8 × 22 inches
Munson-Williams-Proctor Arts Institute, Museum of Art, Utica, New York, Edward W. Root Bequest, 57.110.1

Challenge and Response, ca. 1947
Tempera on composition board
22 × 34¼ inches
Henry Art Gallery, University of Washington, Seattle, Purchase 50.1

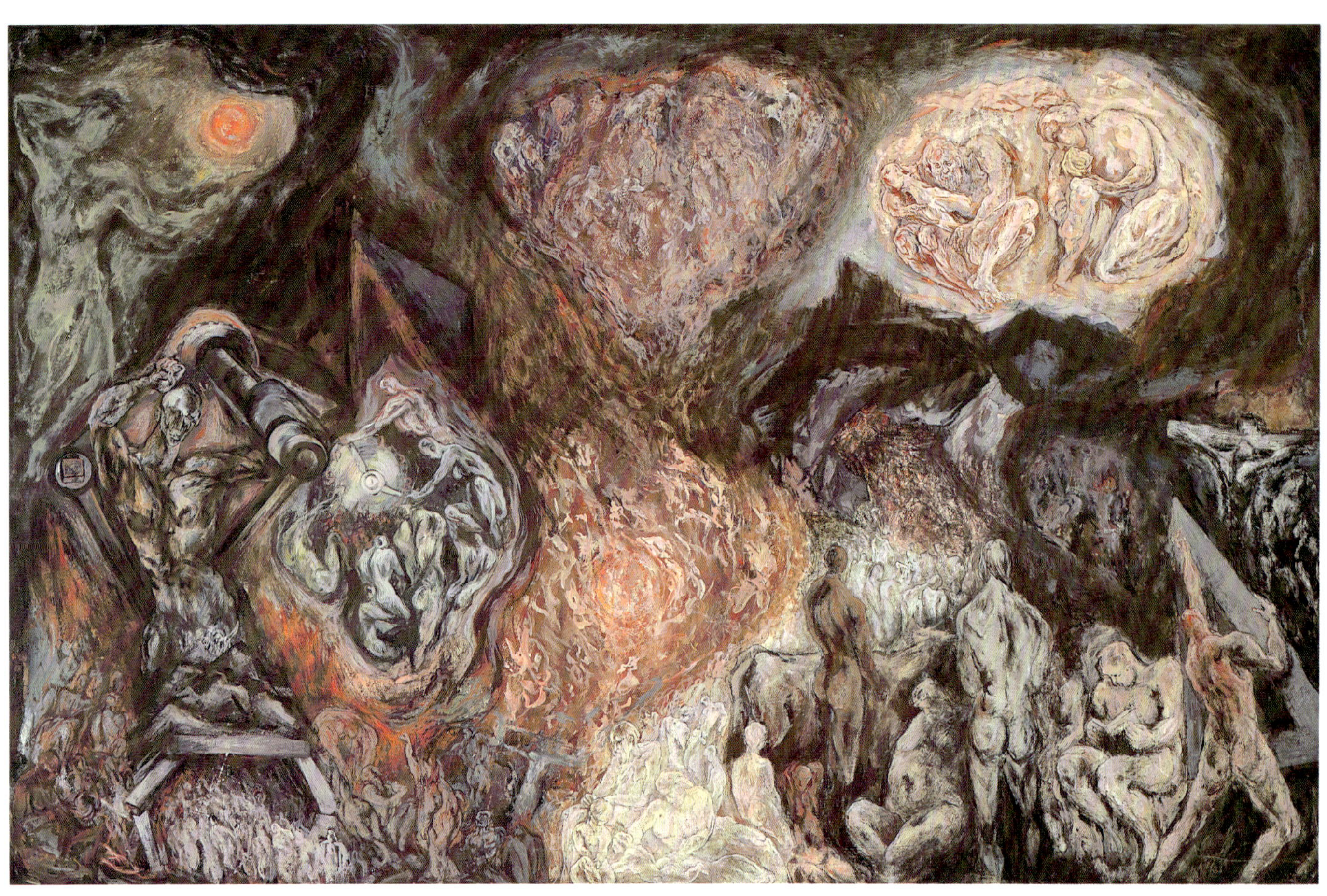

OPPOSITE:

Prism and Dark Globe, 1946
Tempera on board
20⅝ × 35½ inches
Courtesy, Foster/White Gallery

The Quest, ca. 1946
Oil on canvas
28½ × 44½ inches
University of Oregon Museum of Art, Virginia Haseltine Collection of Pacific Northwest Art

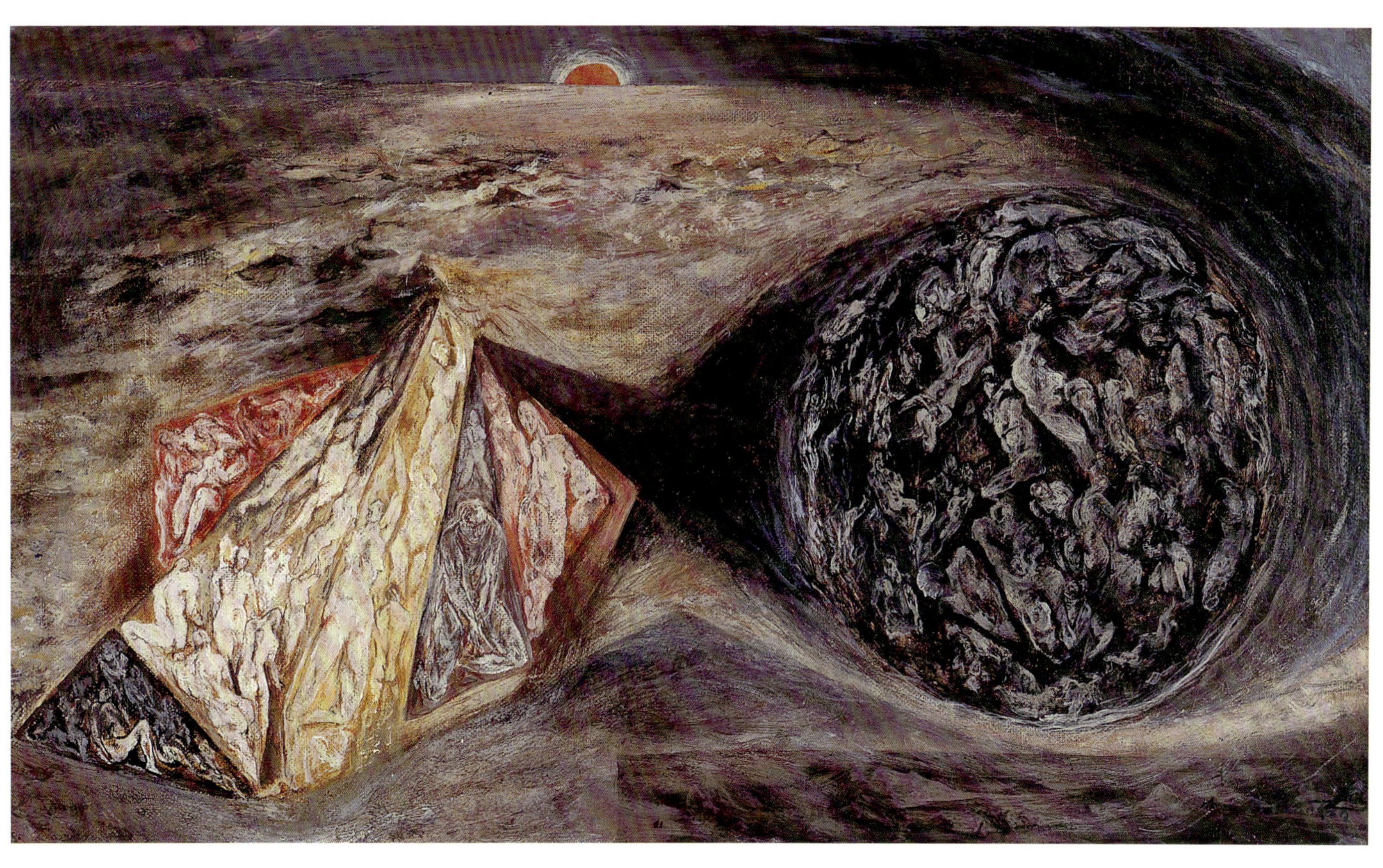

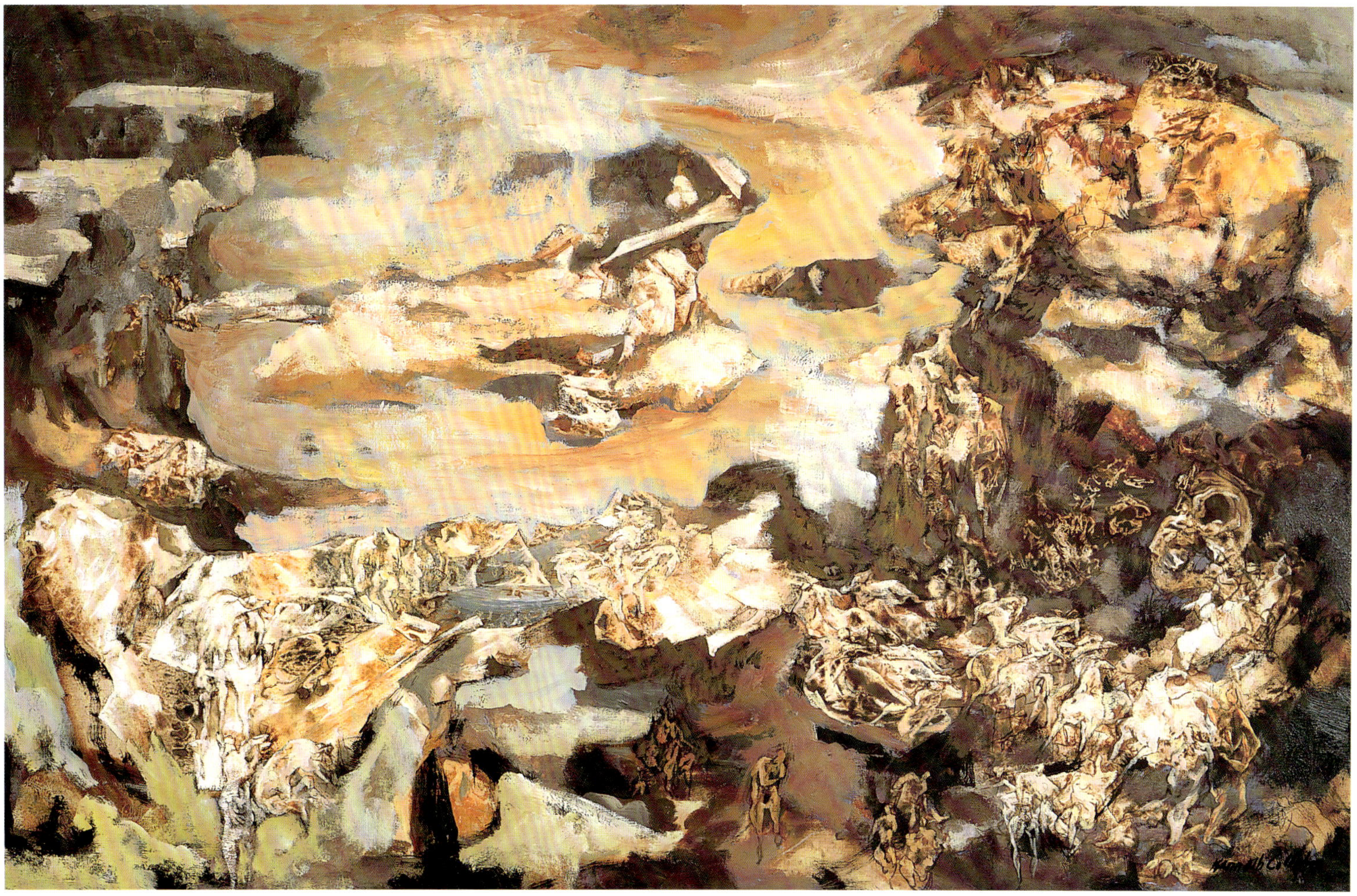

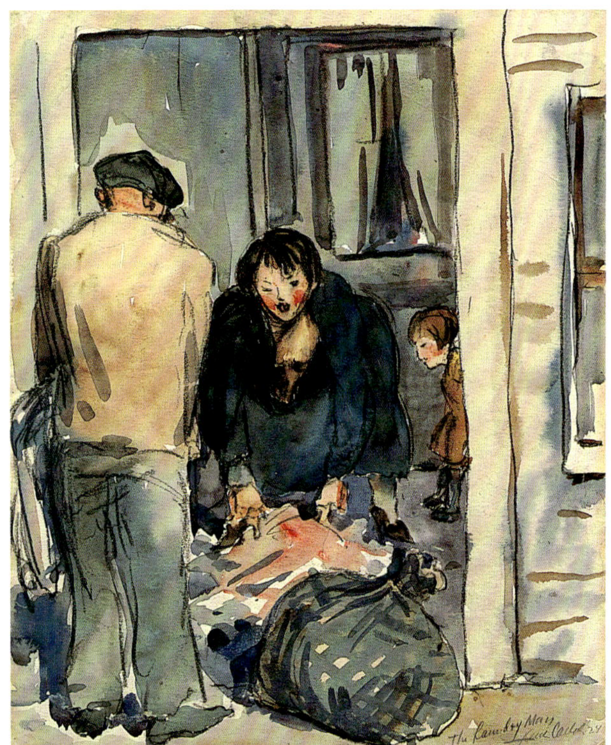

The Laundry Man, 1947
Watercolor on paper
$10^1/_2 \times 9^1/_2$ inches
Private collection

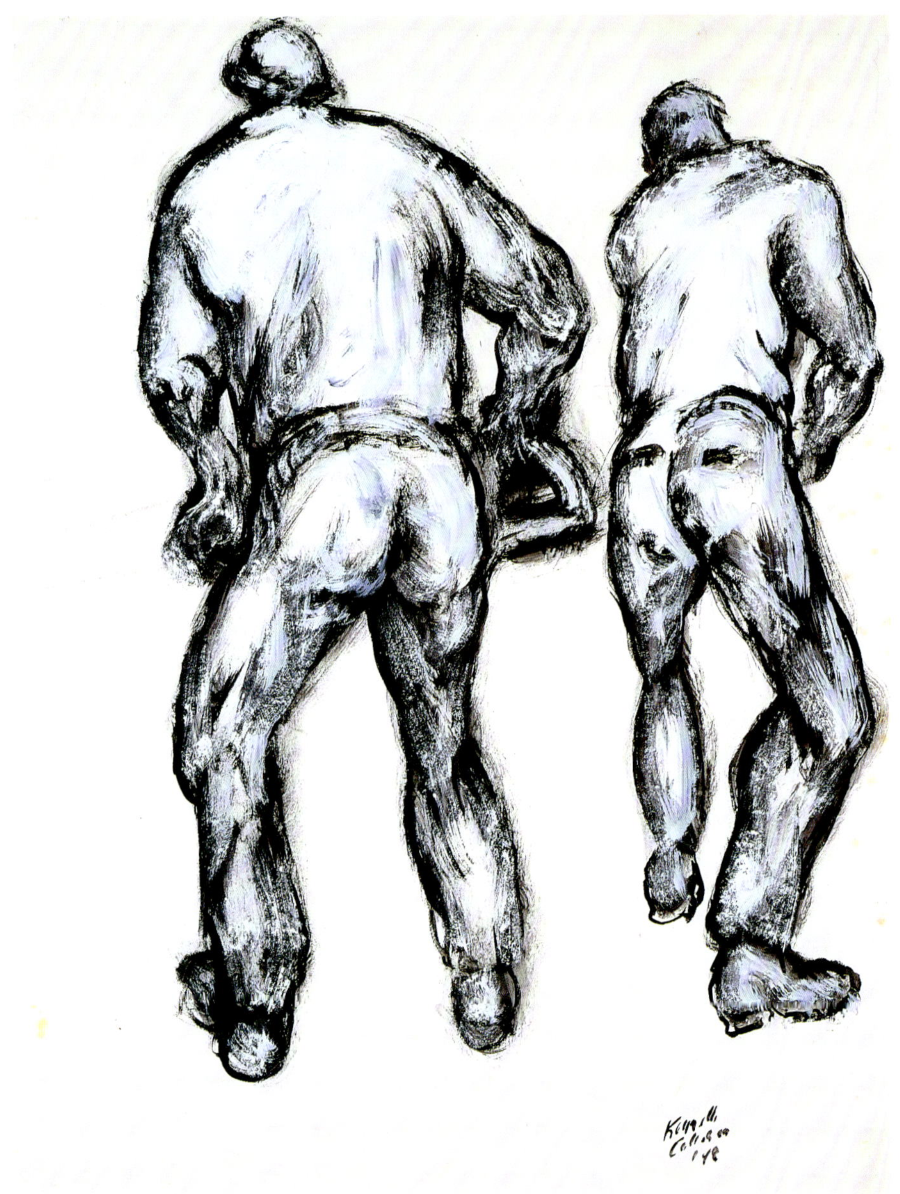

Two Workmen, 1948
Ink and tempera on paper
$26 \times 21^3/_4$ inches
Collection of Neil Goldschmidt and
Ms. Diana Snowden

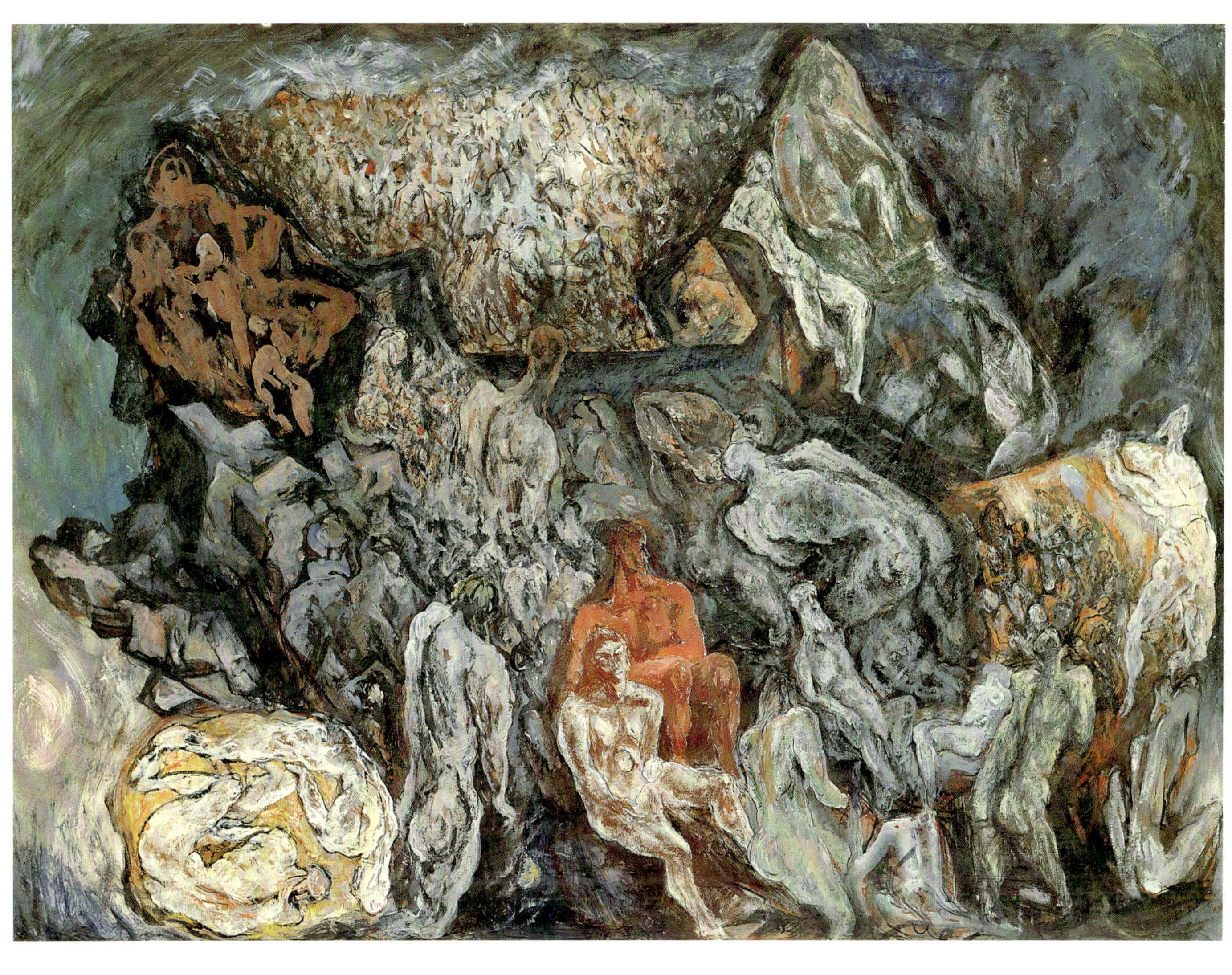

Journey on a Star, 1947
Oil and egg tempera on paper mounted on cardboard
20 × 30 inches
The Phillips Collection, Washington, D.C.

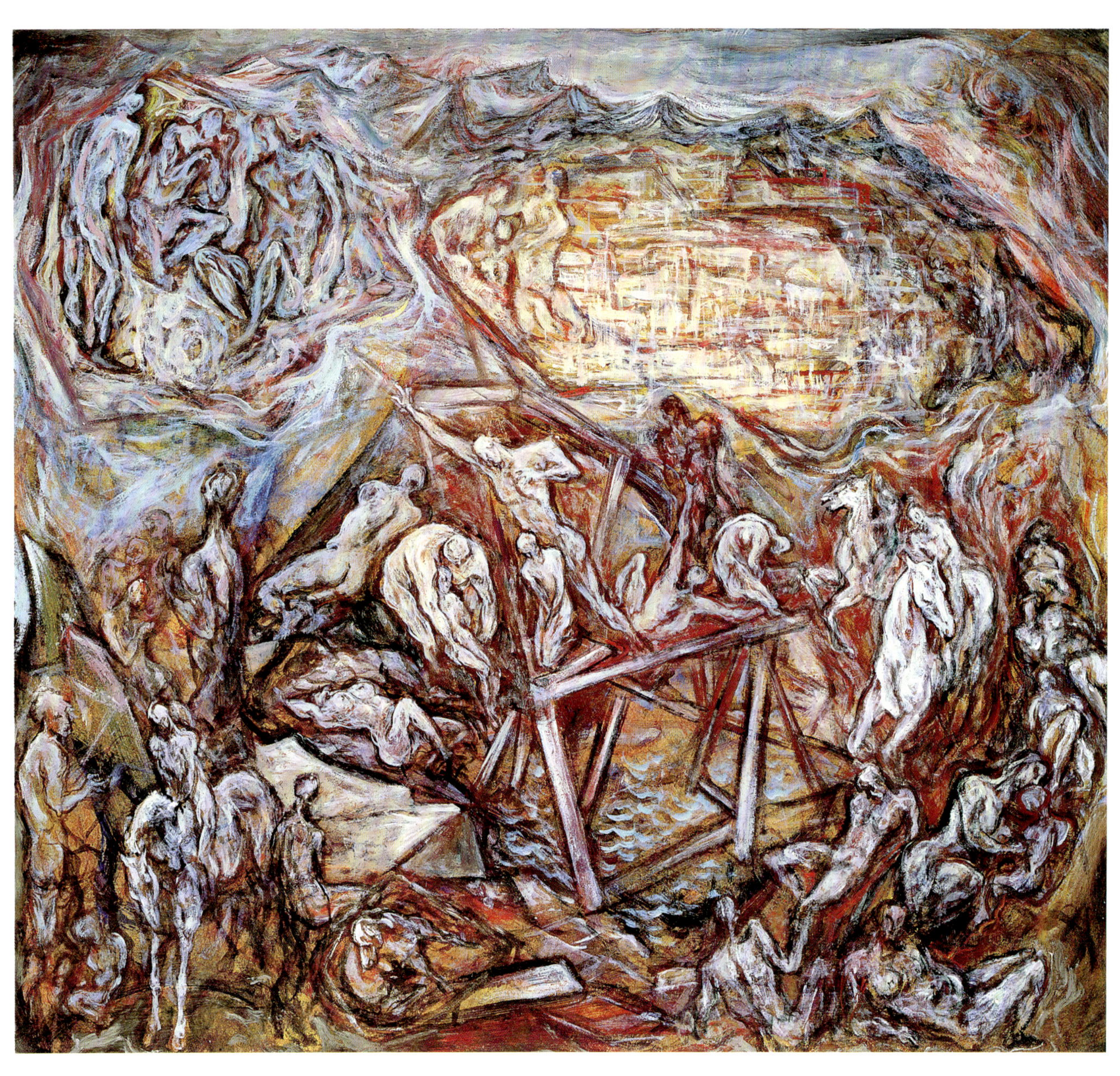

Bridge, 1948
Oil on Masonite
20½ × 23½ inches
Collection of Margaret and Ingolf Noto

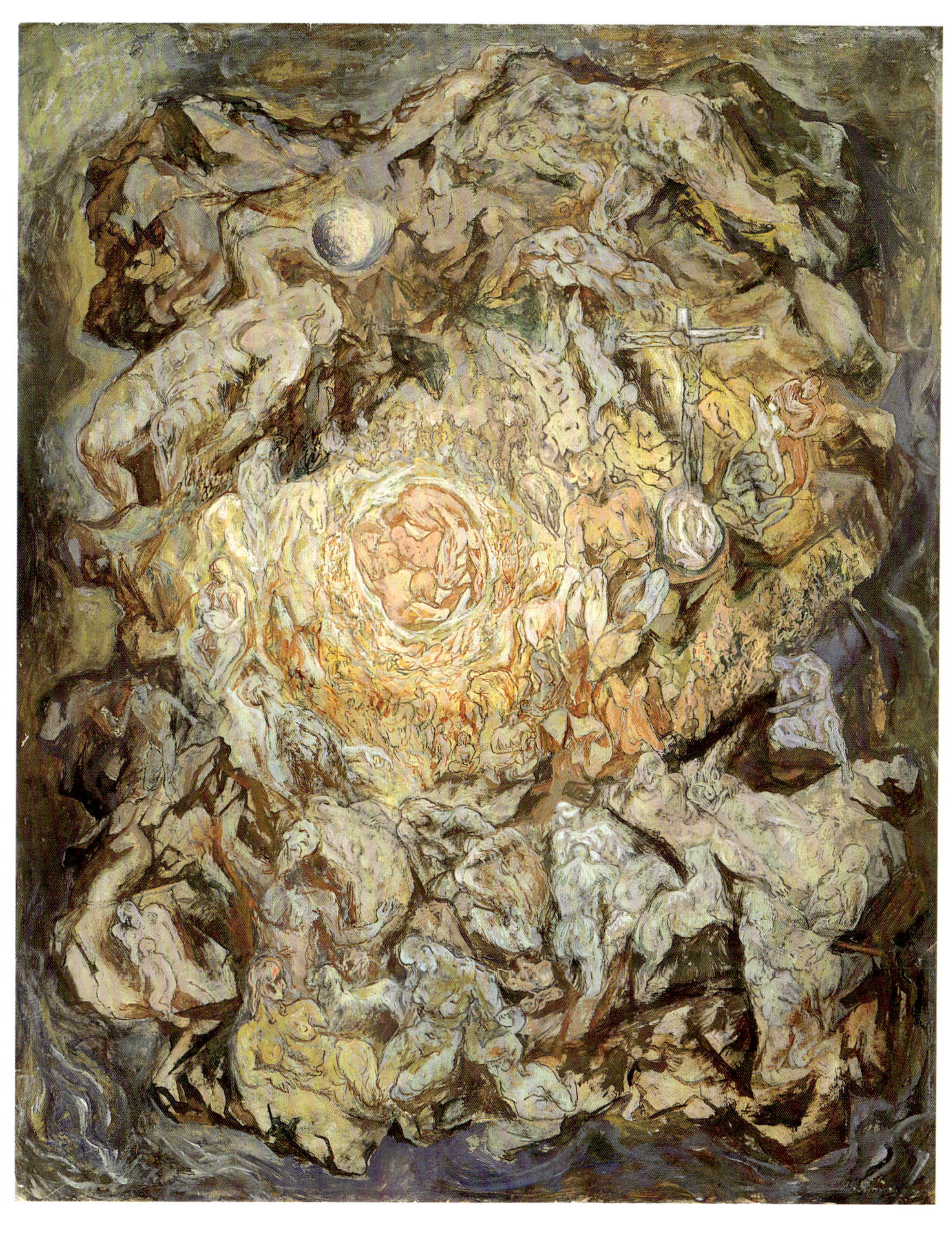

Rock Fragments, 1948
Tempera on panel
17¾ × 14½ inches
Collection of Fred Goldberg

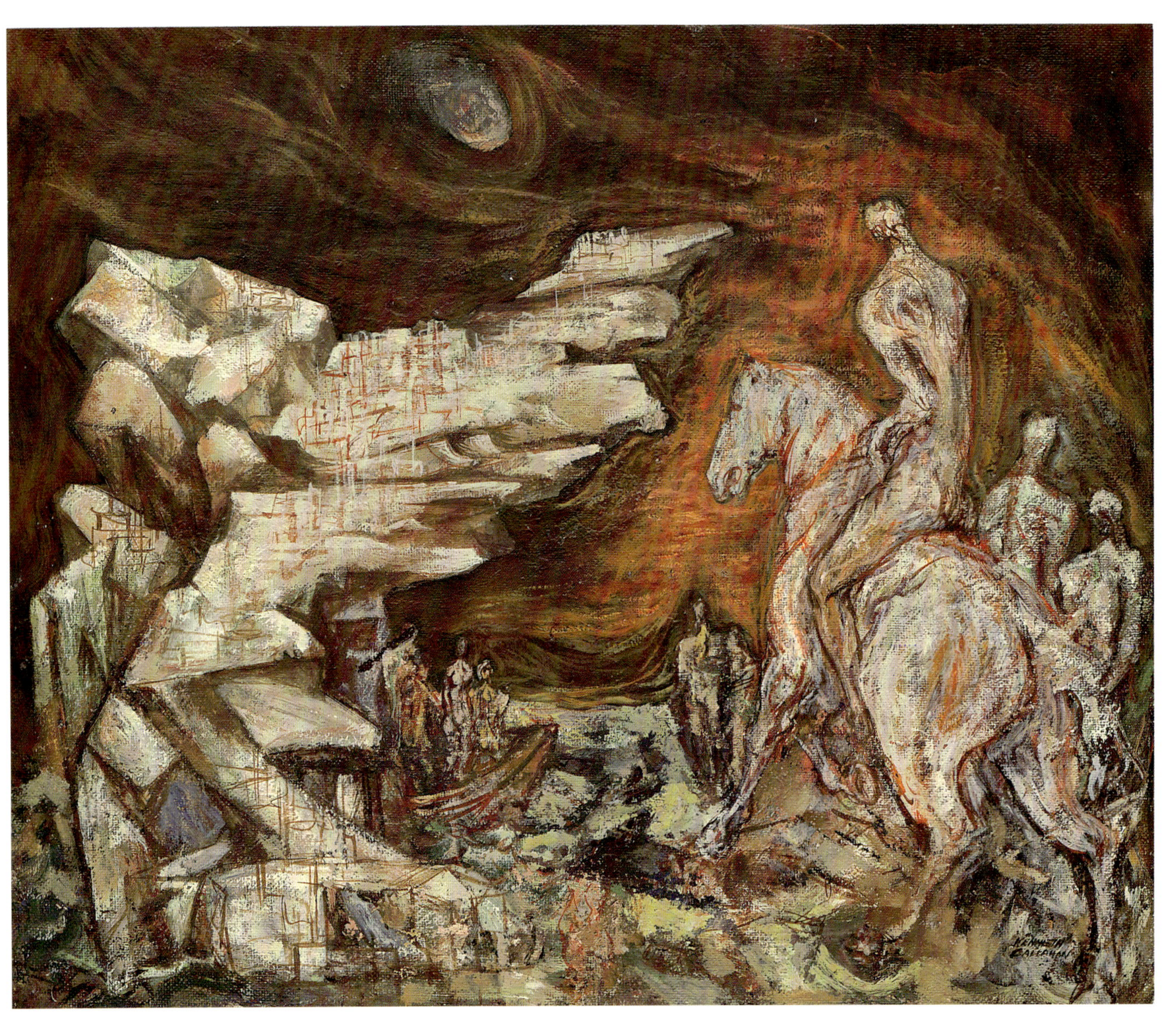

Search #3, 1948
Tempera on Masonite
23 × 27¾ inches
Collection of Charles and Alice Ross

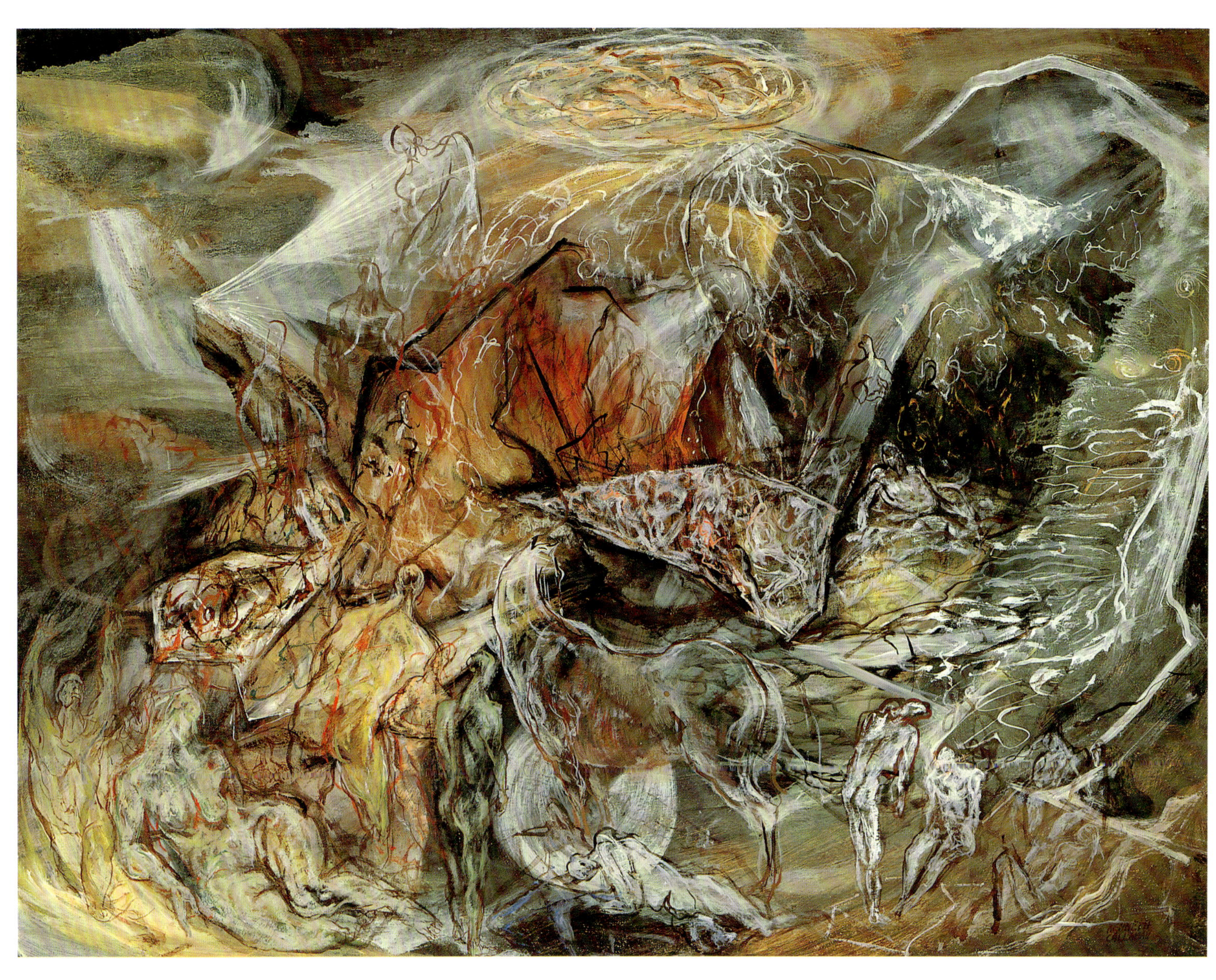

The Tides, 1948–49
Oil on plywood
$23^{3}/_{4} \times 31^{5}/_{8}$ inches
Pennsylvania Academy of the Fine Arts, Philadelphia,
John Lambert Fund, 1950.4

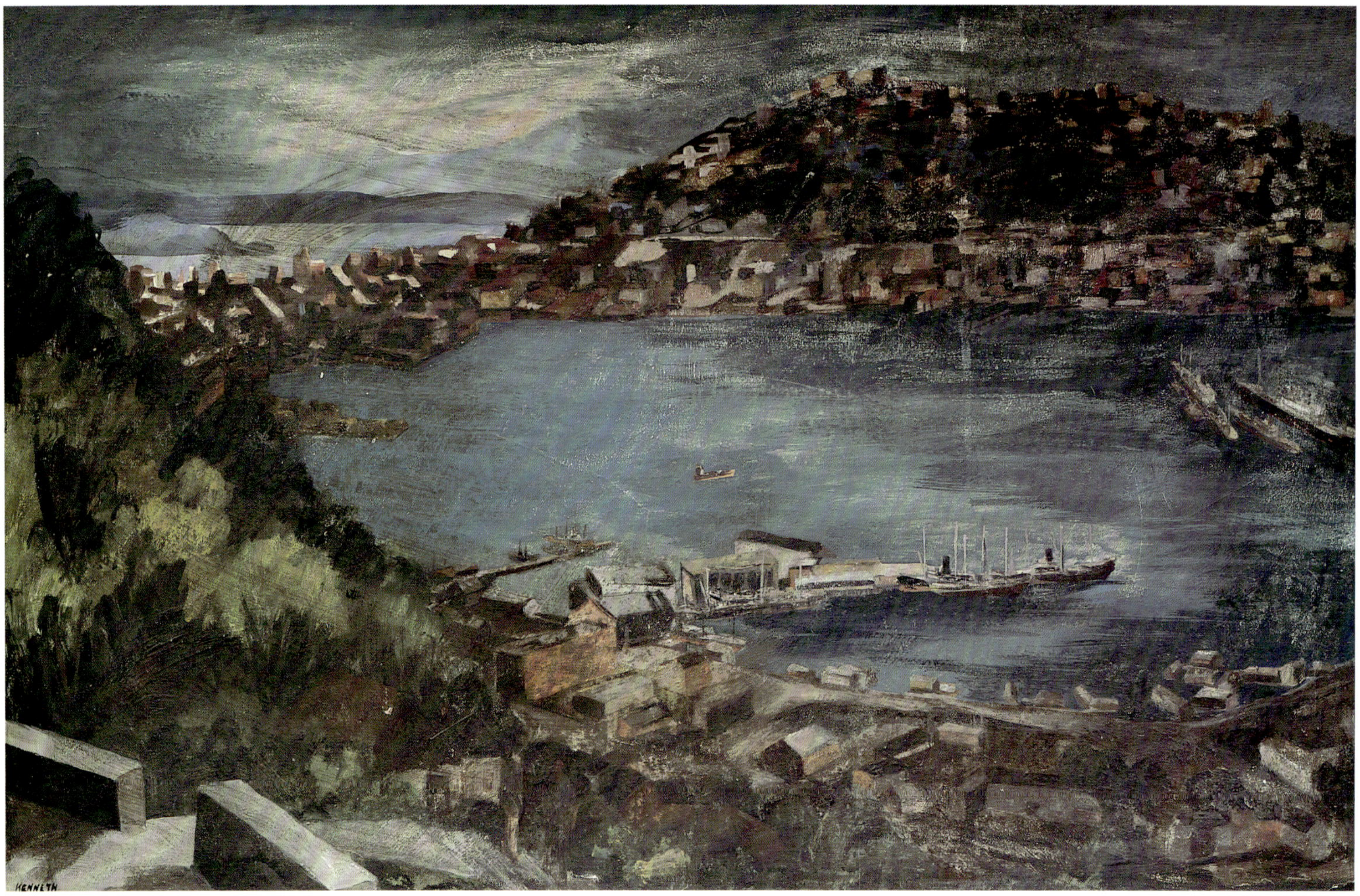

Lake Union from Capitol Hill, 1949
Tempera on board
28 × 45 inches
Collection of John and Irene Tanino

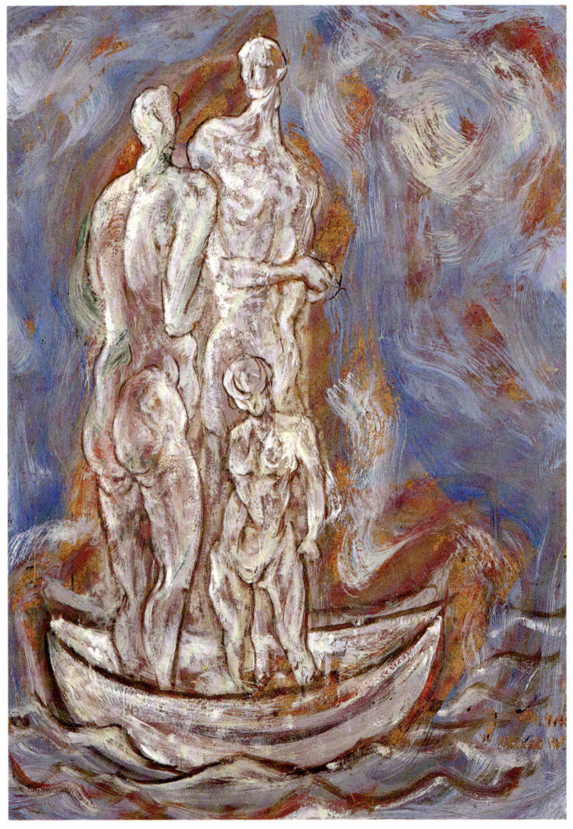

Untitled, ca. 1949
Tempera on hard board
8½ × 11½ inches
Collection of Mikell and Brian T. Callahan

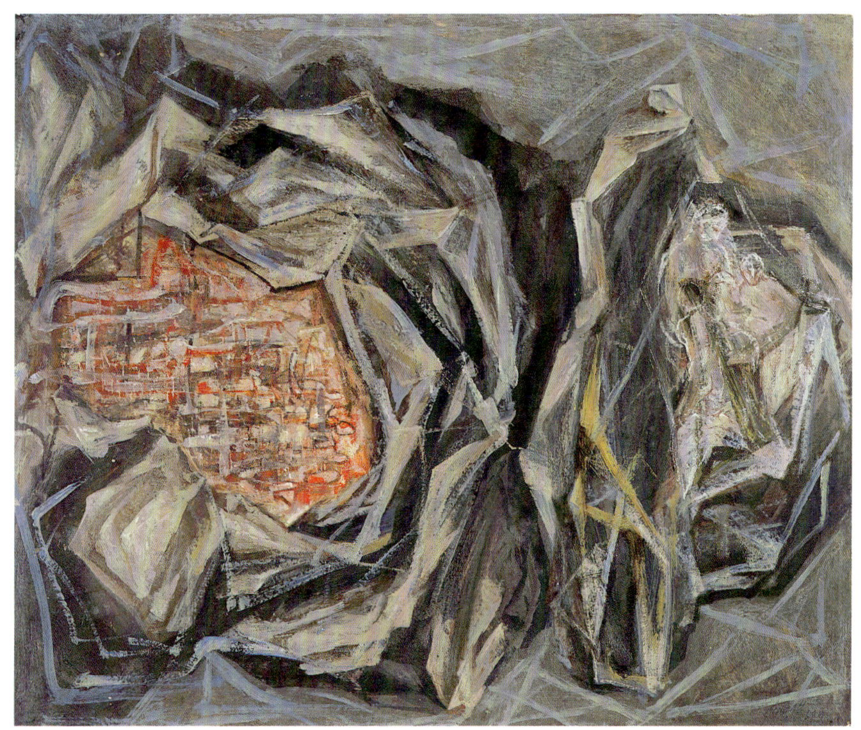

The City, n.d.
Oil on fiber board
$14\frac{5}{8} \times 18$ inches
Addison Gallery of American Art, Phillips Academy, Andover, Massachusetts

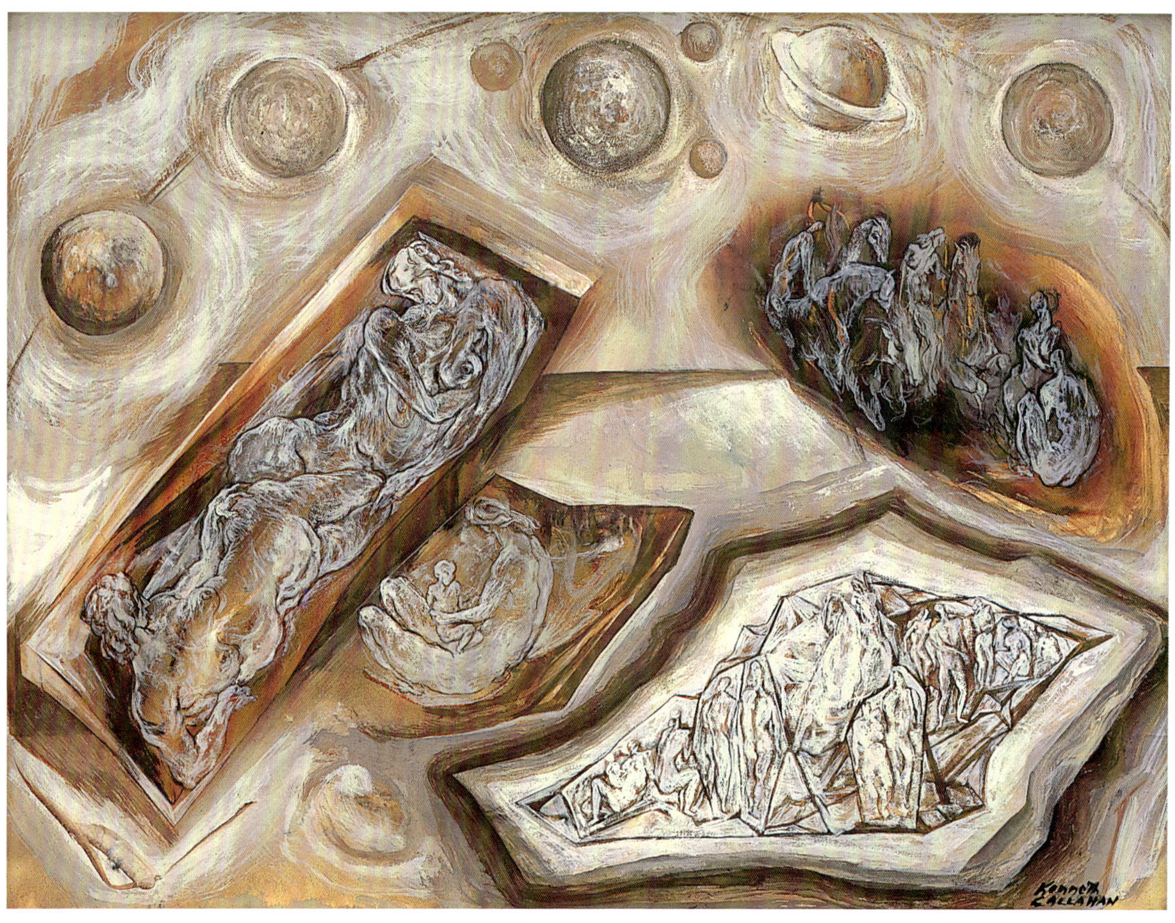

Unknown Sphere, 1949
Tempera on panel
$16\frac{3}{8} \times 22$ inches
Collection of Victoria Ivarsson

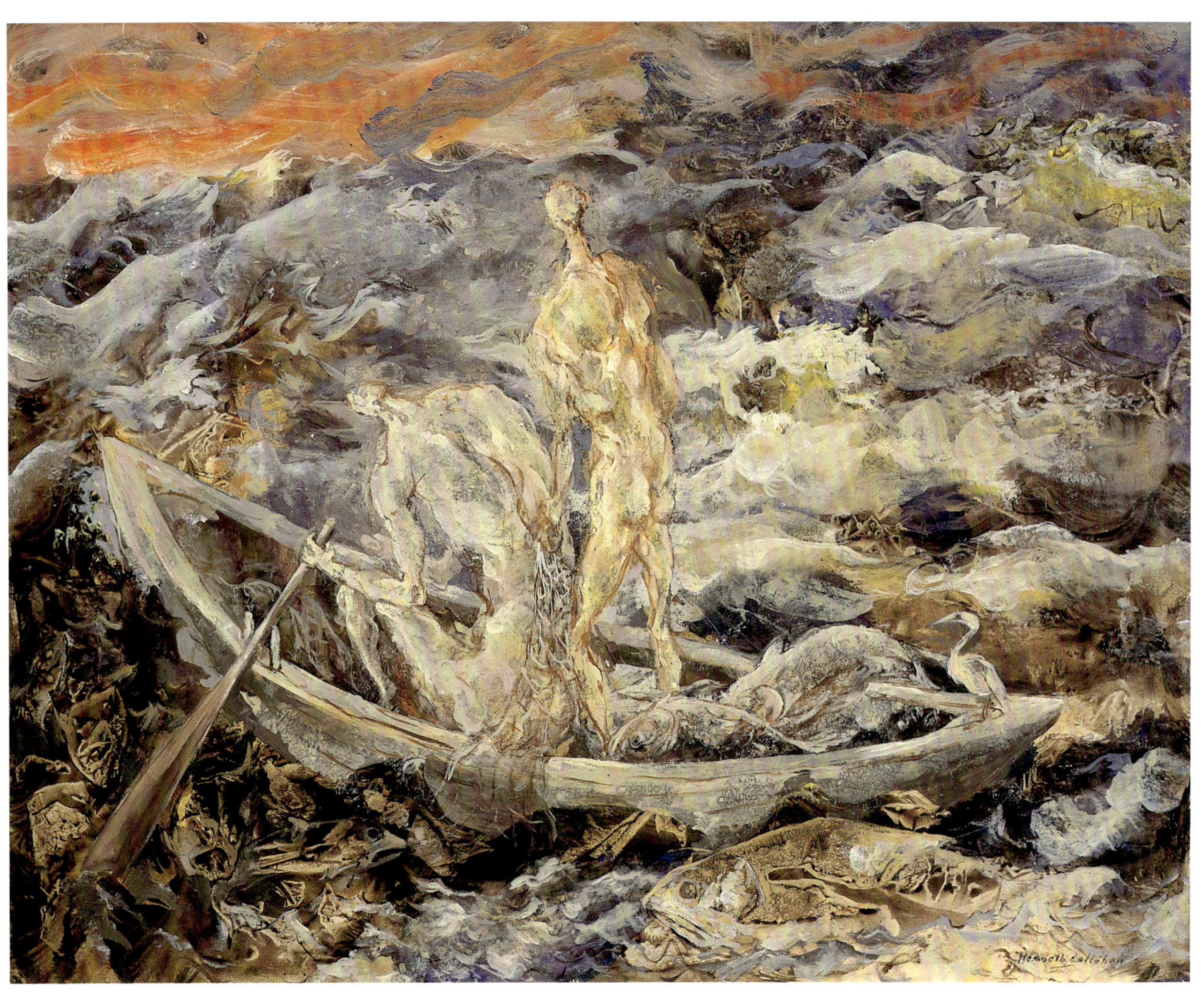

Two Fishermen, ca. 1950s
Tempera and oil on panel
23 × 29 inches
Collection of Alvin and Jacqueline Goldfarb

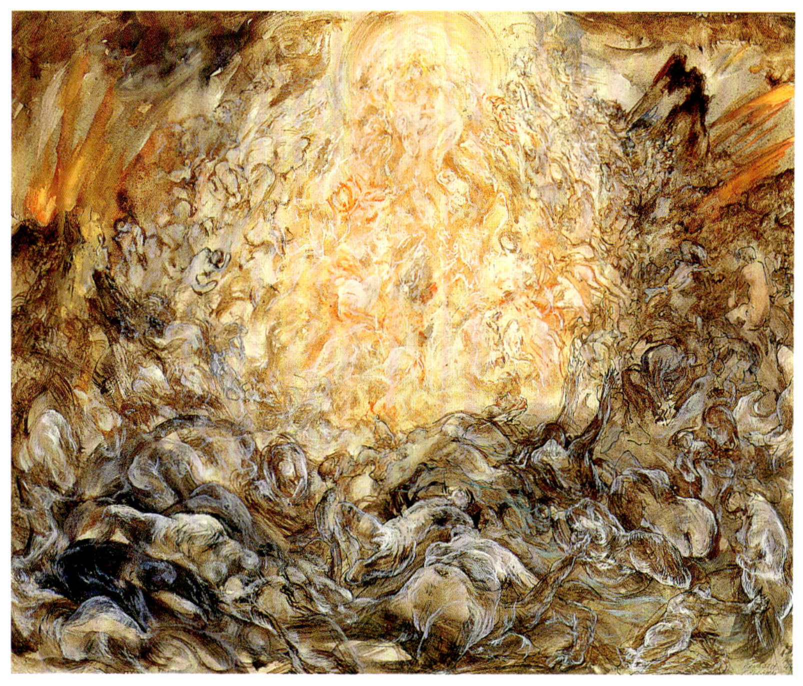

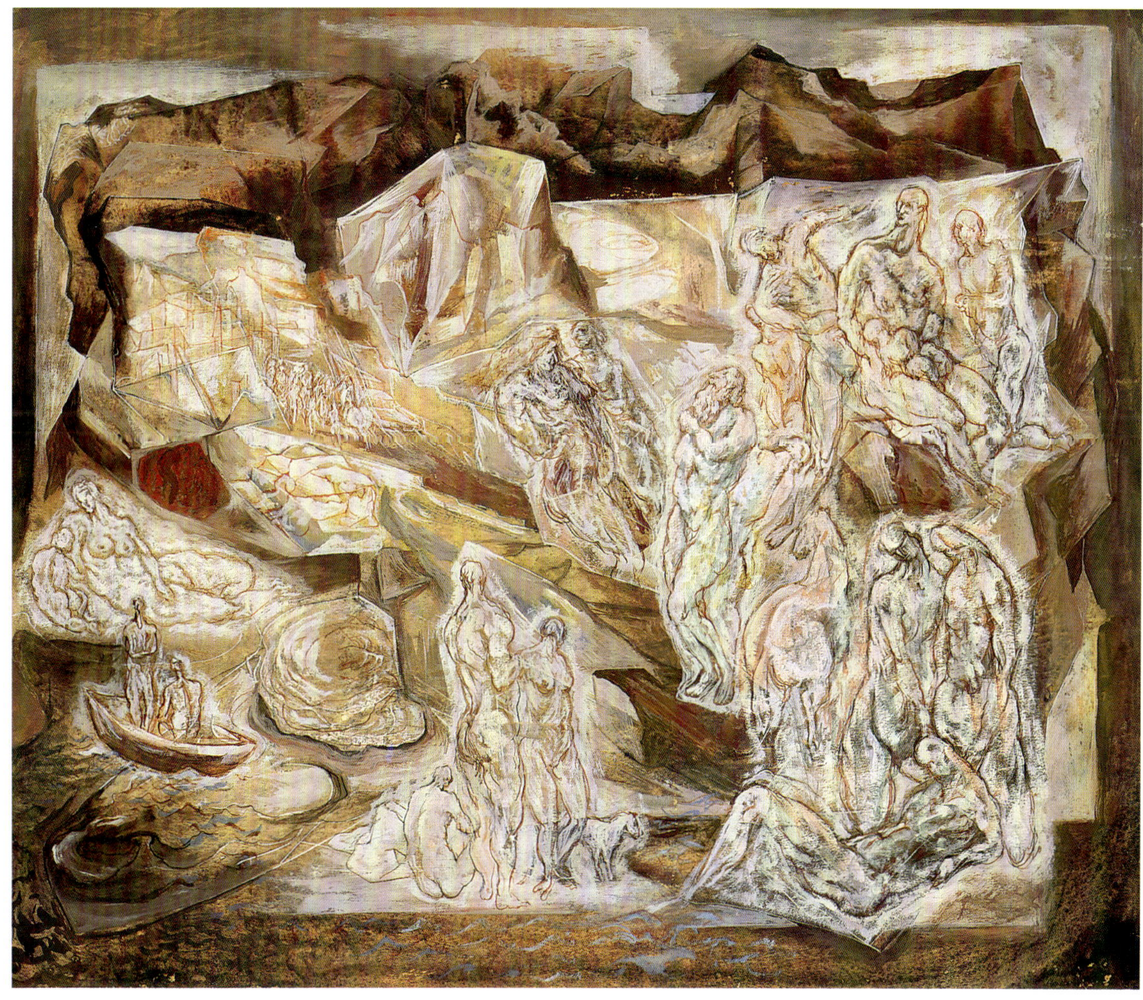

TOP:

Untitled, ca. 1950s
Tempera on board
13¾ × 17½ inches
Collection of Richard and Deanne Rubinstein

BOTTOM:

Crystalline World, 1953
Tempera on panel
20 × 24 inches
Collection of Alvin and Jacqueline Goldfarb

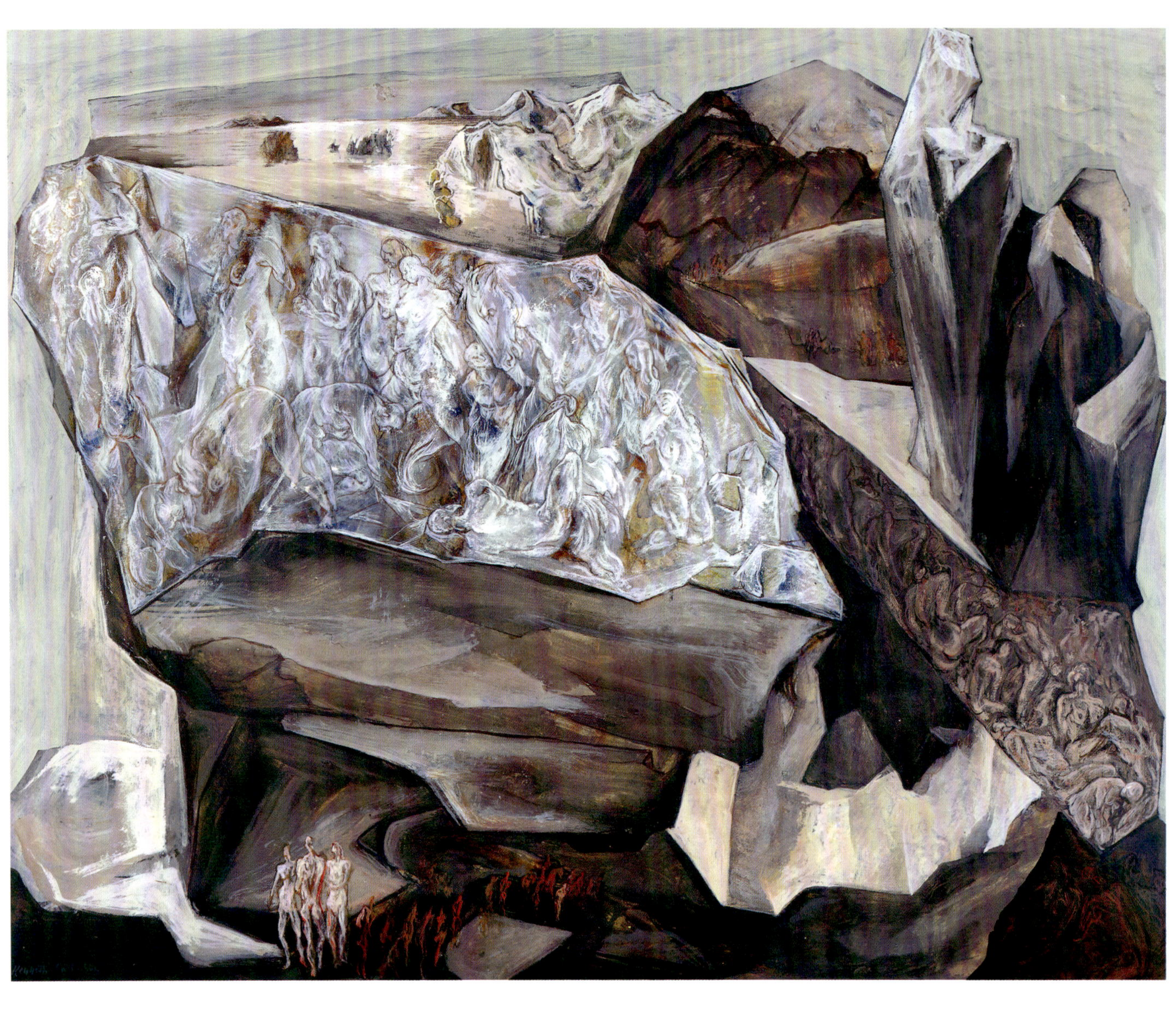

Within the Rocks, 1950
Tempera on paper
22 × 27½ inches
Collection of Mikell and Brian T. Callahan

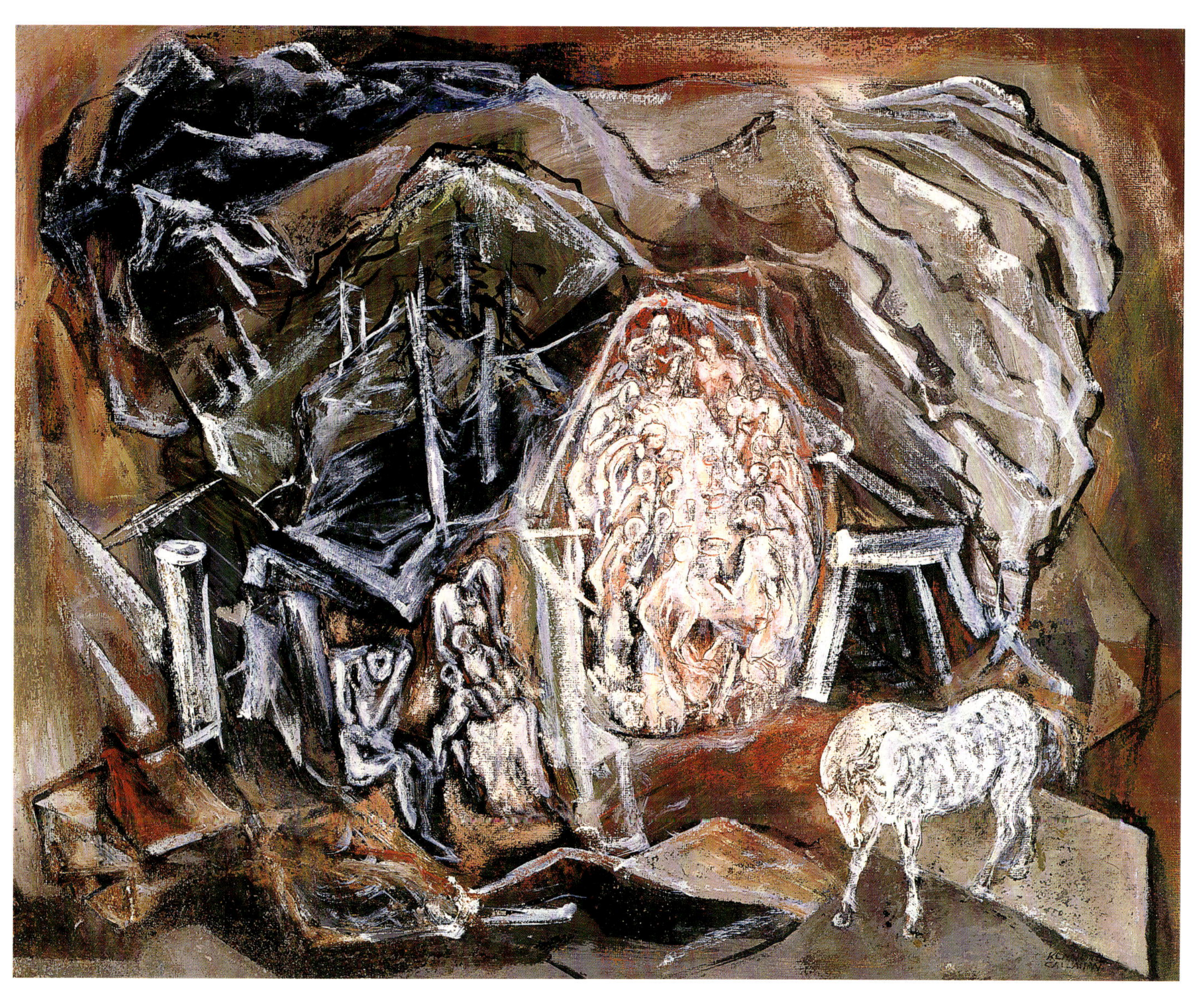

Conclave, 1950
Oil on board
28½ × 34½ inches
Collection of The Laura Russo Gallery

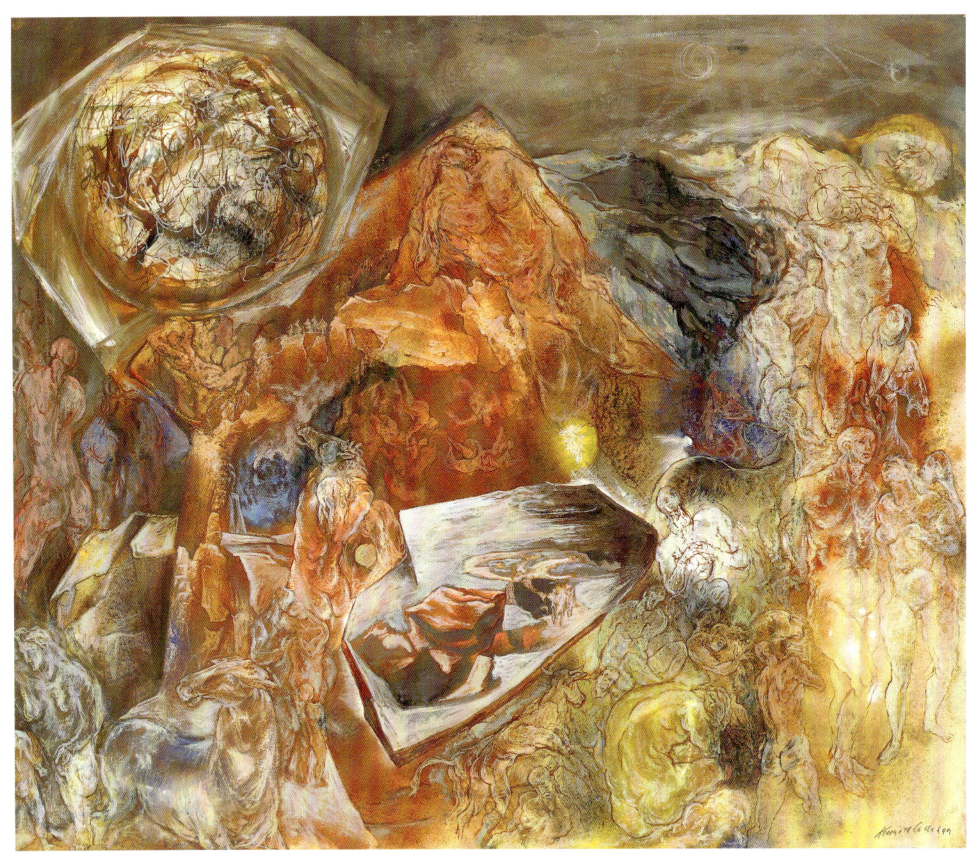

The Cove—Two Worlds, 1952
Tempera on paper
20 × 24 inches
Columbia Museum of Art, Columbia, South Carolina, gift of Emily Winthrop Miles, CMA 1964.15

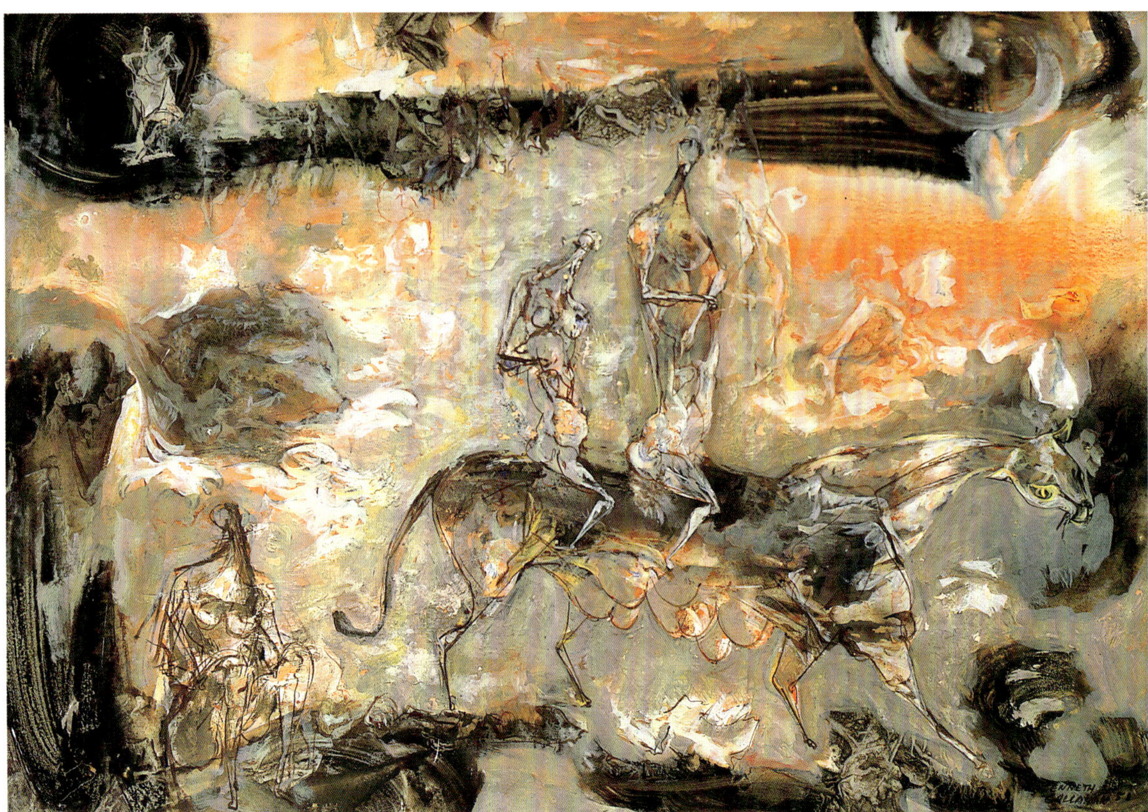

Tiger and Riders, 1952
Tempera and oil on panel
$19^1/_4 \times 27^1/_2$ inches
Collection of Ann S. and John W. Ormsby

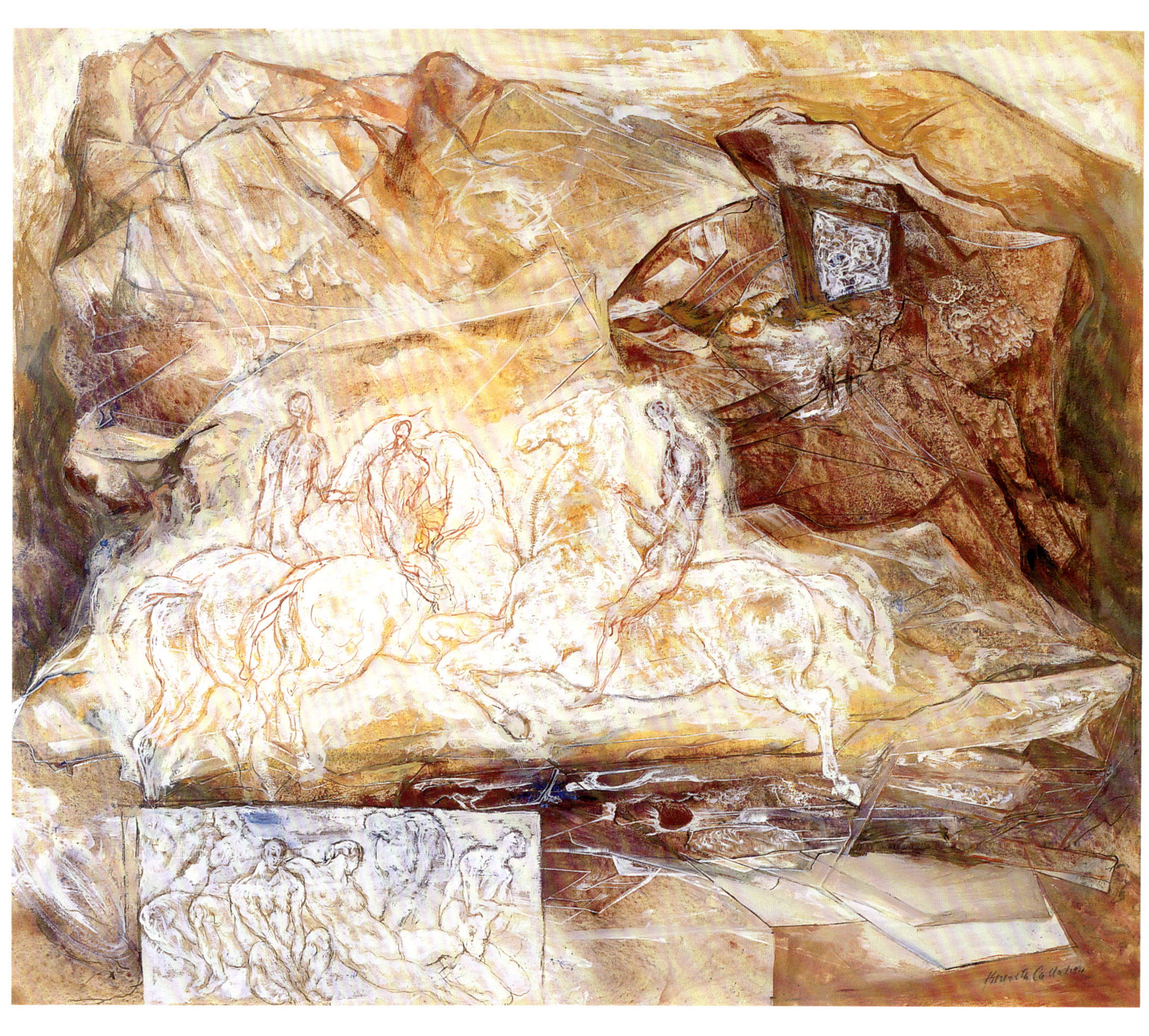

Riders on the Mountain, 1952
Tempera on board
$20^{5}/_{8} \times 24^{5}/_{8}$ inches
The Minneapolis Institute of Arts, bequest of
Emily Winthrop Miles (through Maynard Walker)

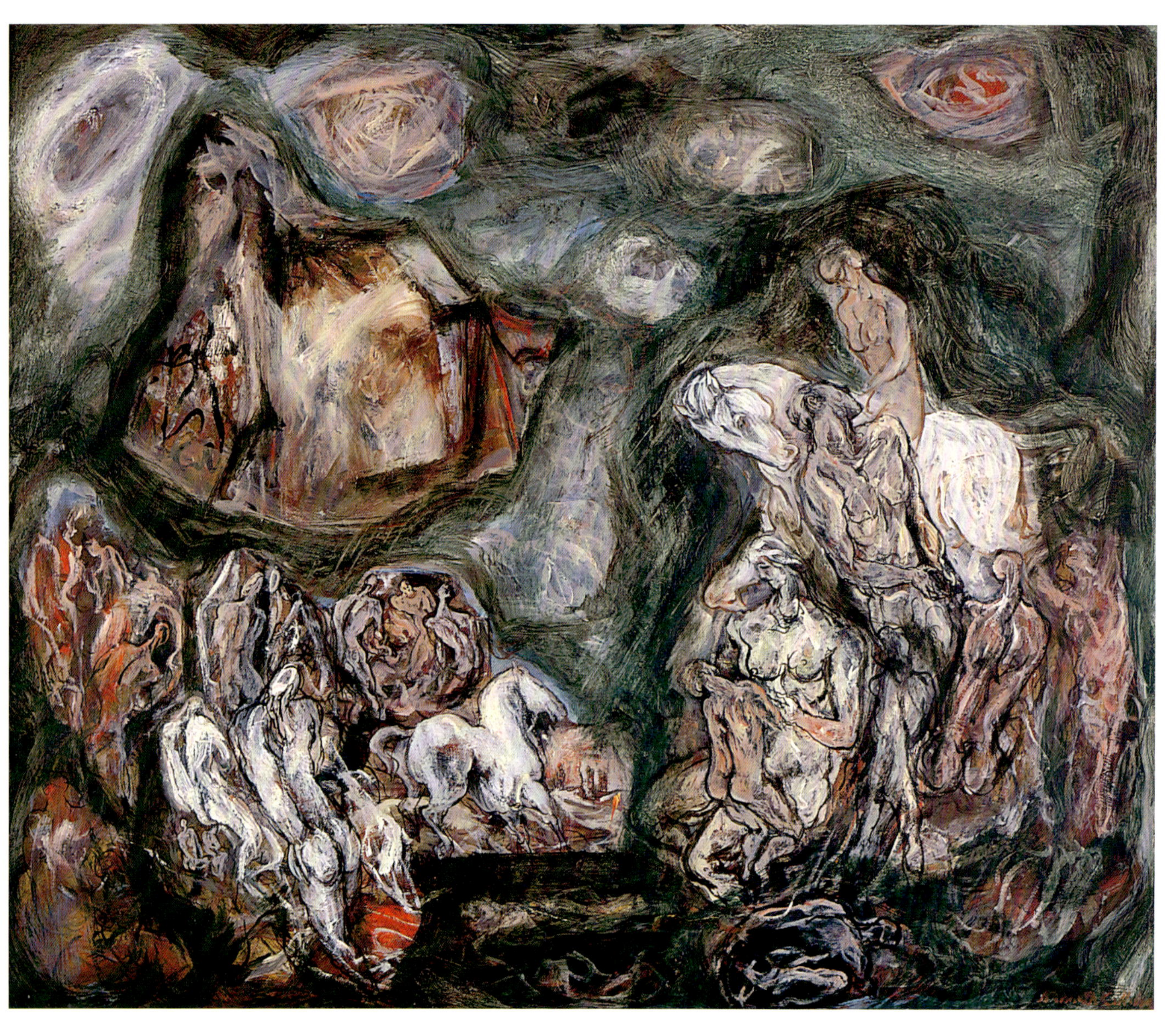

The Islands, ca. 1950–51
Oil on Masonite
23 × 38 inches
The Roland P. Murdock Collection,
Wichita Art Museum, Wichita, Kansas

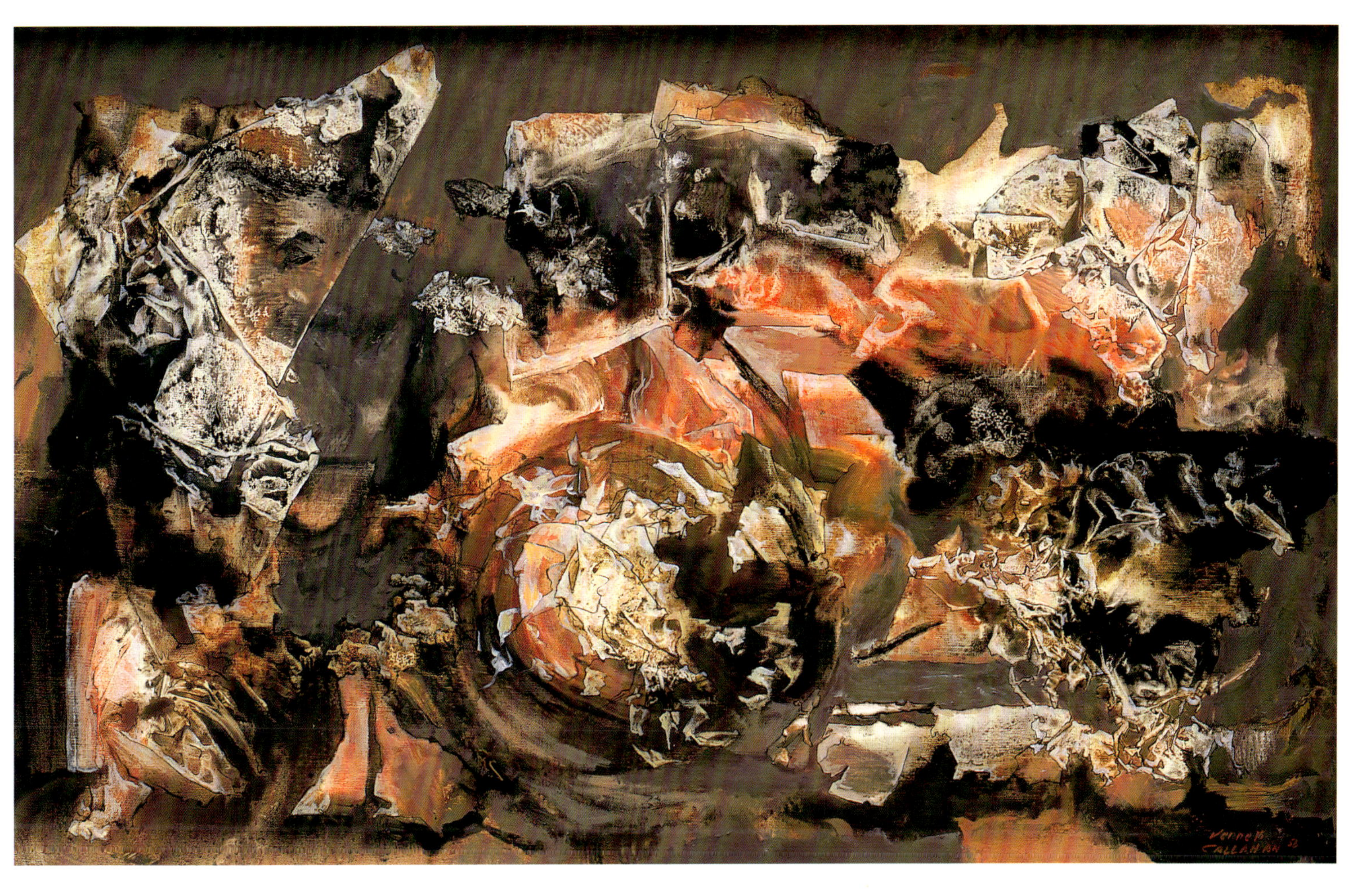

Abstract, 1956
Oil and tempera on panel
27 × 43½ inches
Dr. and Mrs. Nicholas Berman

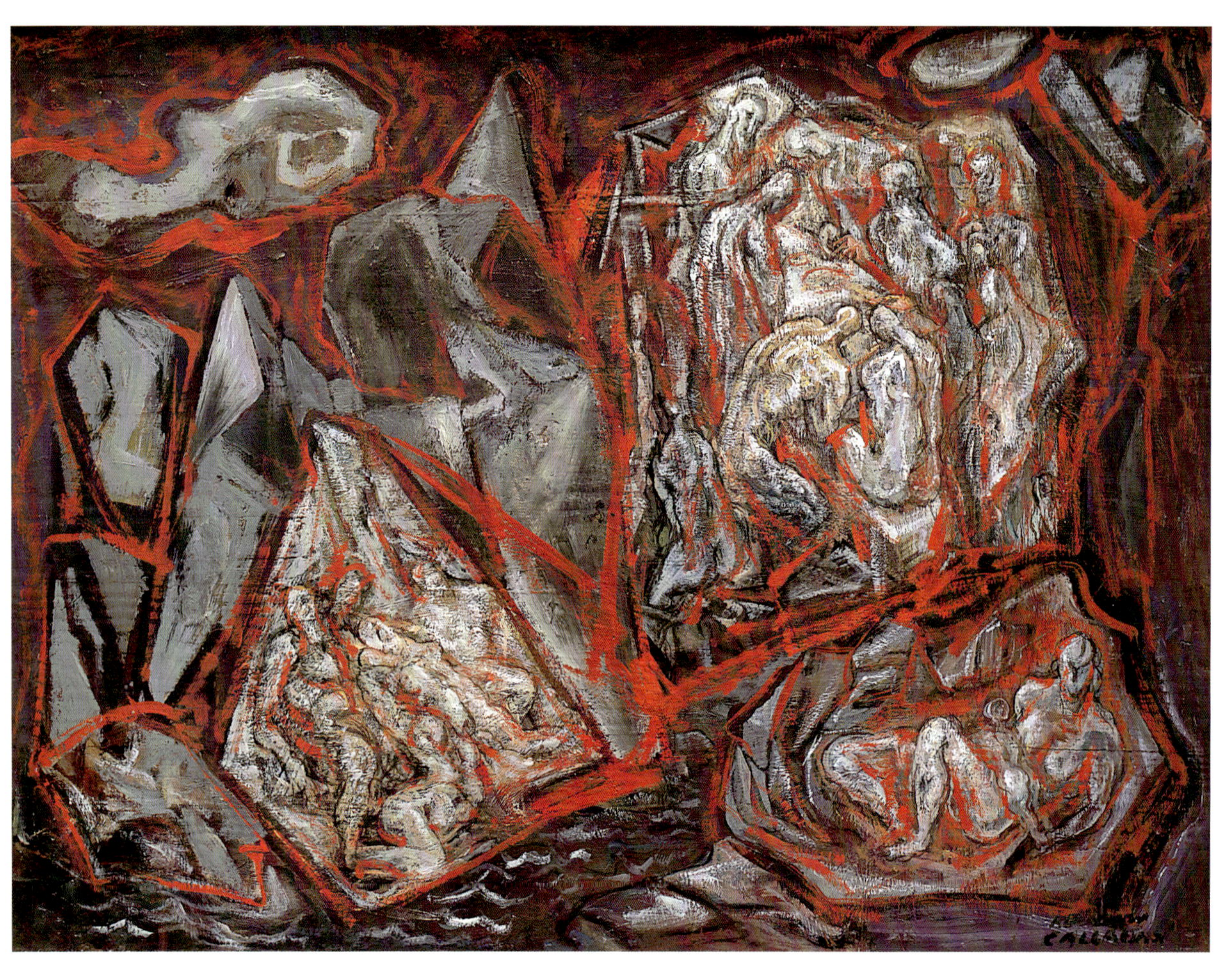

The Supper, 1954
Oil on Masonite
18 × 24 inches
Collection of Mr. and Mrs. Robert M. Sarkis

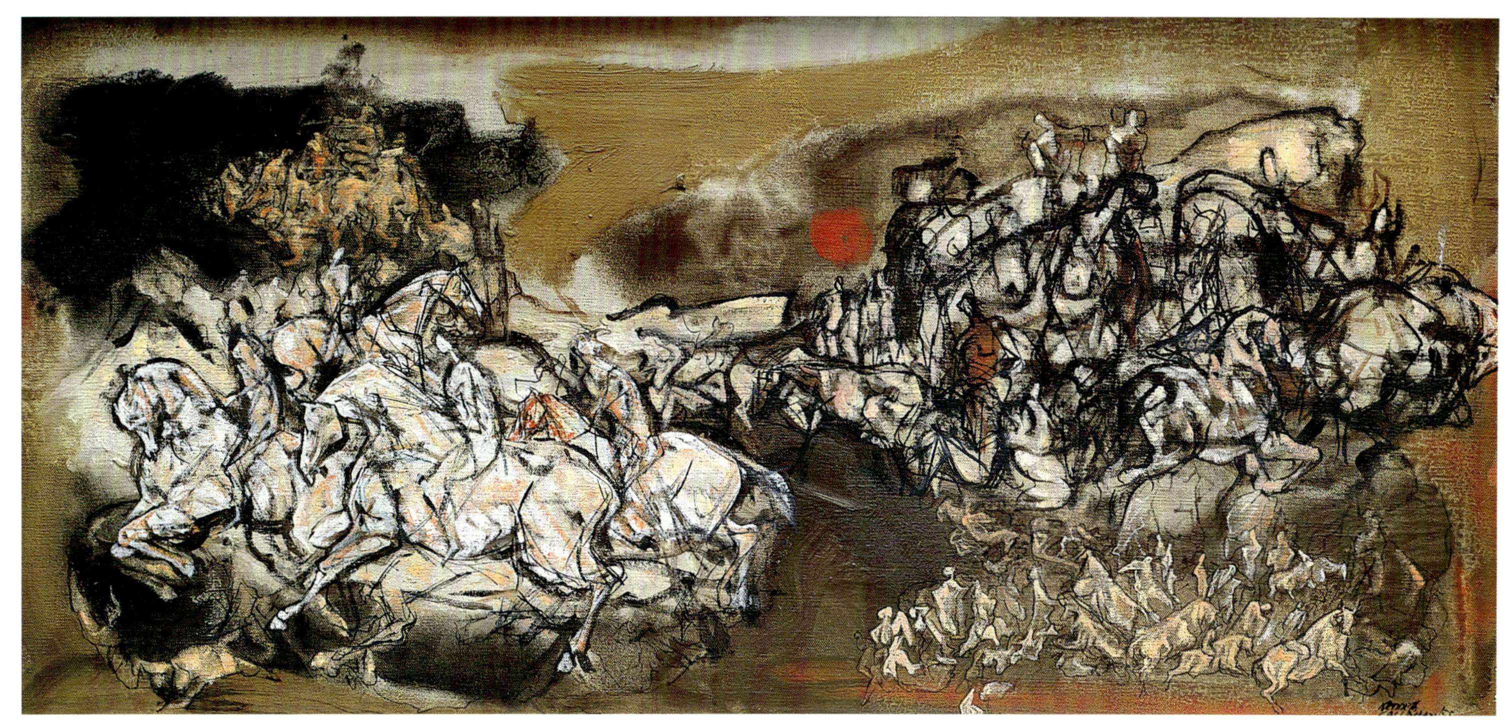

Archaic Battle #2, 1955
Oil on panel
$13^{1}/_{2} \times 29^{1}/_{2}$ inches
Collection of John C. Baxter

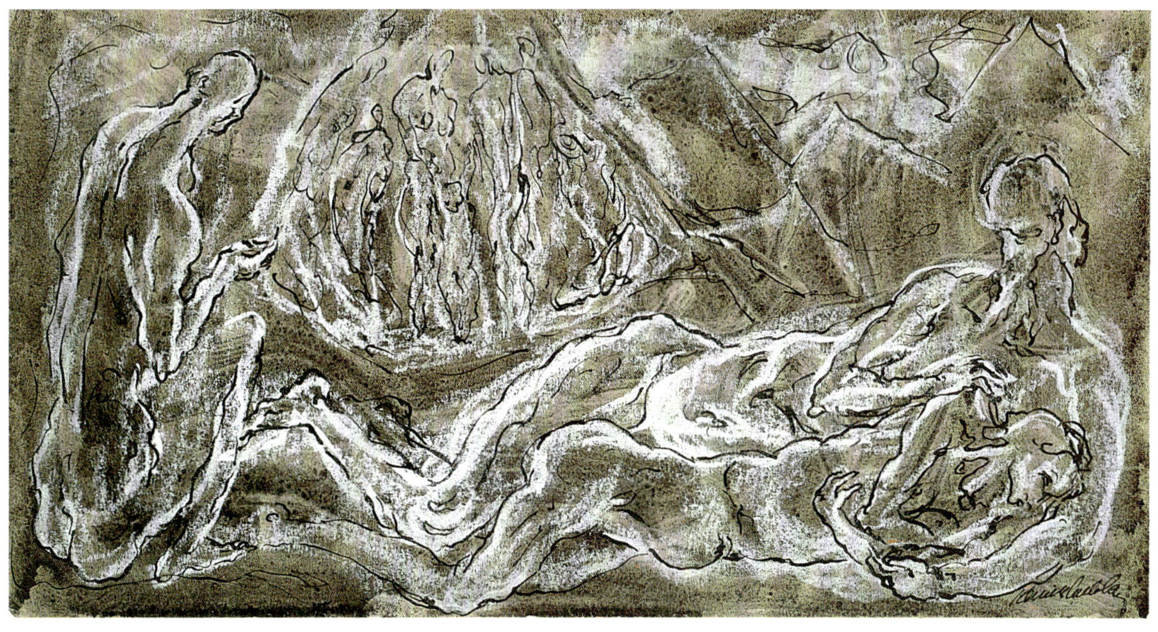

The Prophet, 1955
Ink and chalk drawing on composition board
$6^{7}/_{8} \times 13^{3}/_{8}$ inches
University of Oregon Museum of Art.
Virginia Haseltine Collection of Pacific Northwest Art

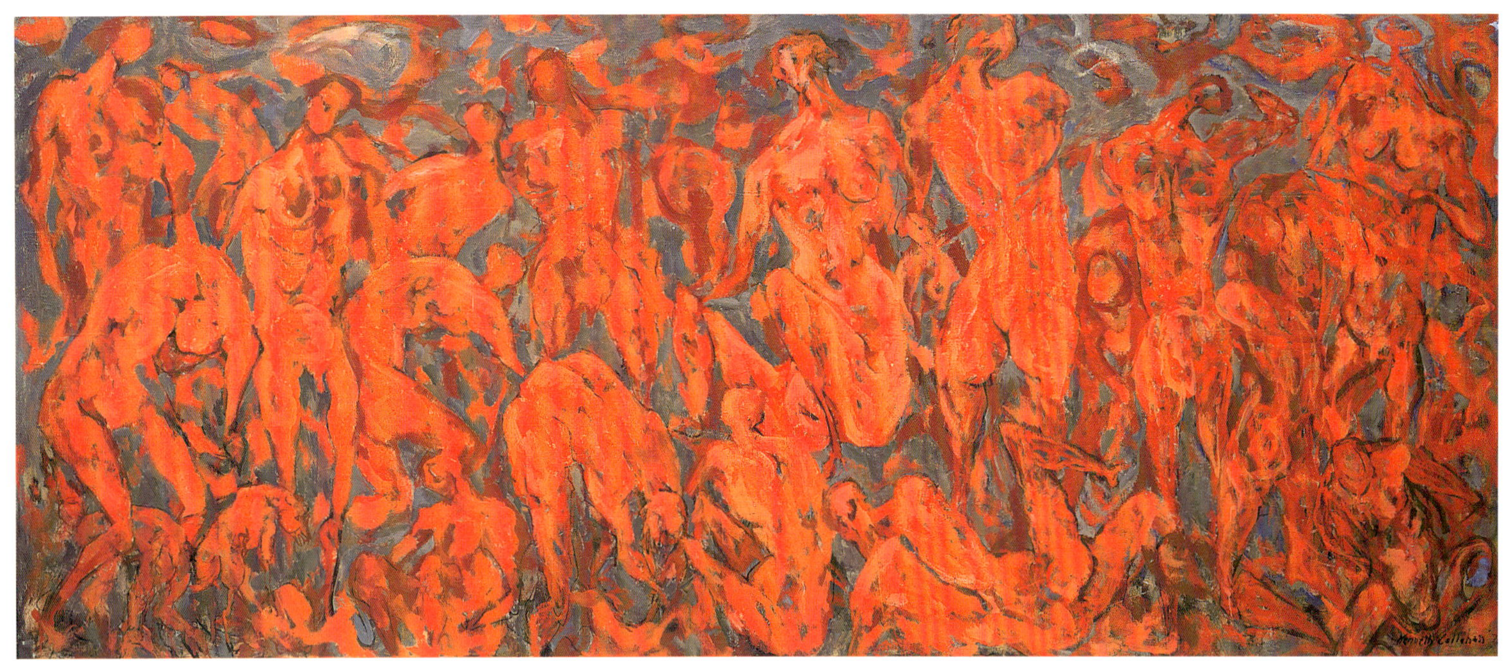

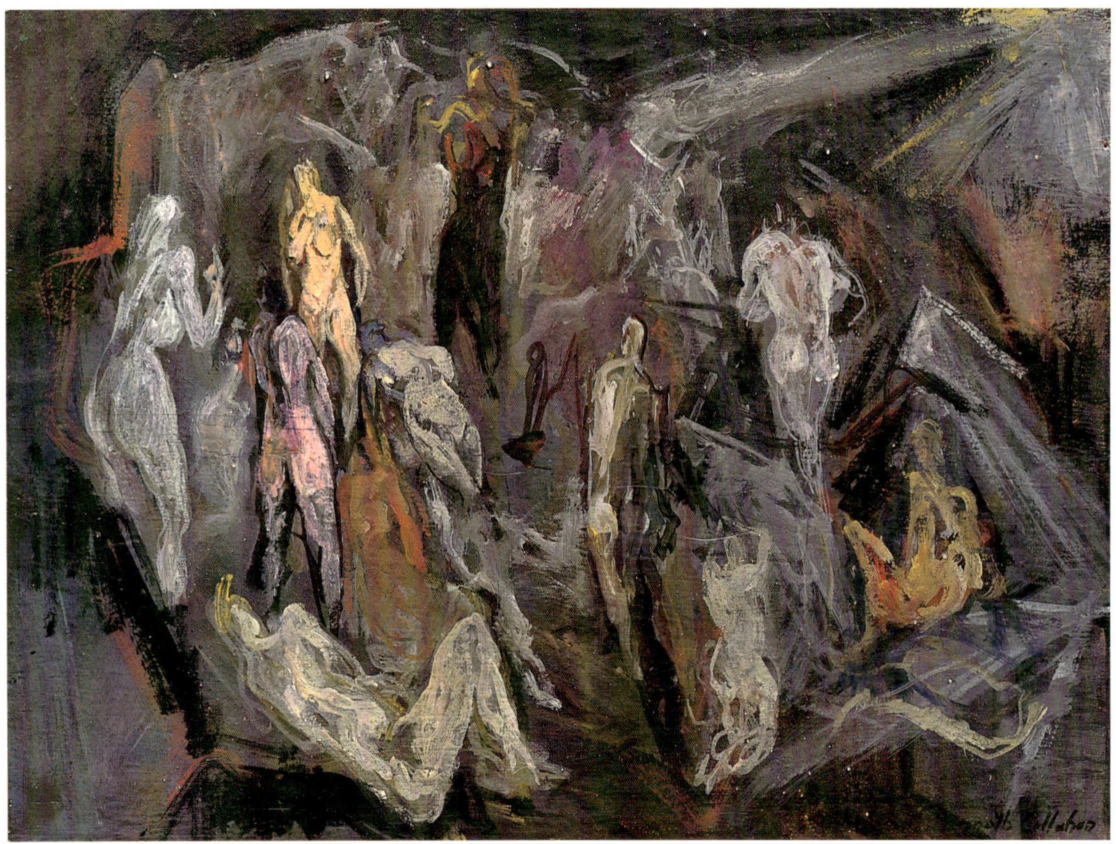

Figure Group, ca. 1950s
Oil and tempera on board
$14\frac{1}{2} \times 20\frac{1}{4}$ inches
Collection of Mrs. William Wesselhoeft

OPPOSITE:

Red Figures, n.d.
Acrylic on Masonite
60 × 150 inches
Collection of Martin Selig

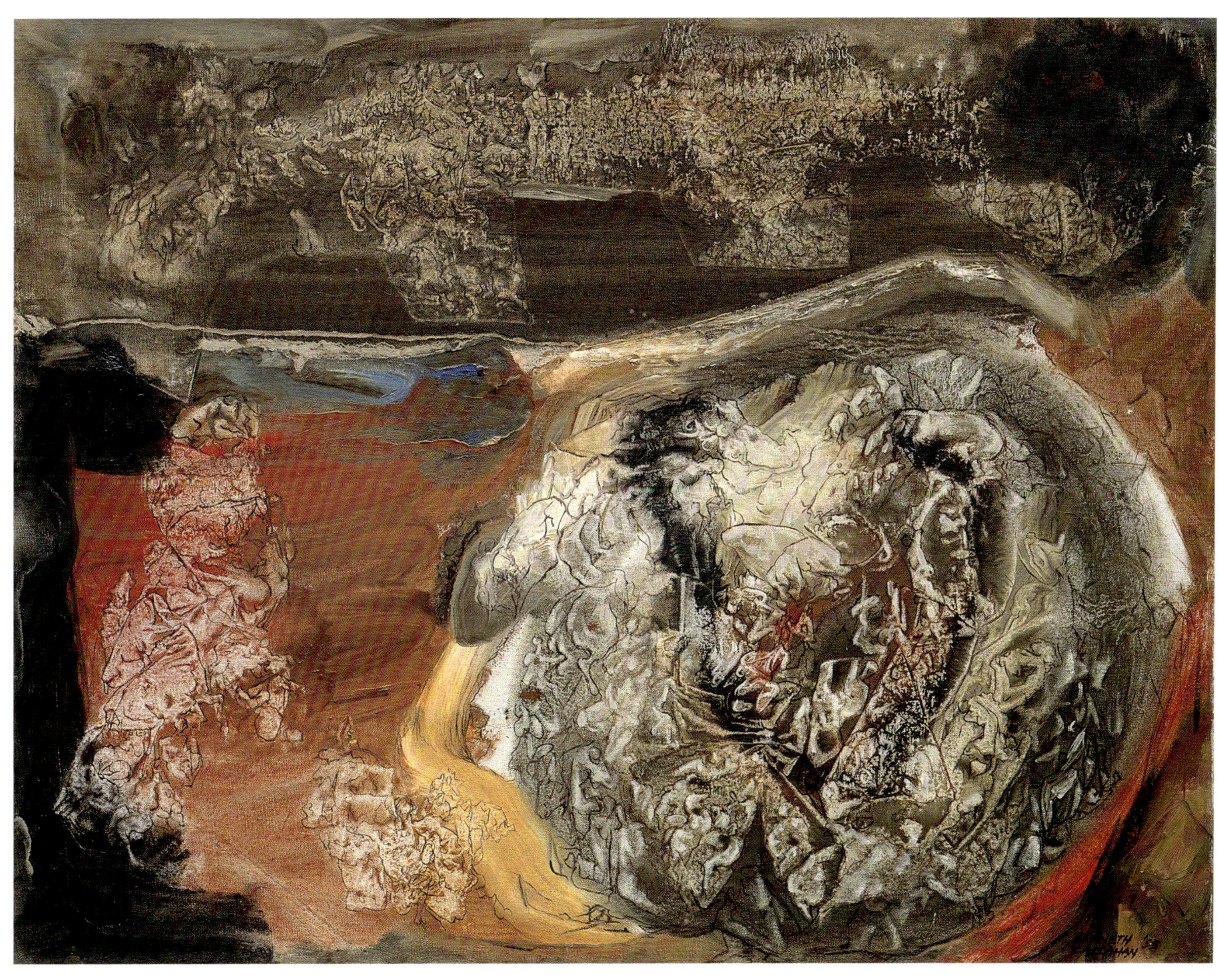

Vortex, 1955
Oil and tempera on canvas
$22^{3}/_{4} \times 29^{1}/_{2}$ inches
Collection of Martin Selig

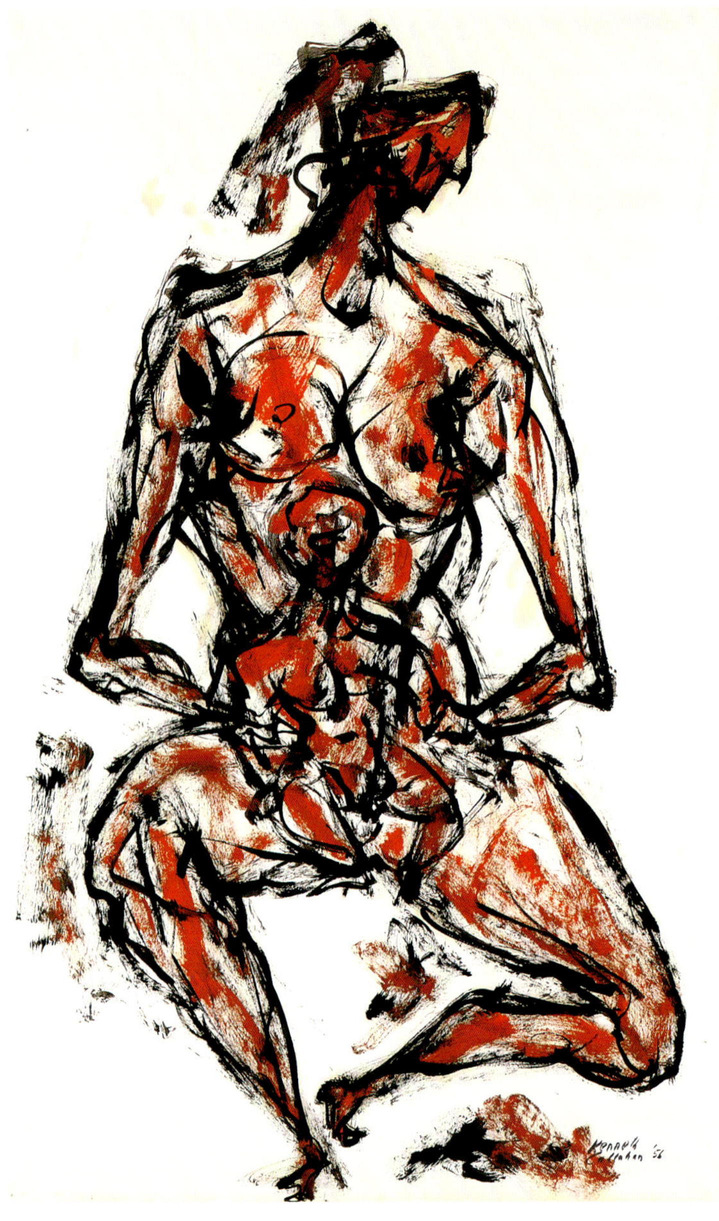

Untitled [*Nude, frontal*], 1956
Oil on paper
37 × 24 inches
Collection of Richard and Deanne Rubinstein

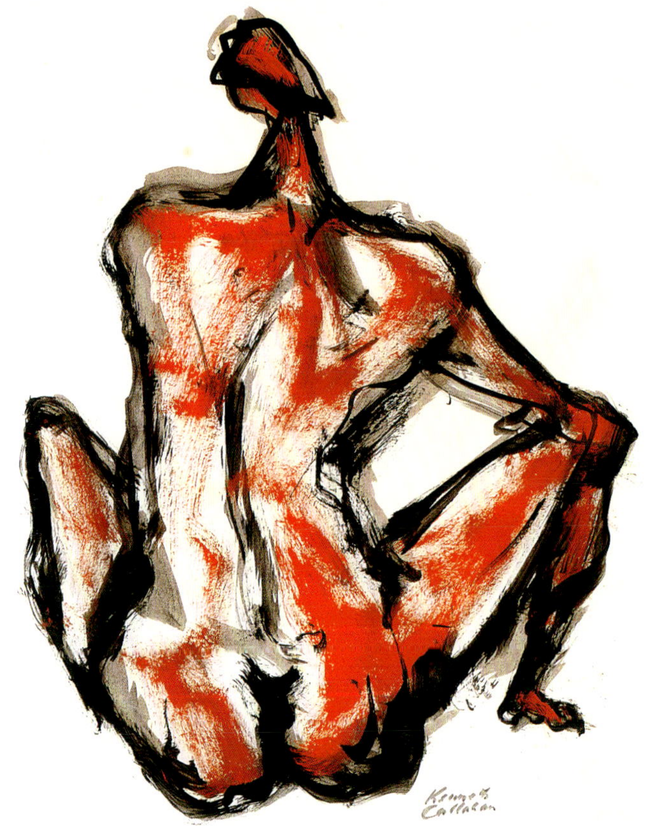

Untitled [*Nude*], ca. 1956
Oil on paper
16 × 13 inches
Collection of Richard and Deanne Rubinstein

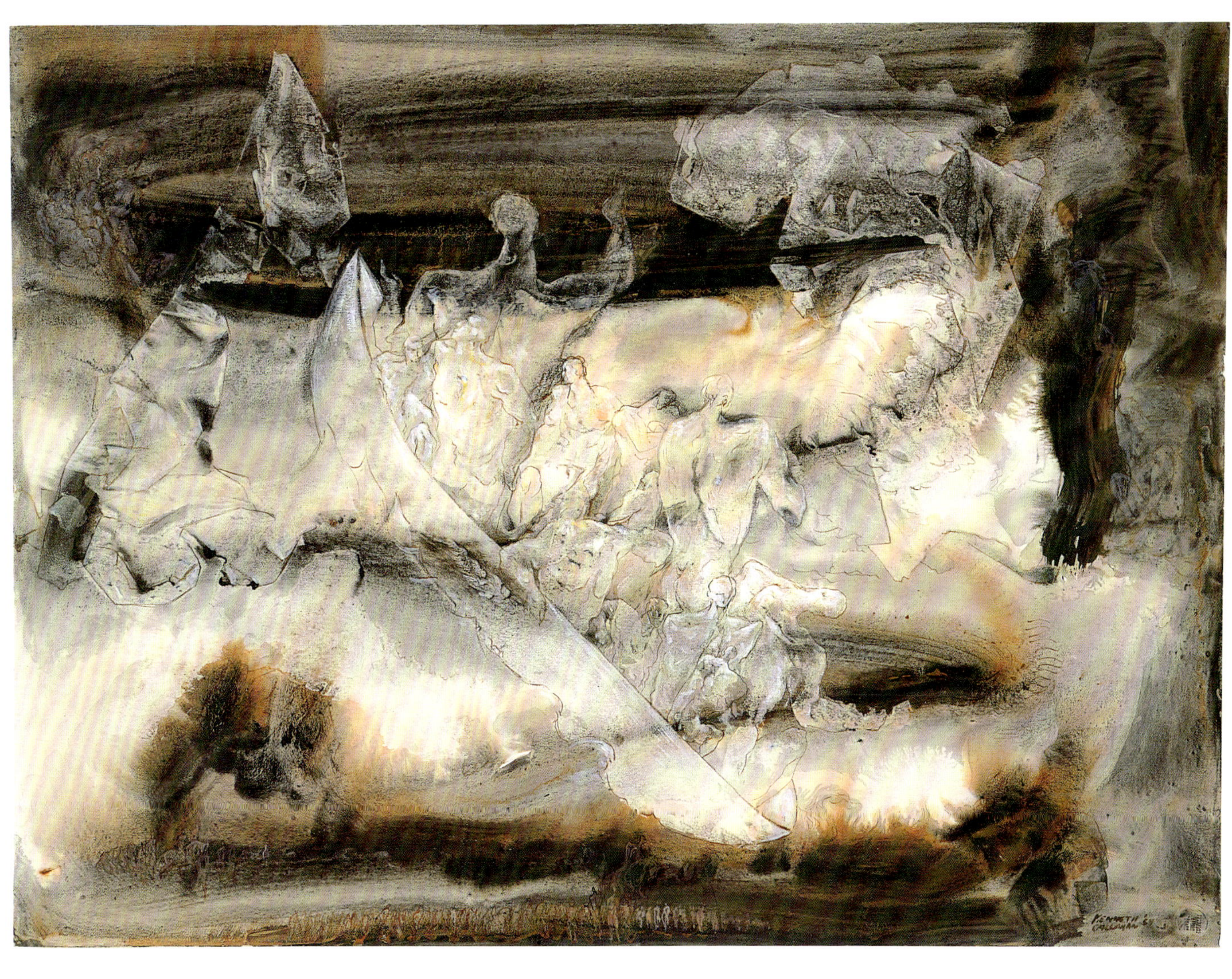

Argonauts #2, 1954
Watercolor on paperboard
$21\frac{7}{8} \times 29\frac{7}{8}$ inches
Hirshhorn Museum and Sculpture Garden,
Smithsonian Institution, gift of Joseph H.
Hirshhorn, 1966

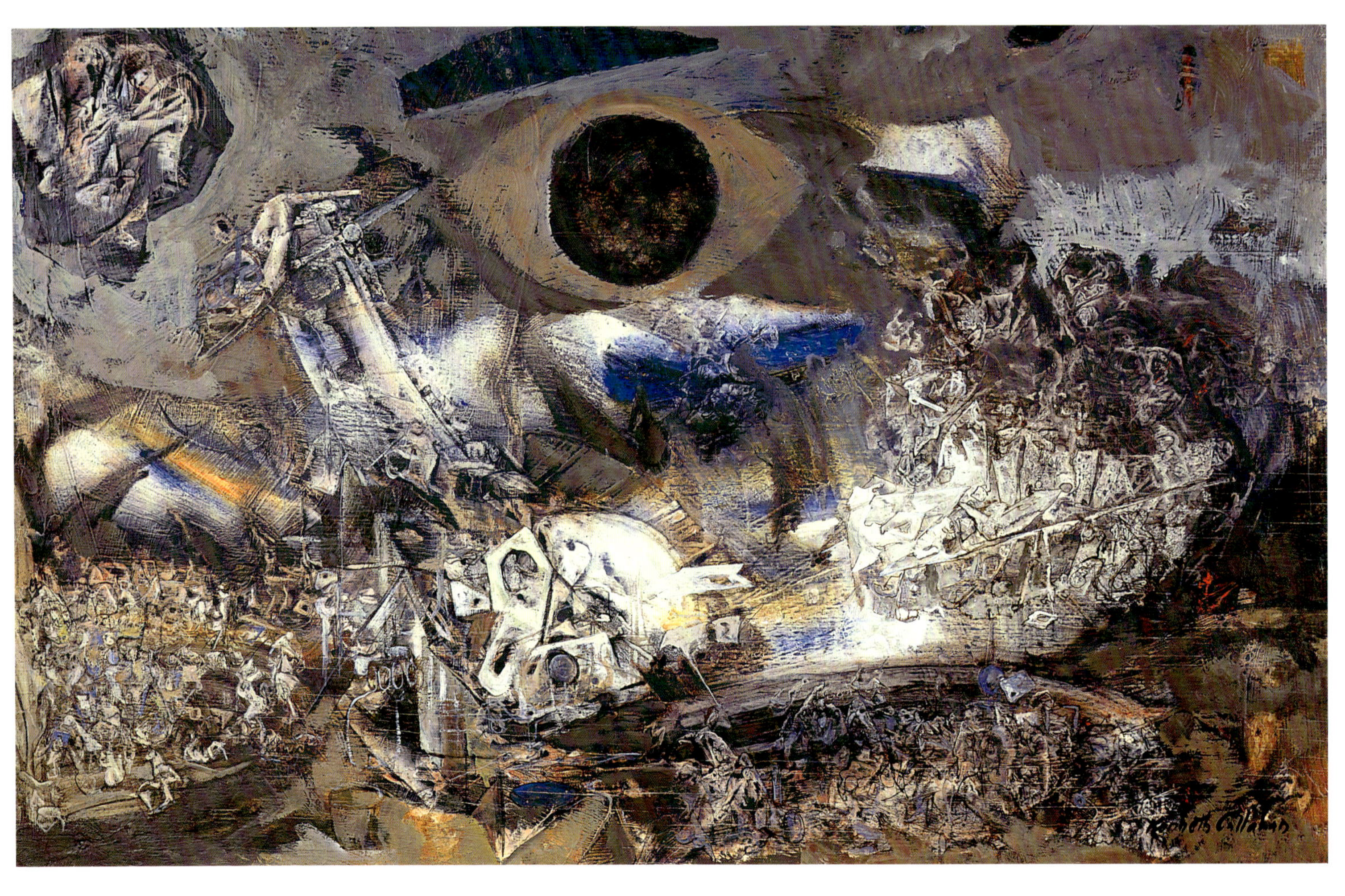

Multitudes, ca. 1957
Oil on panel
26 × 41½ inches
Nora Eccles Harrison Museum of Art,
gift of the Marie Eccles Caine Foundation

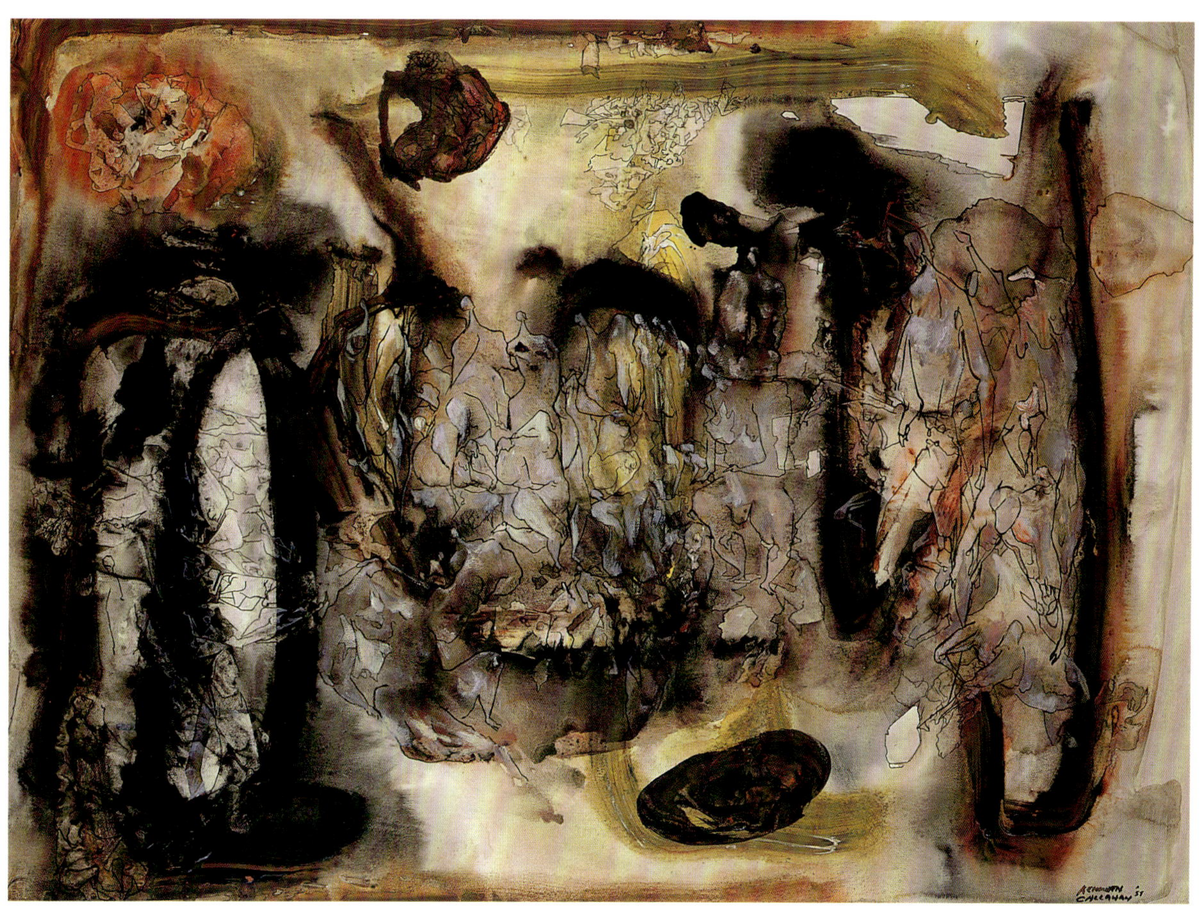

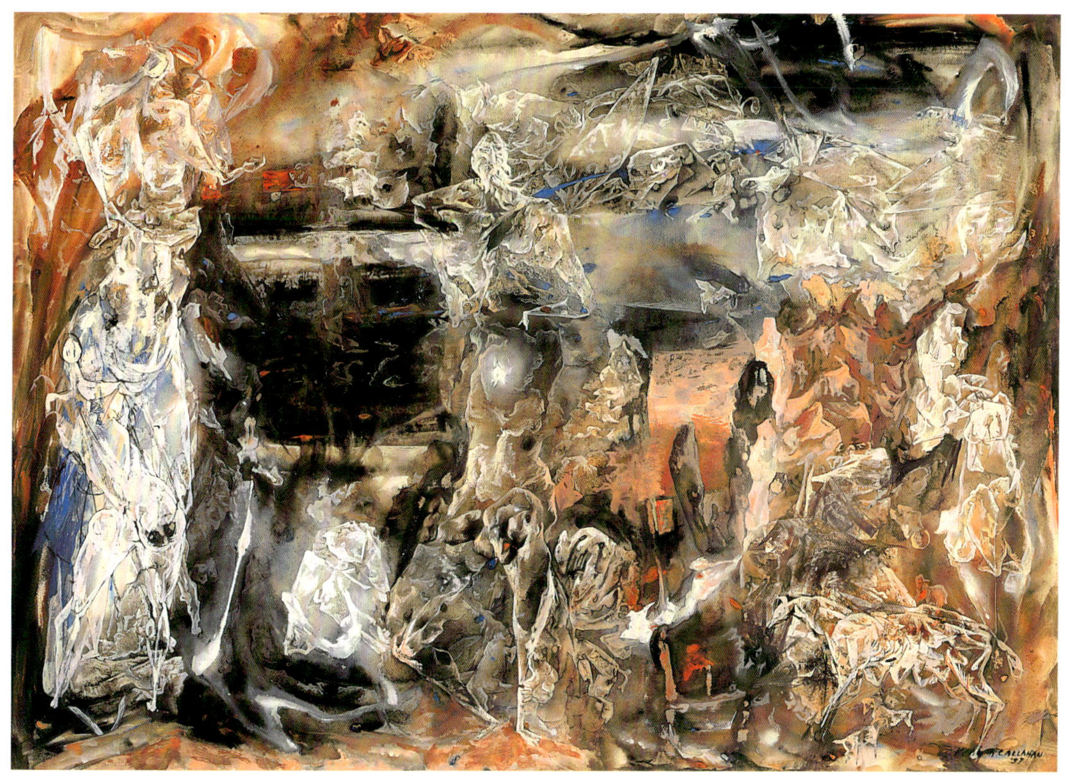

TOP:
The Dancers, 1958
Tempera on paper
22 × 30 inches
Courtesy, Kraushaar Galleries, New York

BOTTOM:
Temptation of St. Anthony, 1957
Tempera on paper
19¾ × 28¼ inches
Portland Art Museum, bequest of Emily Winthrop Miles

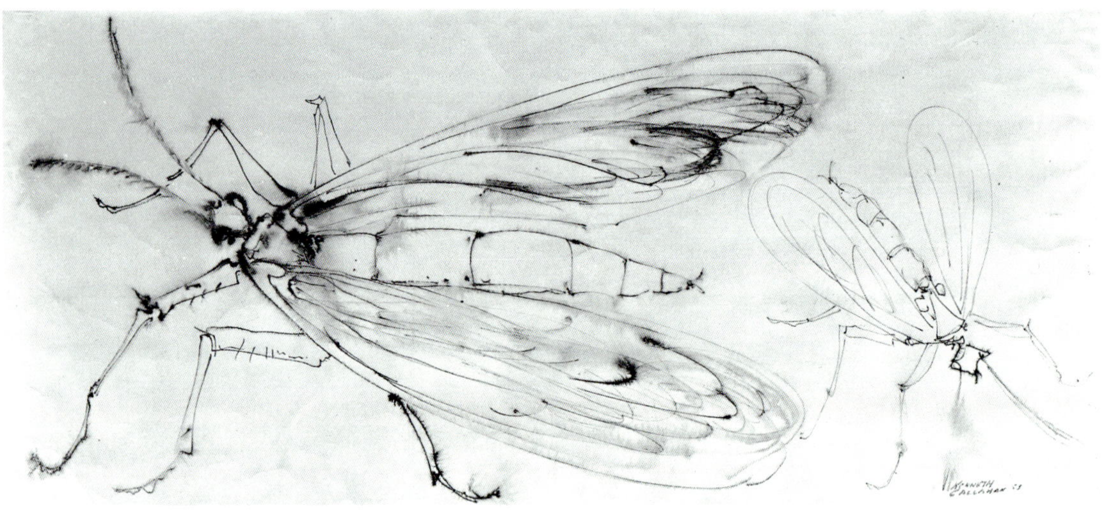

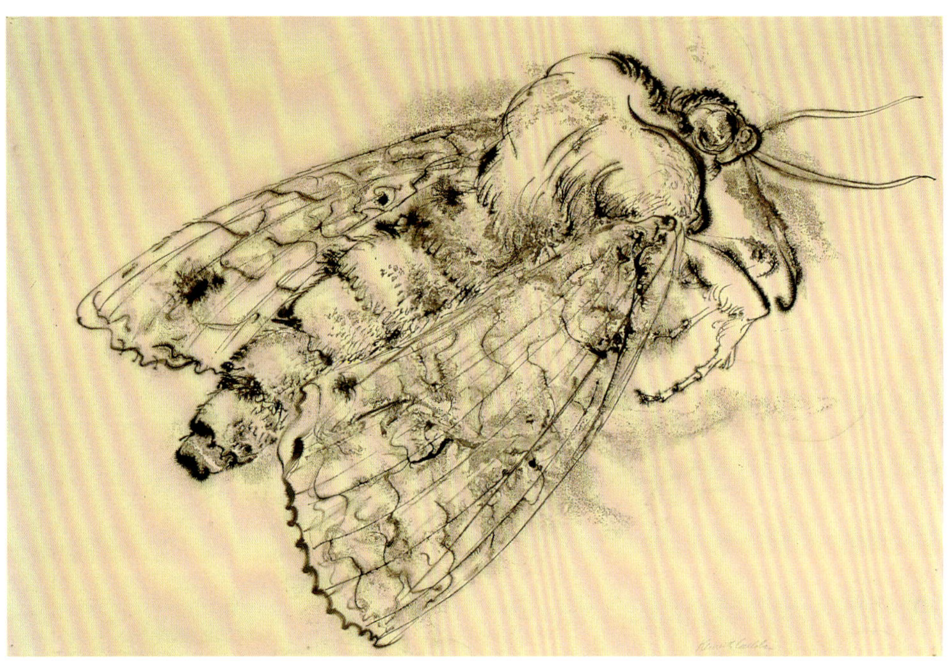

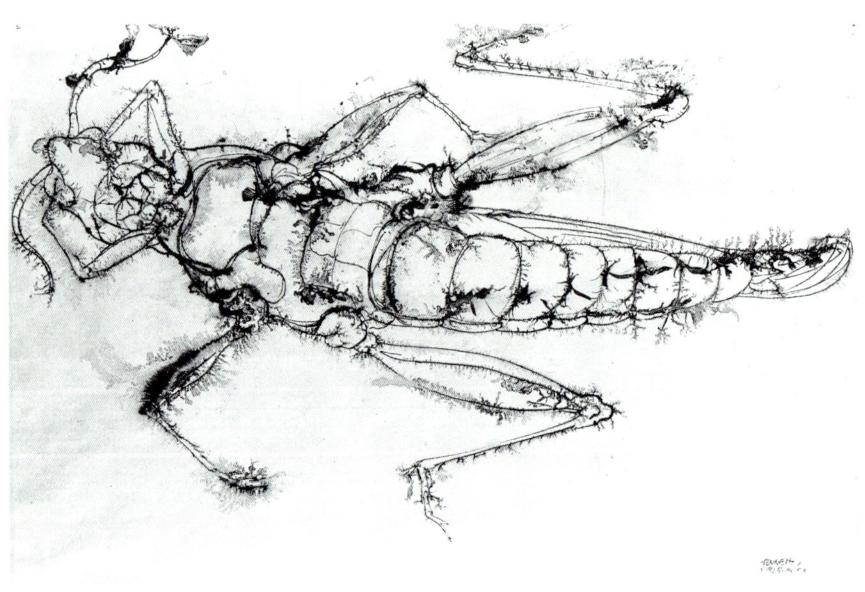

TOP TO BOTTOM:

Maine Flies, 1959
Pen and ink on wove paper
16½ × 37¾ inches
The Detroit Institute of Arts, Founders Society Purchase, Director's Discretionary Fund

Great Moth, n.d.
Pen, ink wash, and charcoal on dampened paper
25 × 36 inches
Santa Barbara Museum of Art, bequest of Emily Winthrop Miles

Dead Grasshopper, 1953
Ink on beige laid paper
24½ × 38⅛ inches
Solomon R. Guggenheim Museum, New York

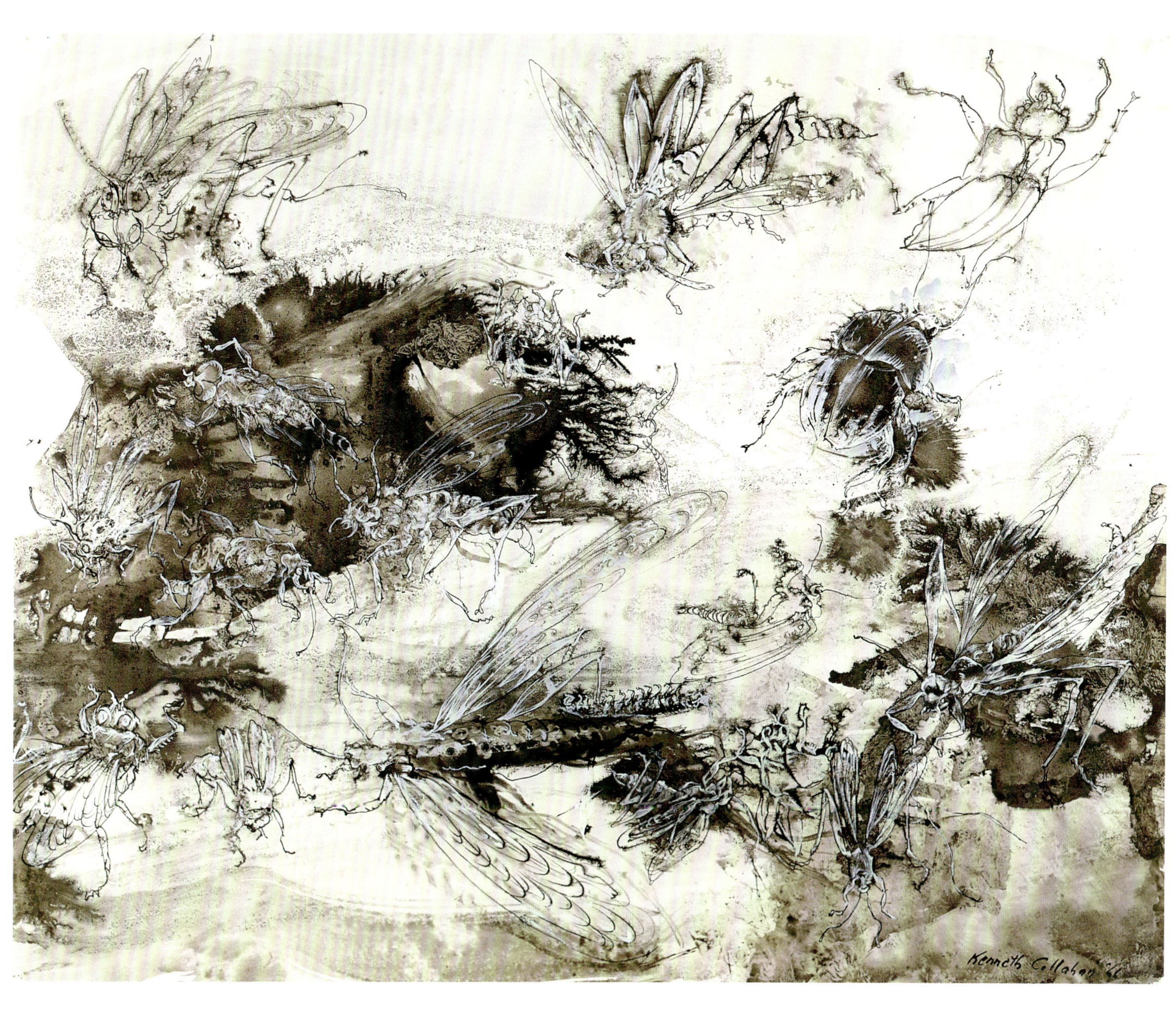

Many Insects, 1966
Gouache and ink on paper
22½ × 28½ inches
Kalamazoo Institute of Arts

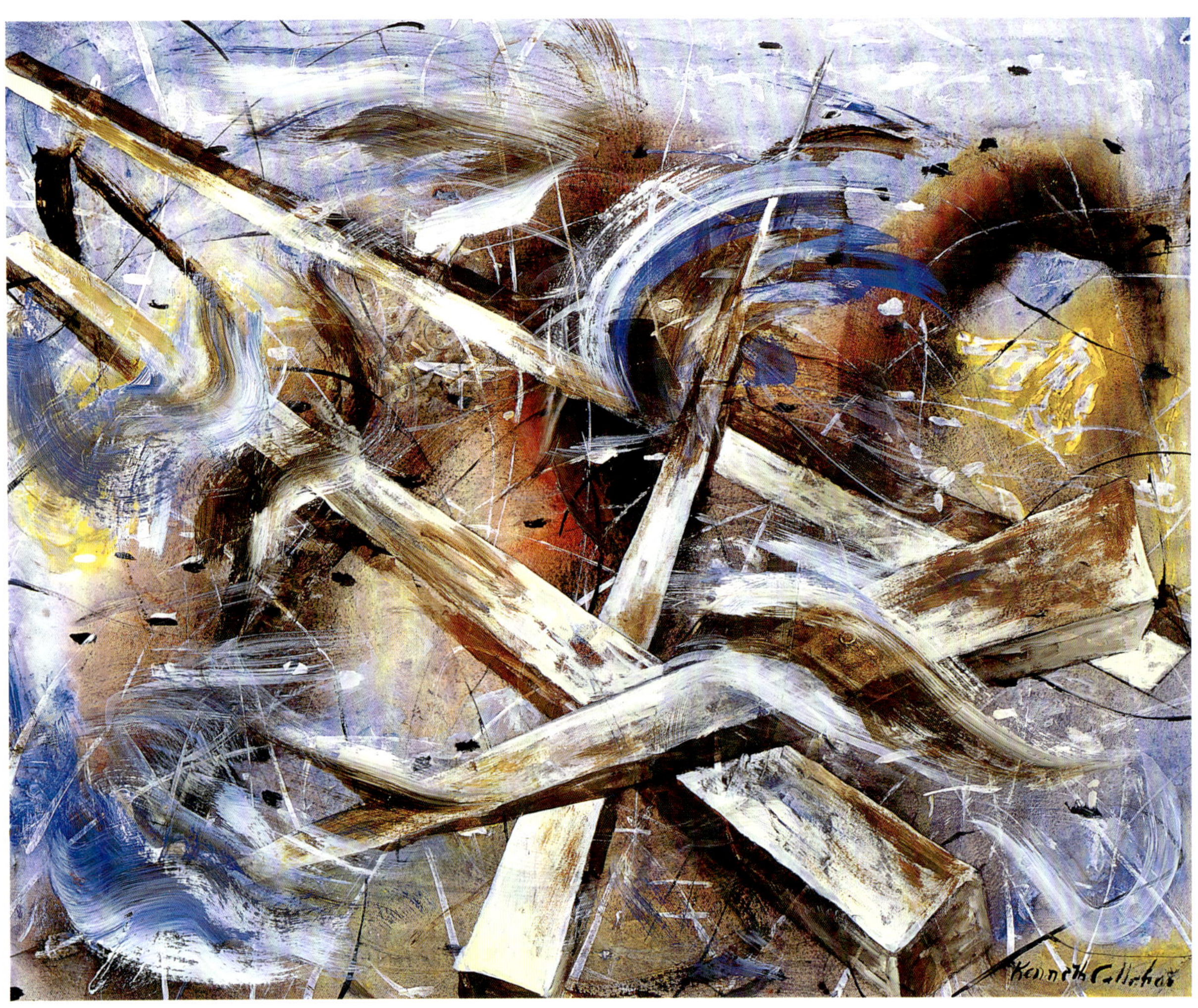

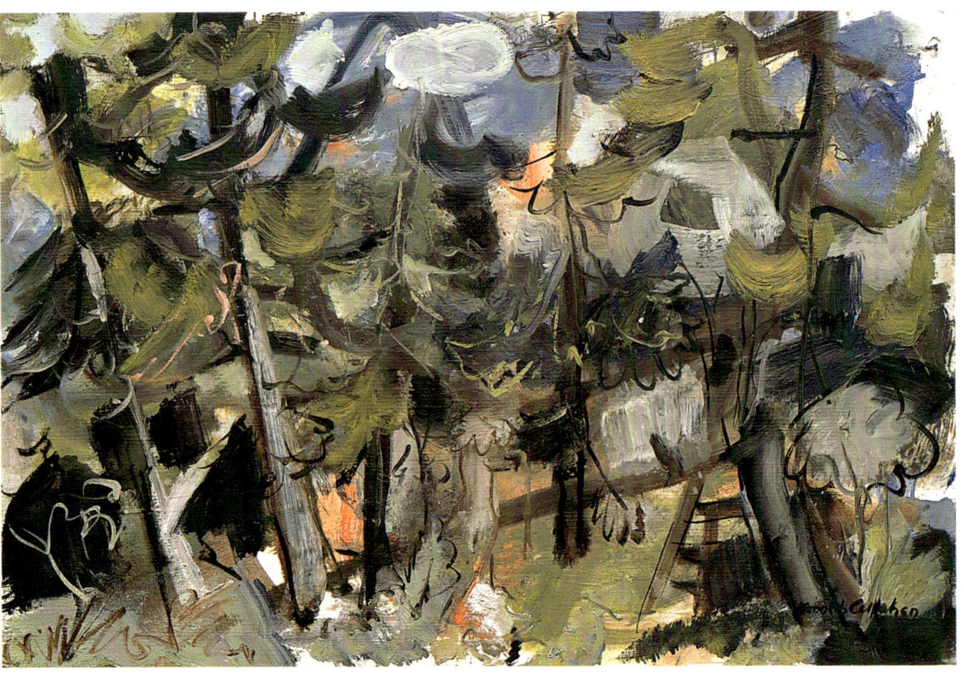

TOP:

Restless Sea, ca. 1960s
Tempera on paper on panel
32 × 40 inches
Collection of Susan Elle Stubblefield

BOTTOM:

The Farm, ca. 1960s
Tempera and oil on Masonite
24 × 36 inches
Collection of Charles and Alice Ross

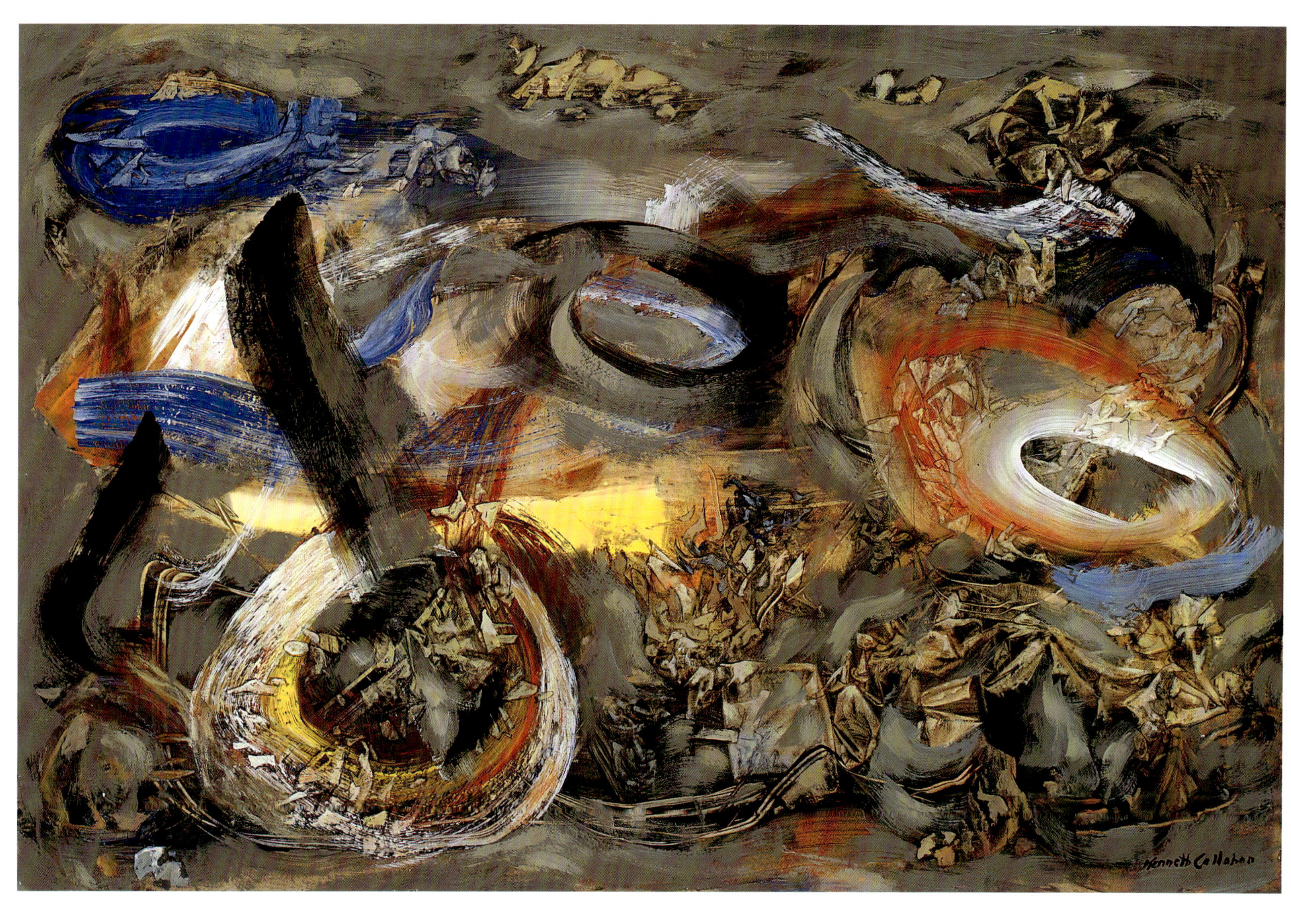

Untitled, ca. 1960s
Oil on canvas
42 × 63 inches
Collection of Becky and Jack Benaroya

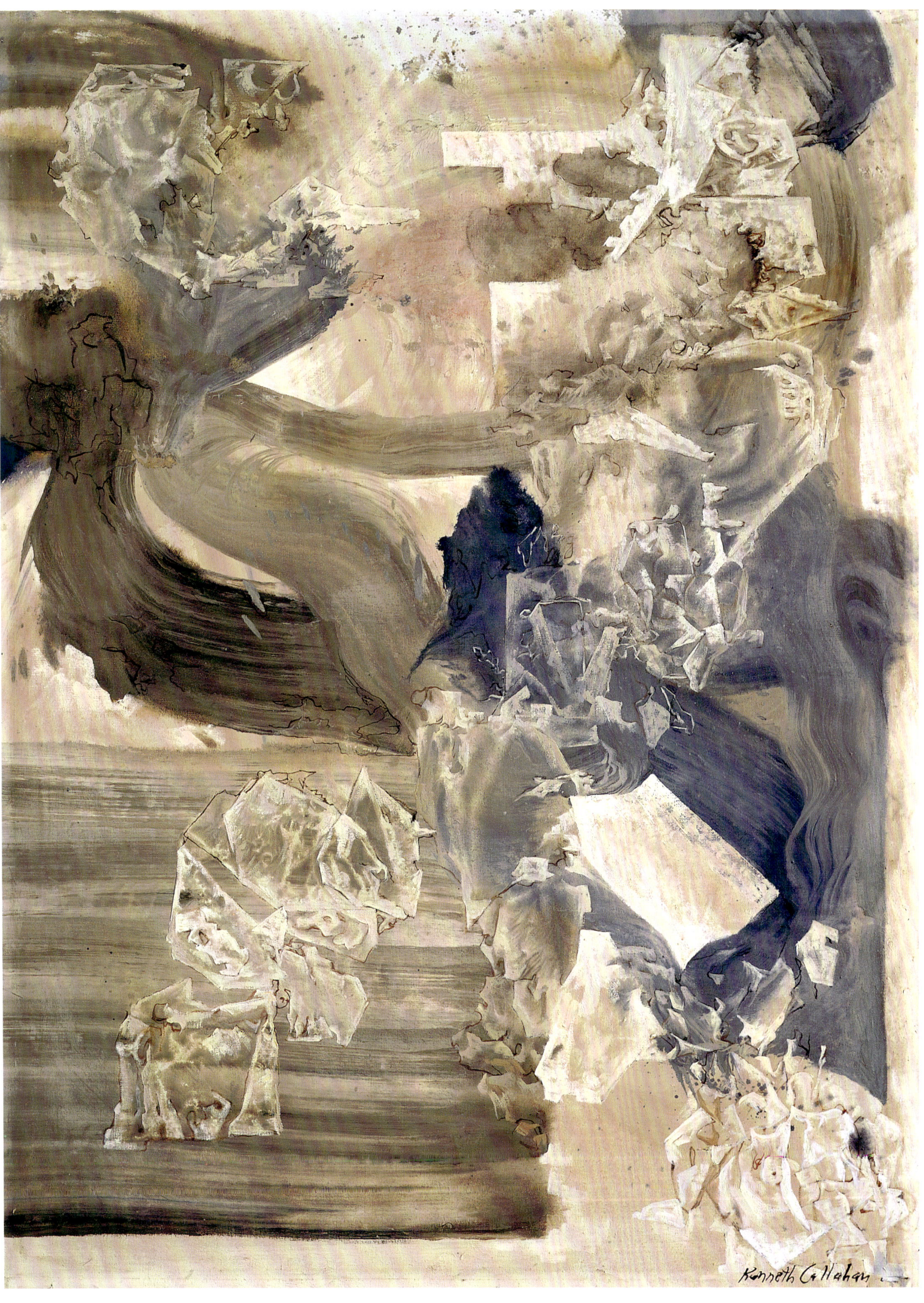
Kenneth Callahan

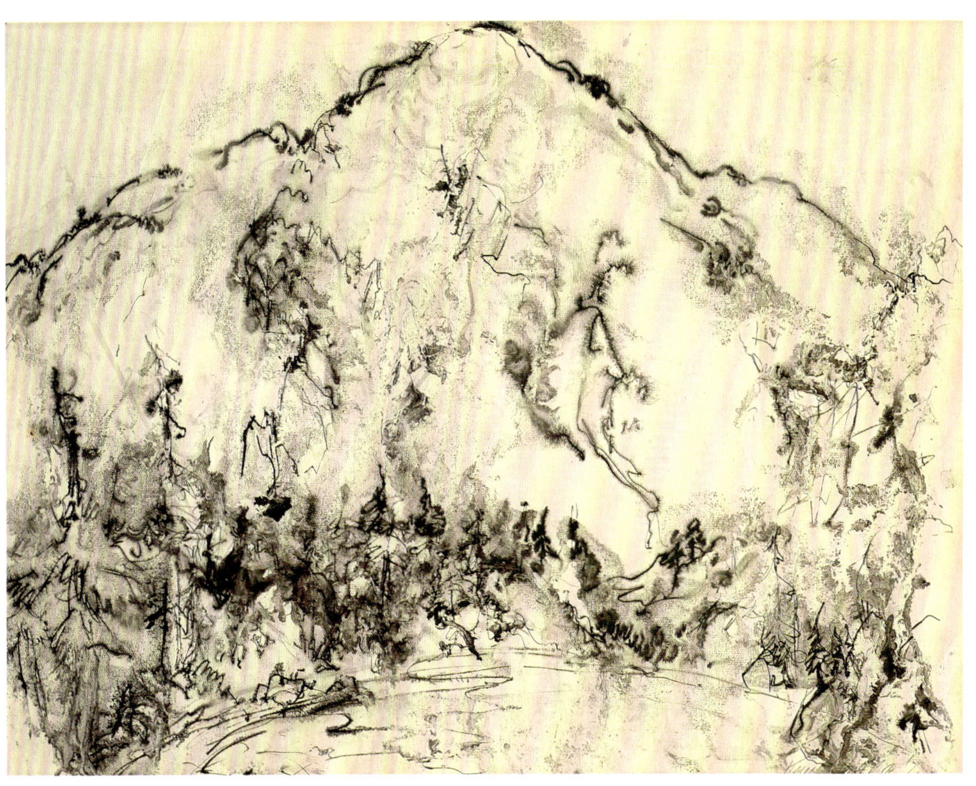

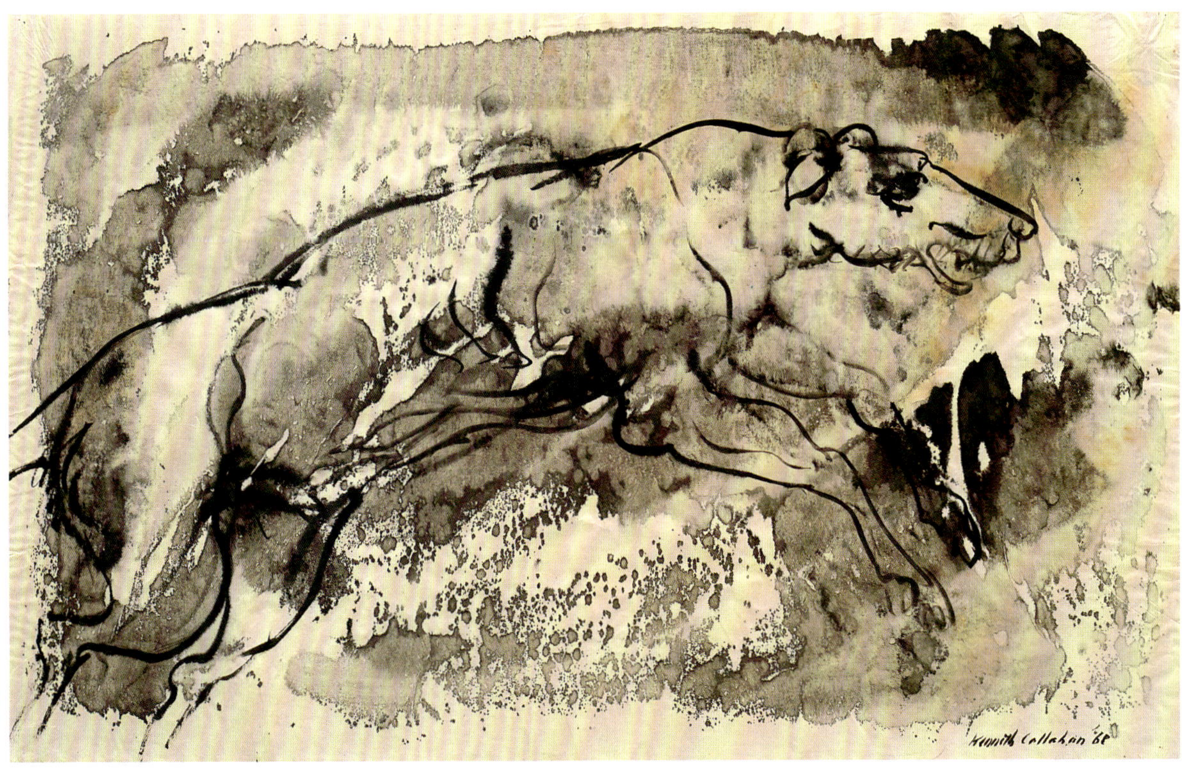

OPPOSITE:

Fragmented World, 1960
Tempera on board
45 × 34 inches
Collection of Mr. and Mrs. Gordon Cochran

TOP:

Mountain Drawing, 1960
Ink on paper
18½ × 24½ inches
Collection of Alvin and Jacqueline Goldfarb

BOTTOM:

Tiger, 1968
Sumi ink on paper
24 × 38 inches
Dr. and Mrs. Nicholas Berman

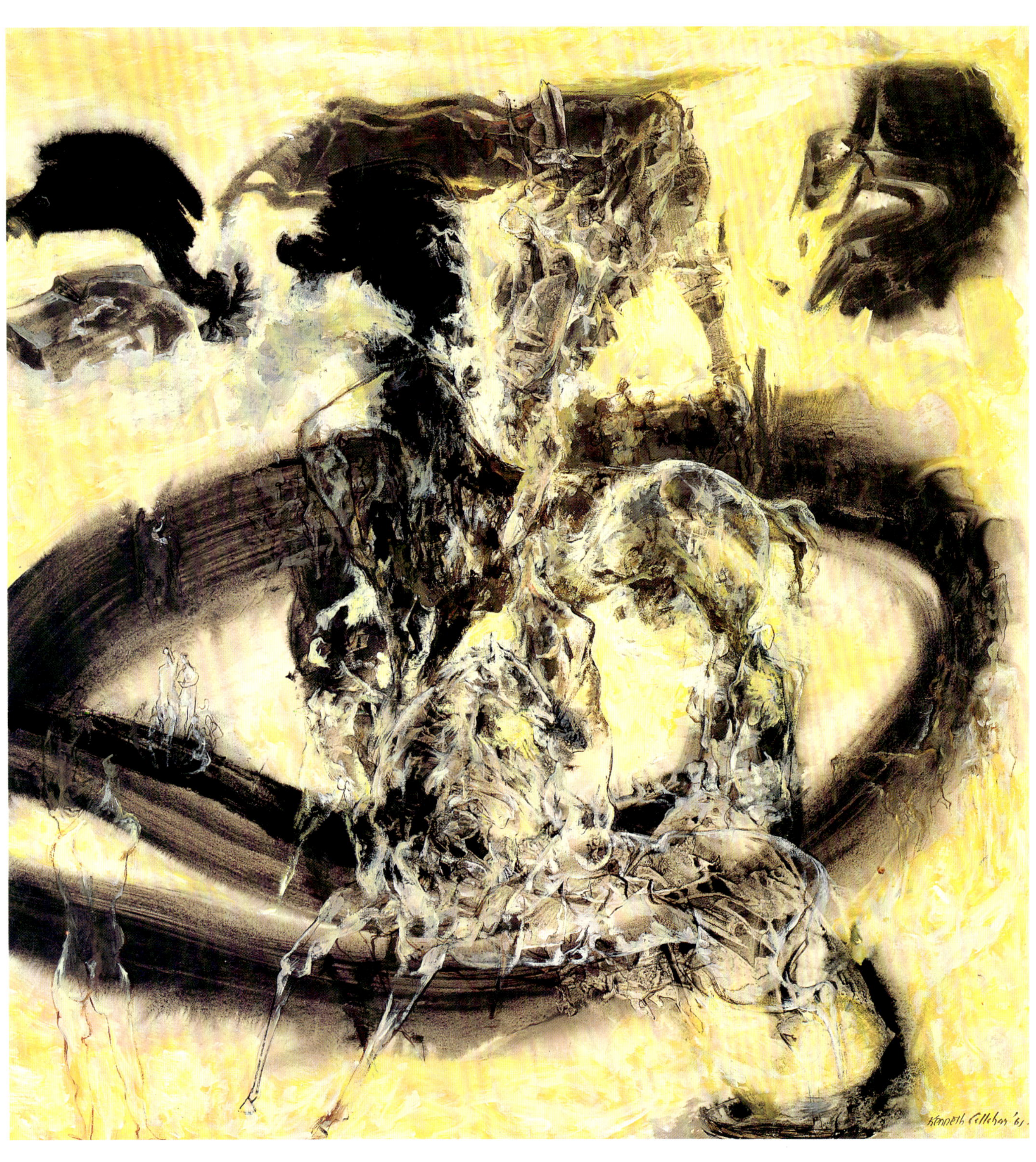

Noon Soliloquy, 1961
Tempera on paper
43 × 41½ inches
Collection of Cyrus and Anita Tsui

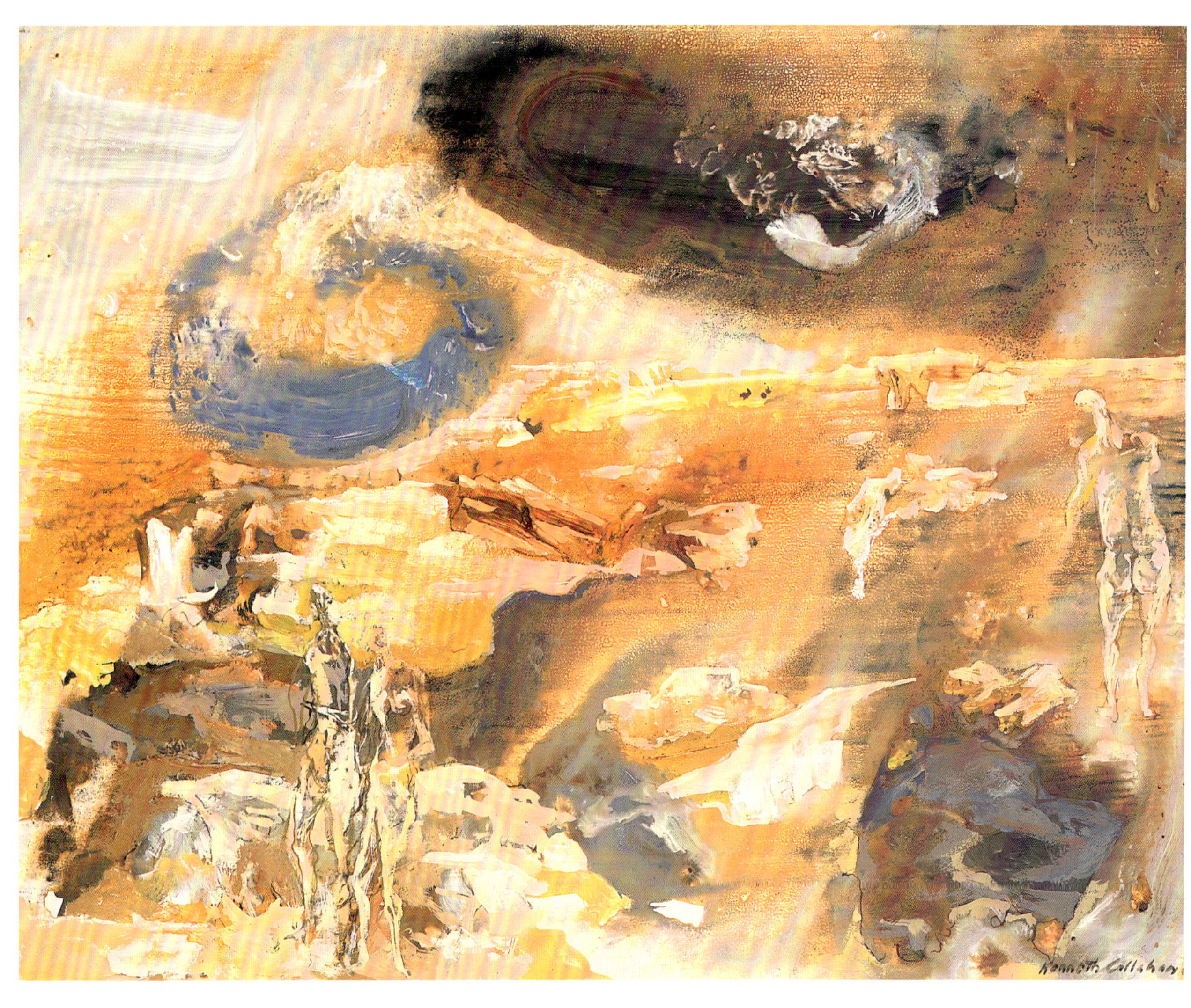

Desert Landscape, 1962
Oil on canvas
13 × 16½ inches
University of Oregon Museum of Art,
Virginia Haseltine Collection of Pacific Northwest Art

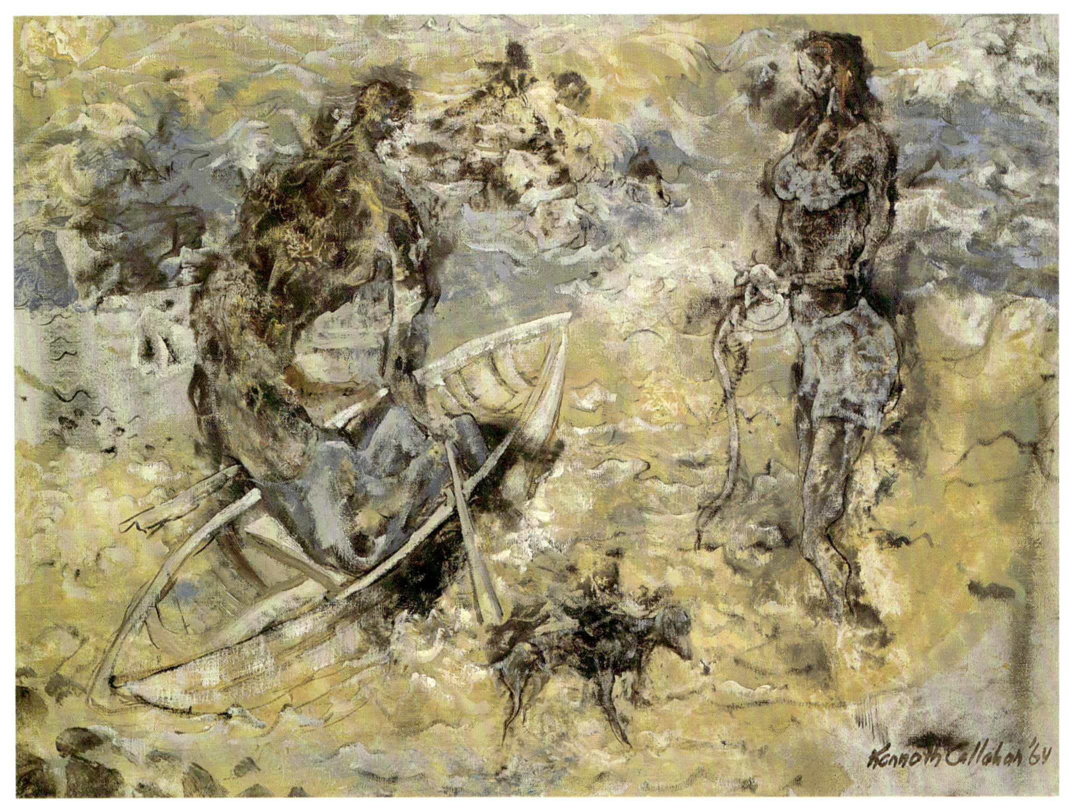

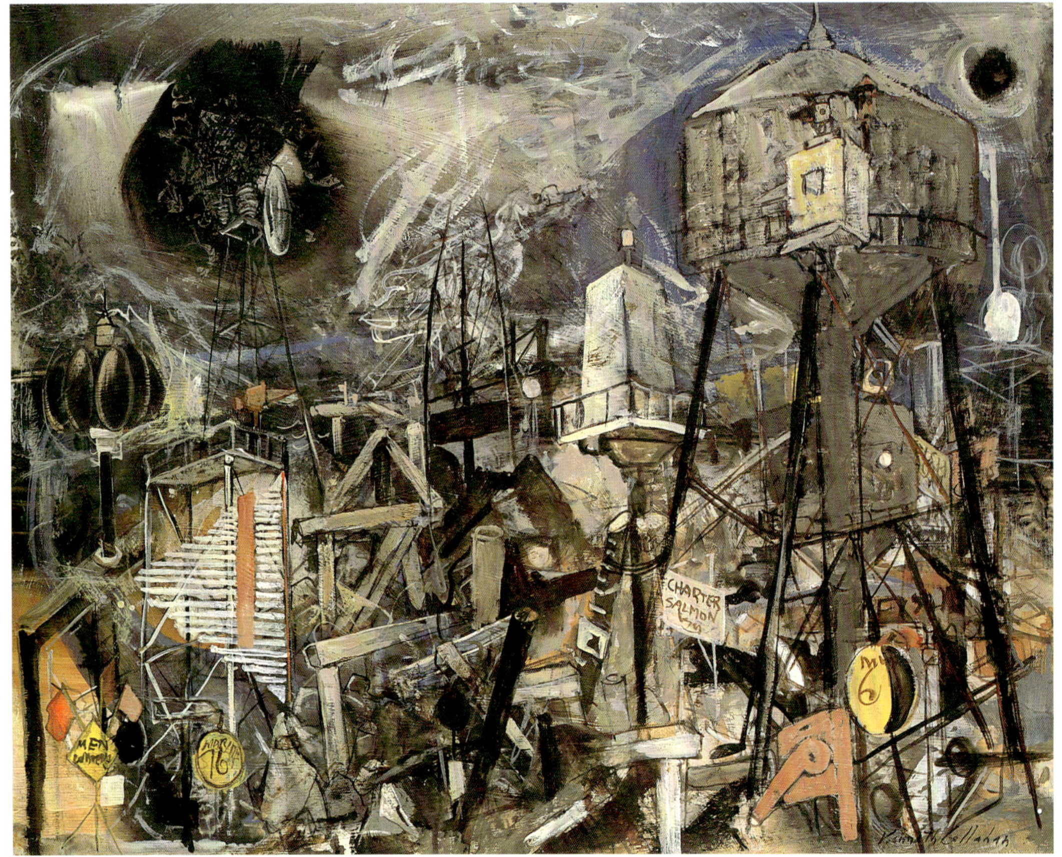

TOP:

The Fisherman, 1964
Oil and tempera on panel
21 × 28 inches
Collection of Manfred and Karen Laband

BOTTOM:

Ilwaco Harbor #2, 1964
Tempera on panel
23 × 29 inches
Collection of Carolyn and Guy Glenn

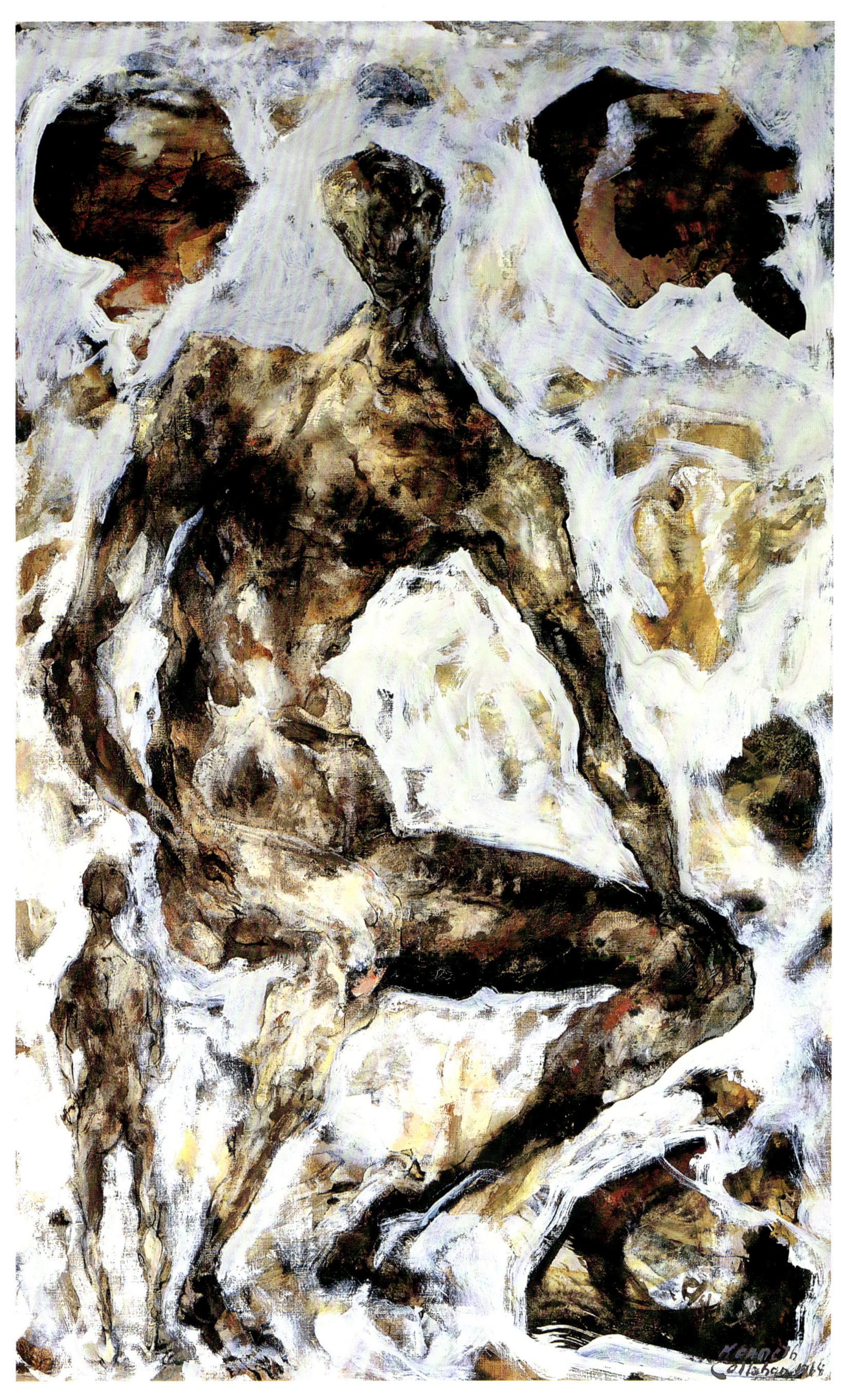

The Waiters, 1964
Oil on canvas
43 × 27 inches
Corcoran Gallery of Art, Washington, D.C.,
Gift of the Friends of the Corcoran Gallery of Art, 67.1

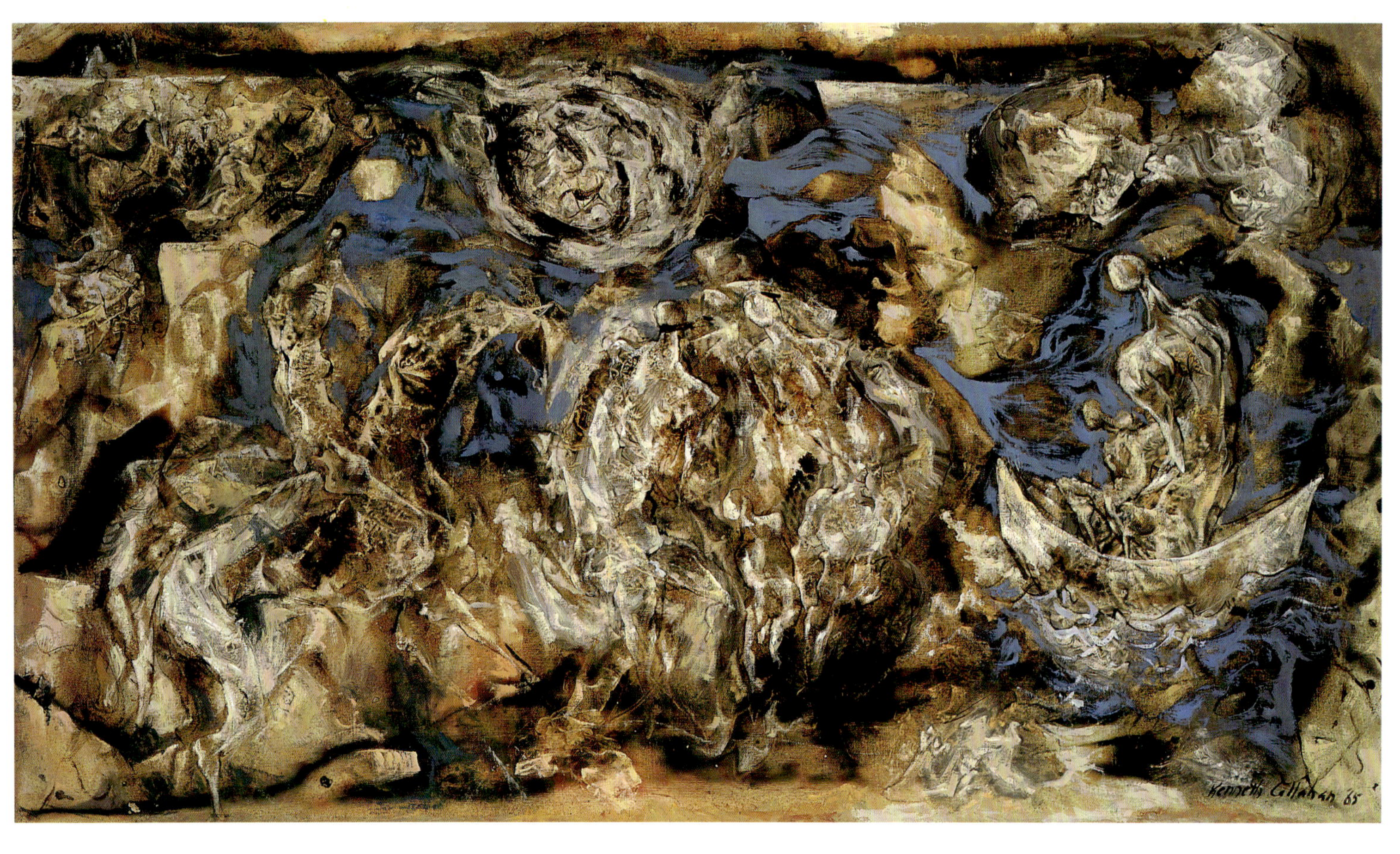

The Meeting, 1965
Tempera on canvas on board
39½ × 61½ inches
Safeco Collection, Seattle

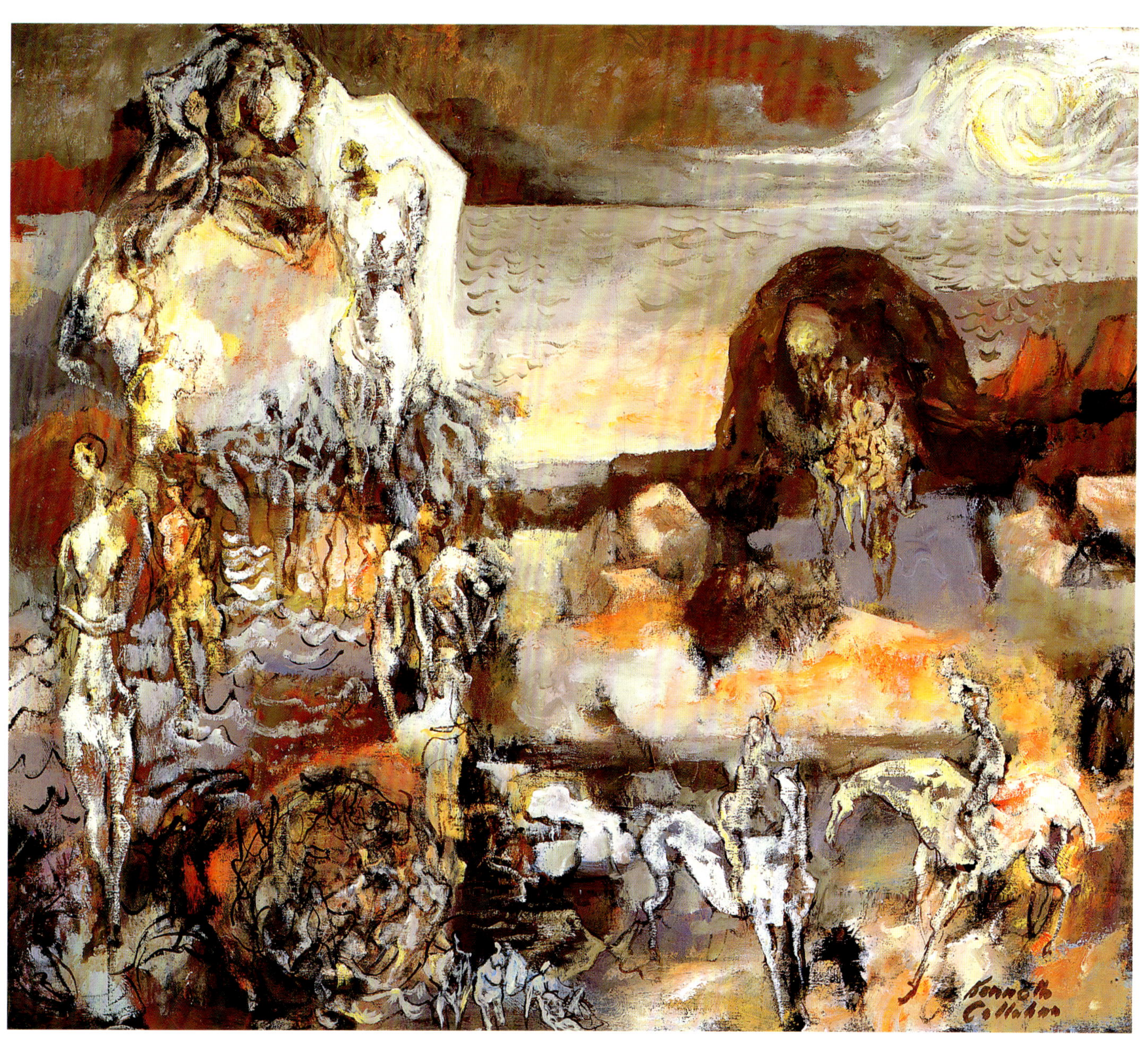

Untitled, ca. 1965
Oil on canvas on board
30 × 34 inches
Private collection

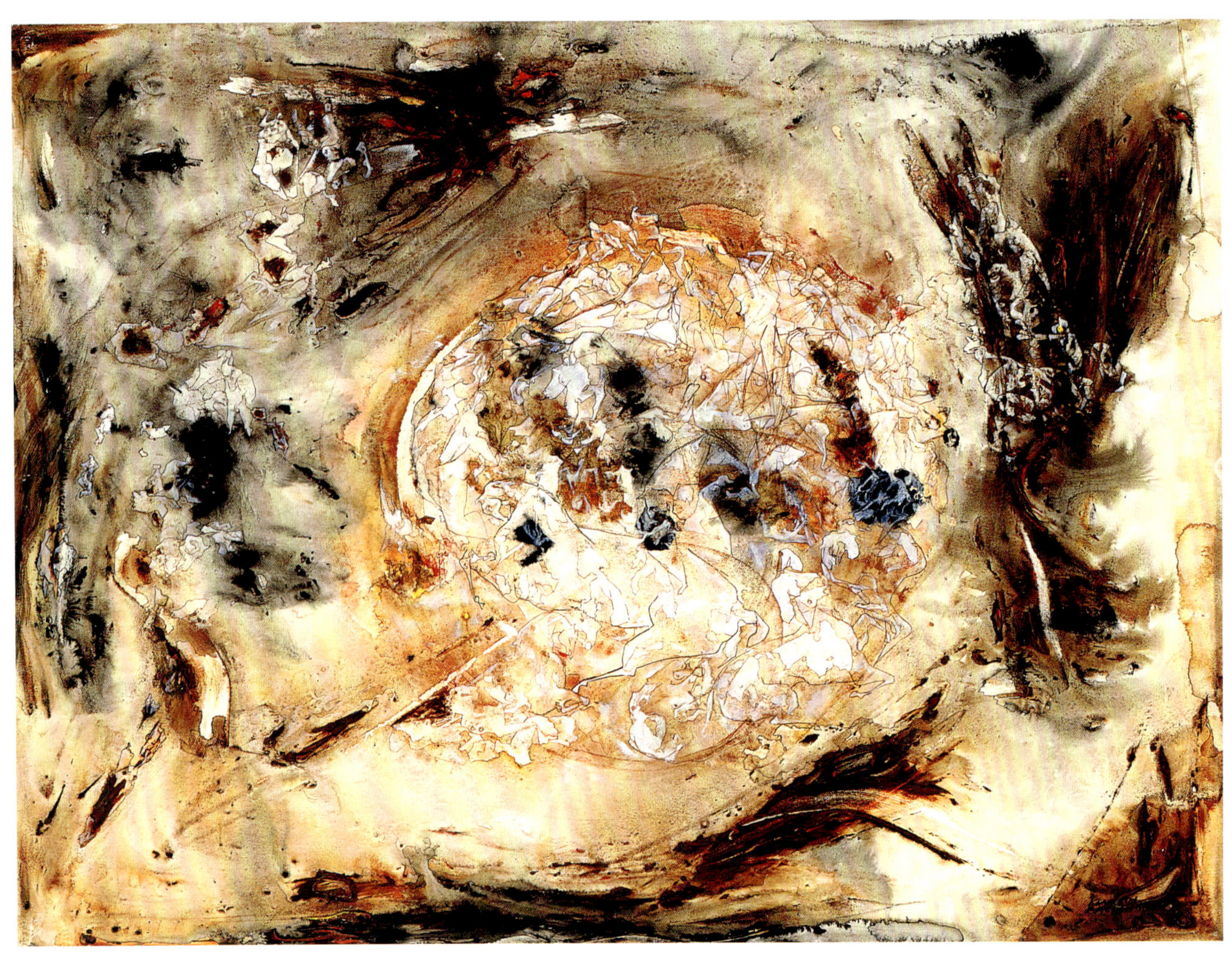

November, 1968
Tempera on board
$23\frac{1}{2} \times 31\frac{1}{2}$ inches
Courtesy, The Laura Russo Gallery

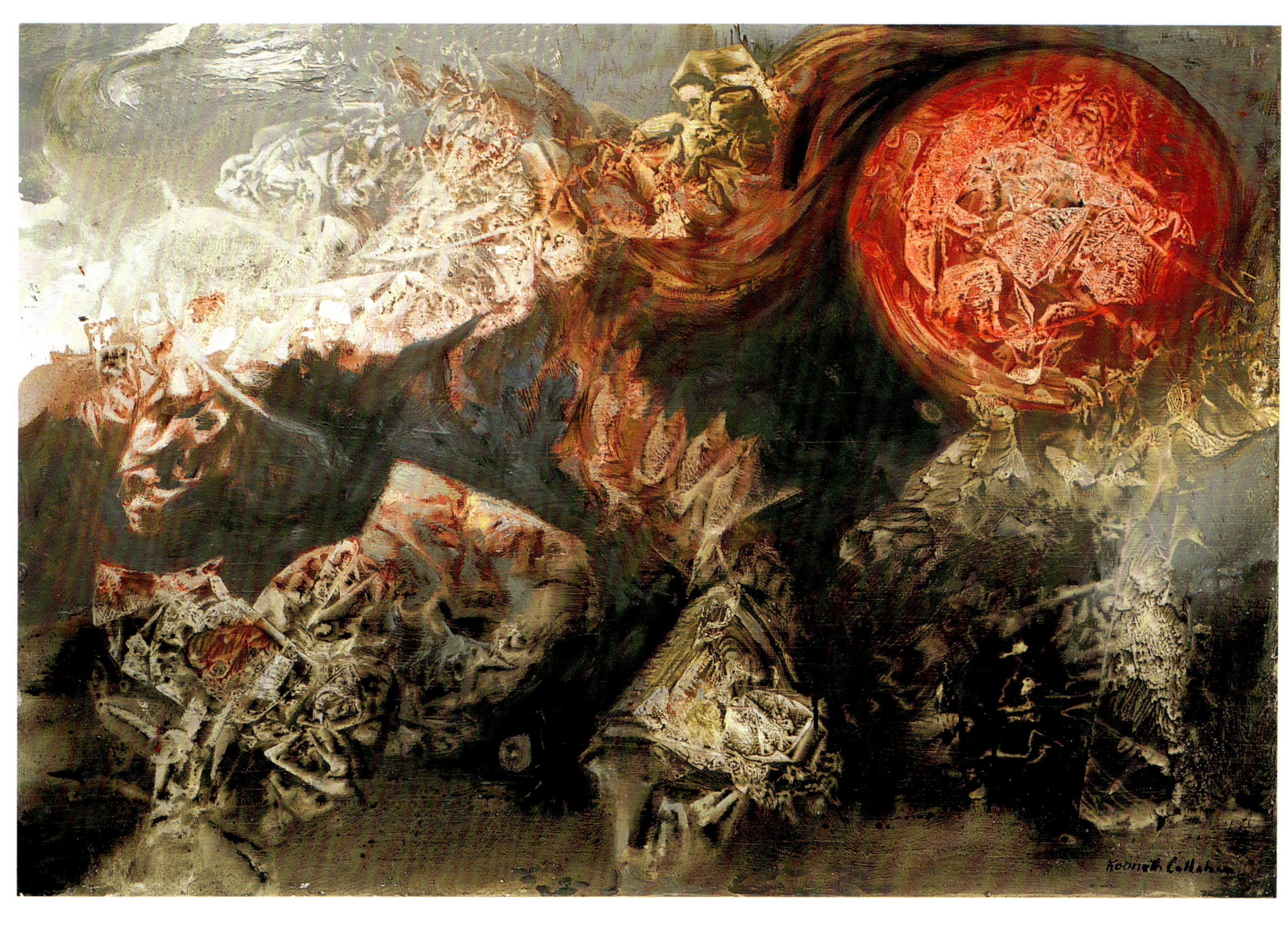

Fiery Globe, ca. 1967–68
Oil on board
29 × 40 inches
Seattle Arts Commission

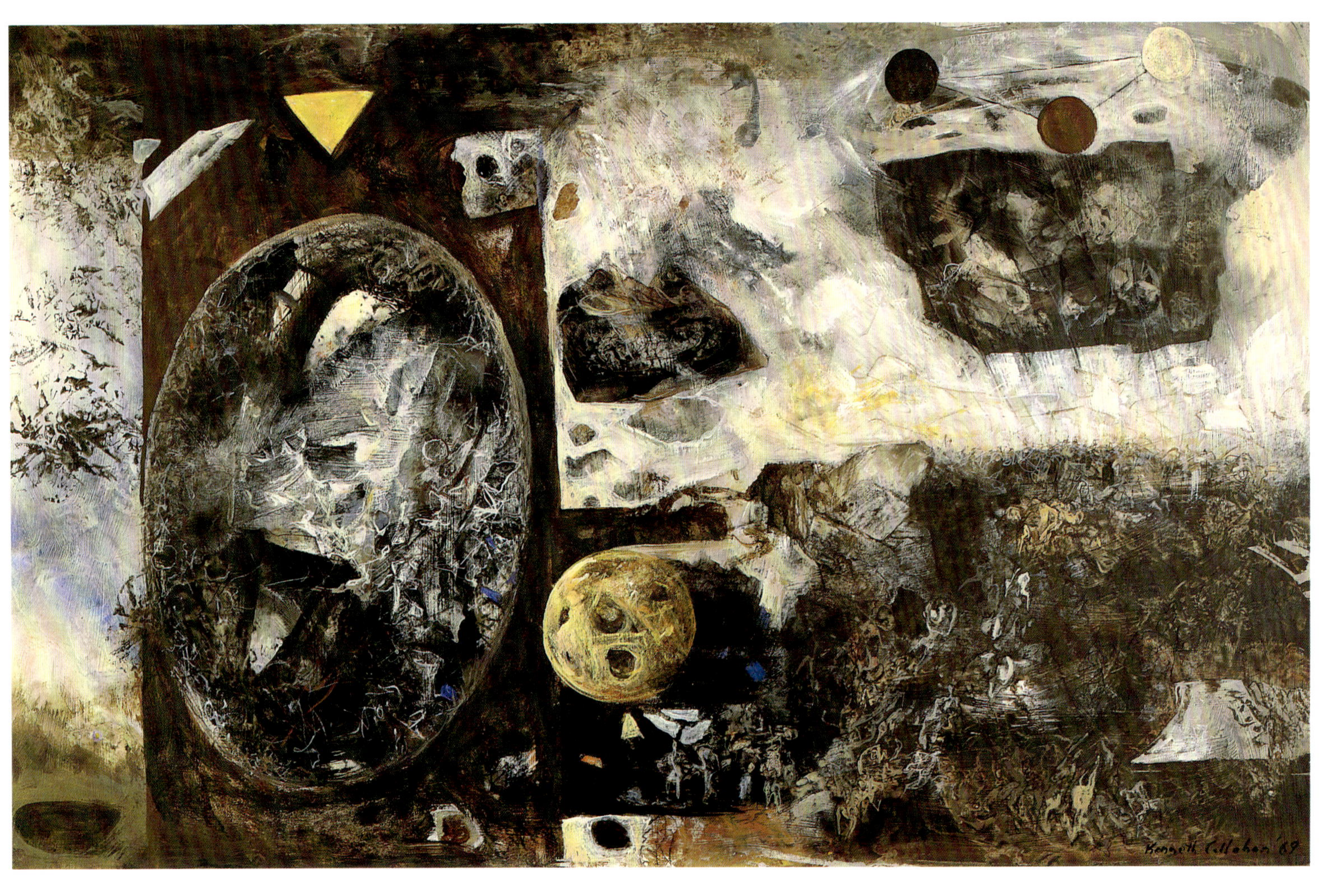

Fractured Egg, 1969
Oil and tempera on board
30⅛ × 48 inches
Neuberger Museum of Art, Purchase College, State University of New York, gift of Roy R. Neuberger

OPPOSITE:
Susanna and the Elders, ca. 1960s
Tempera on paper on board
16 × 18 inches
Collection of Dr. and Mrs. Stanley W. Jackson, Bethany, Connecticut

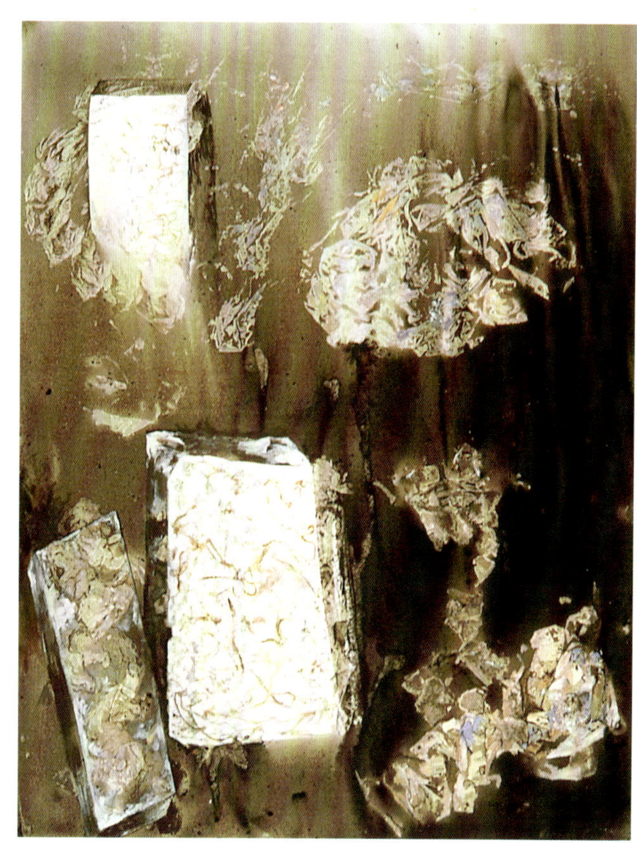

The Tablets, 1968
Tempera on paper on board
28½ × 22½ inches
New Britain Museum of American Art

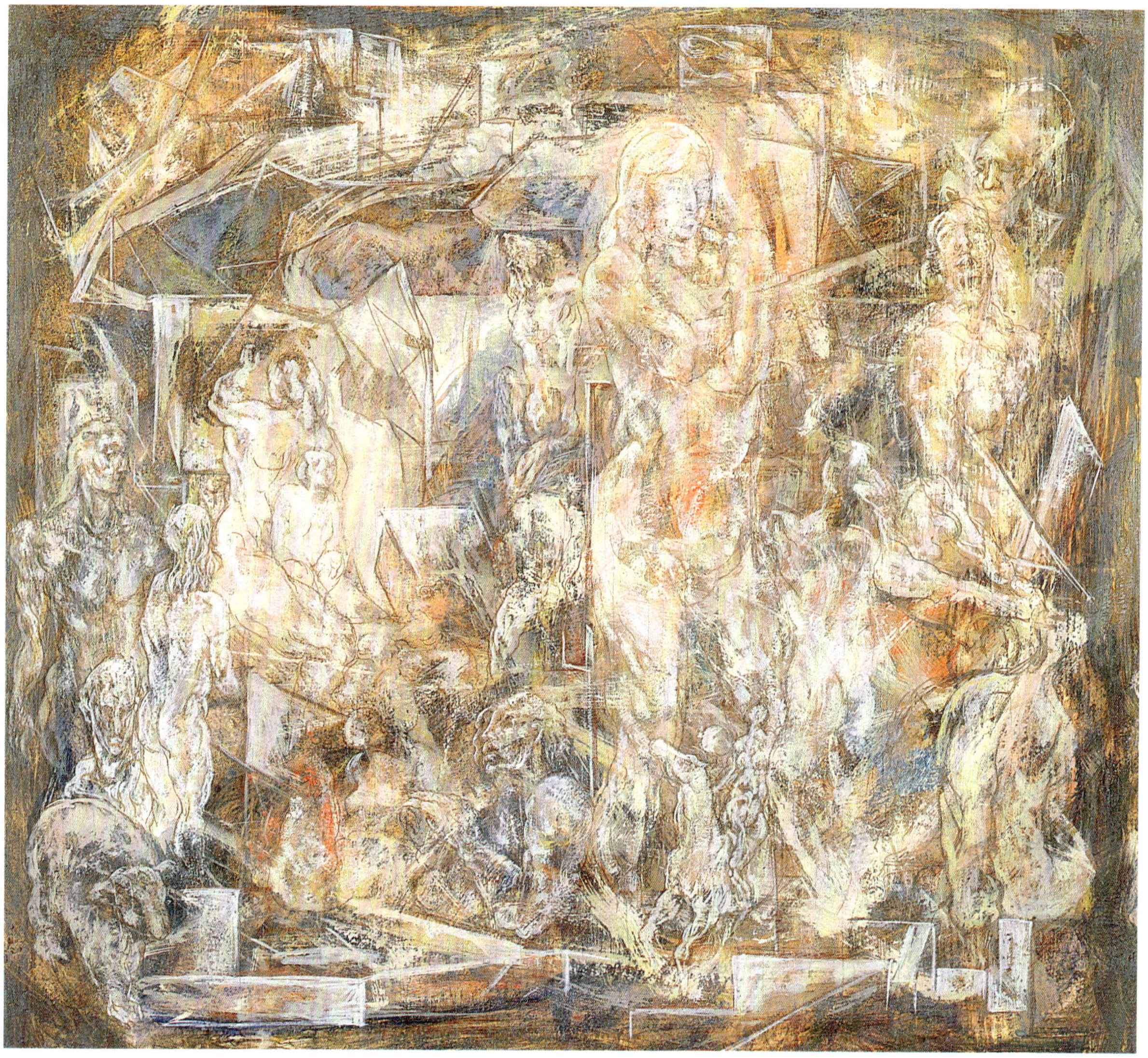

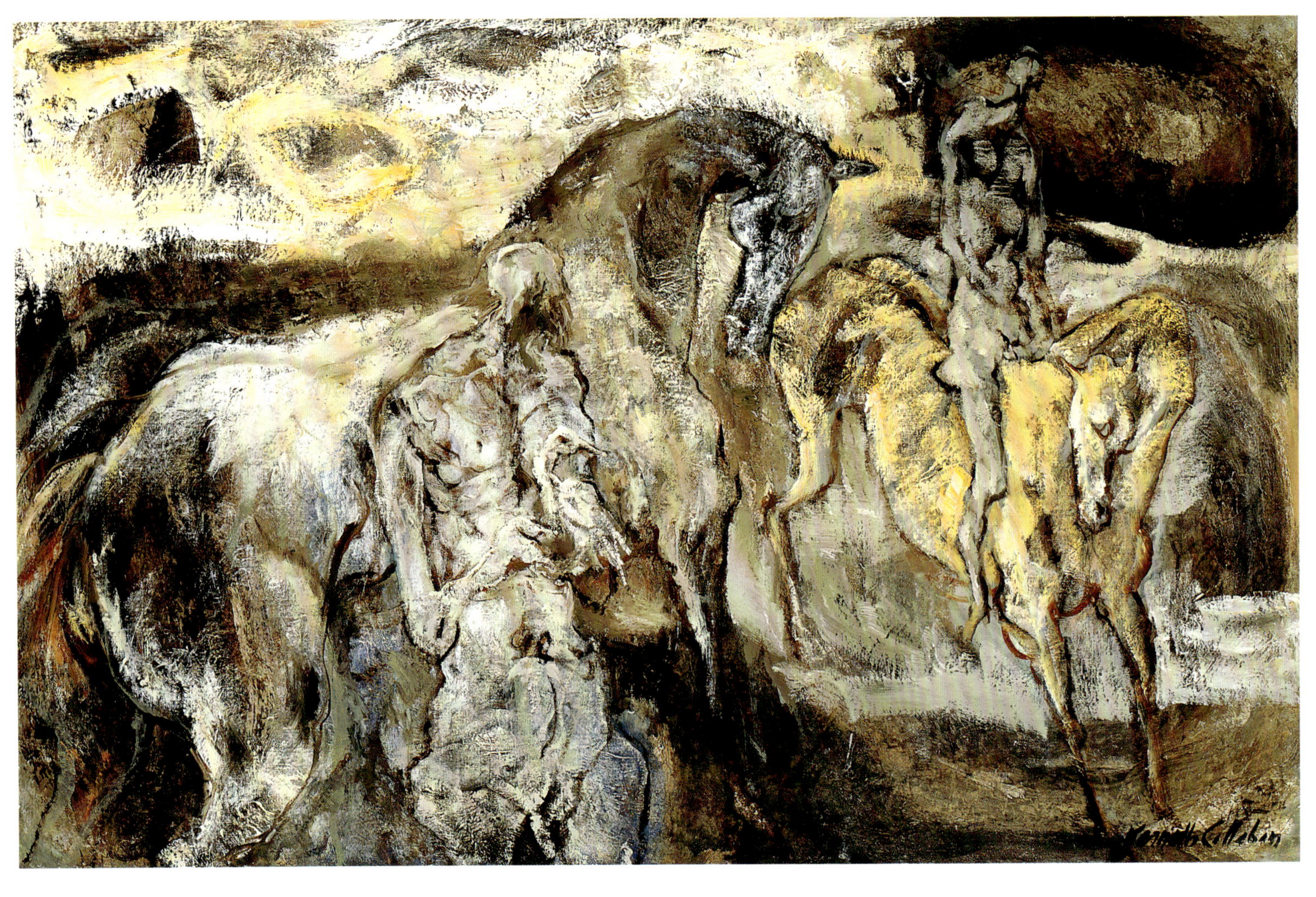

The Meeting, 1969
Oil on canvas
35 × 51 inches
Collection of Gerry and Barbara Pratt

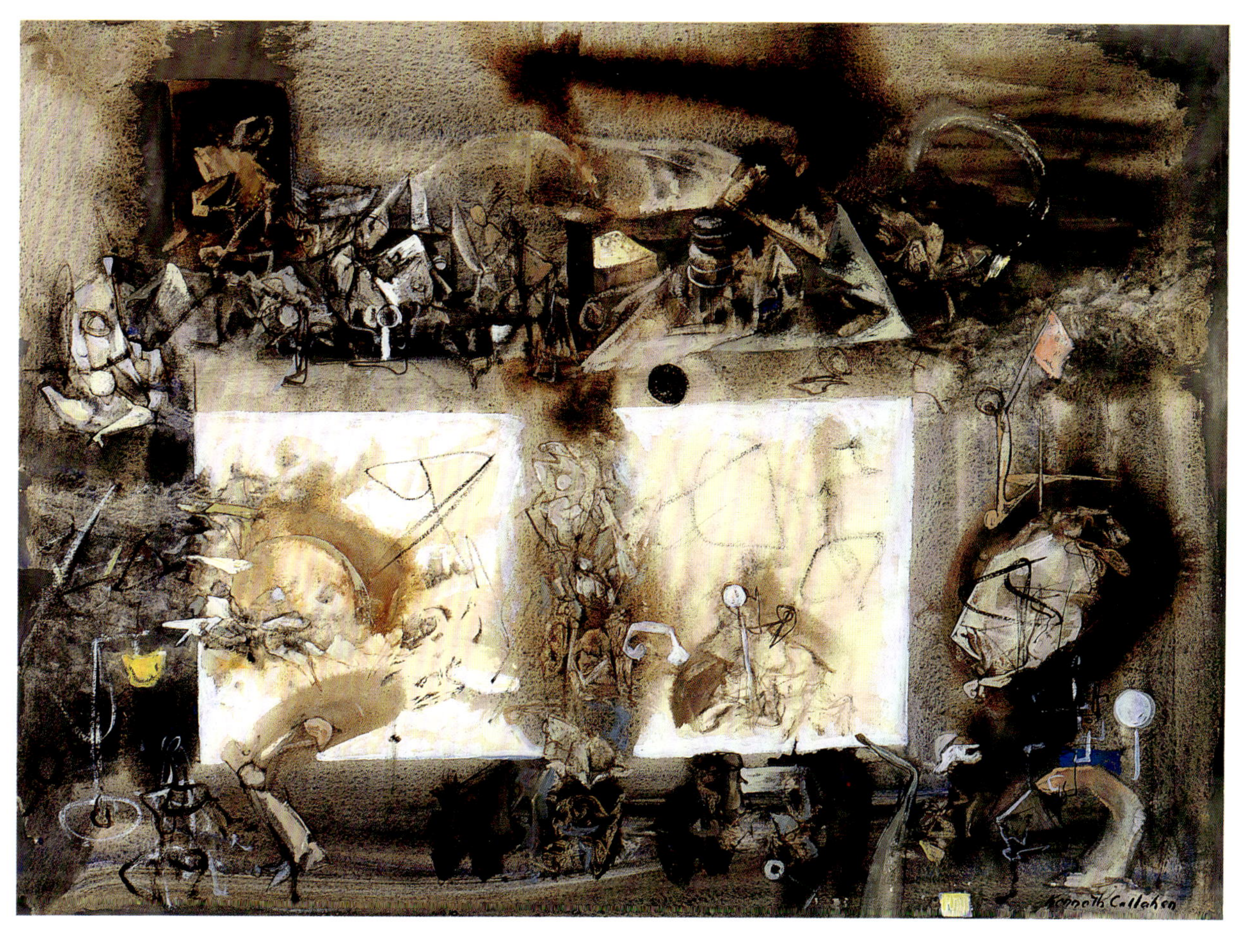

Prepared Table, 1969
Oil and tempera on cardboard on plywood
$22\frac{3}{8} \times 31$ inches
New Orleans Museum of Art, gift of the Childe Hassam Fund of the American Academy of Arts and Letters

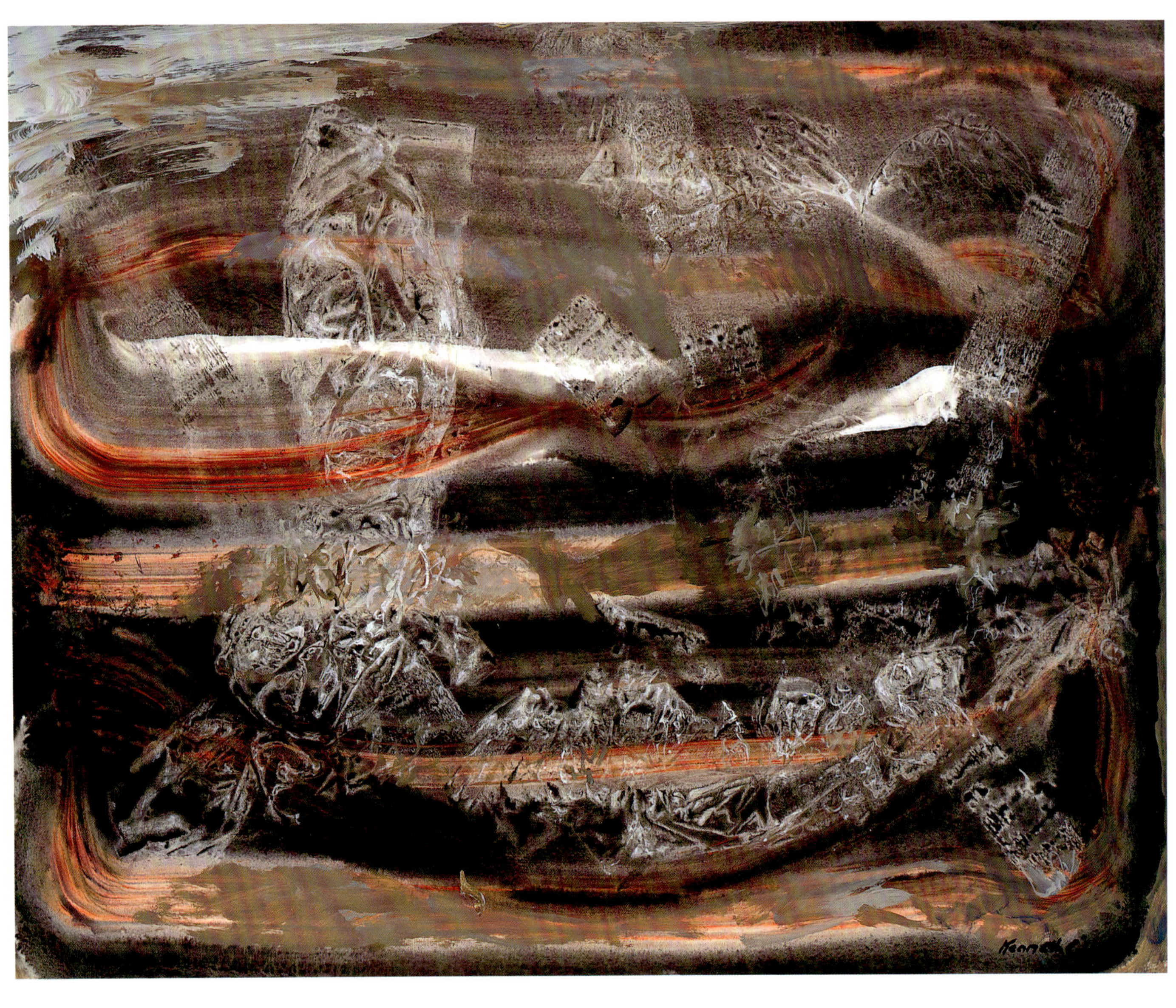

Untitled, ca. 1970s
Acrylic on paper
36 × 44 inches
Collection of Becky and Jack Benaroya

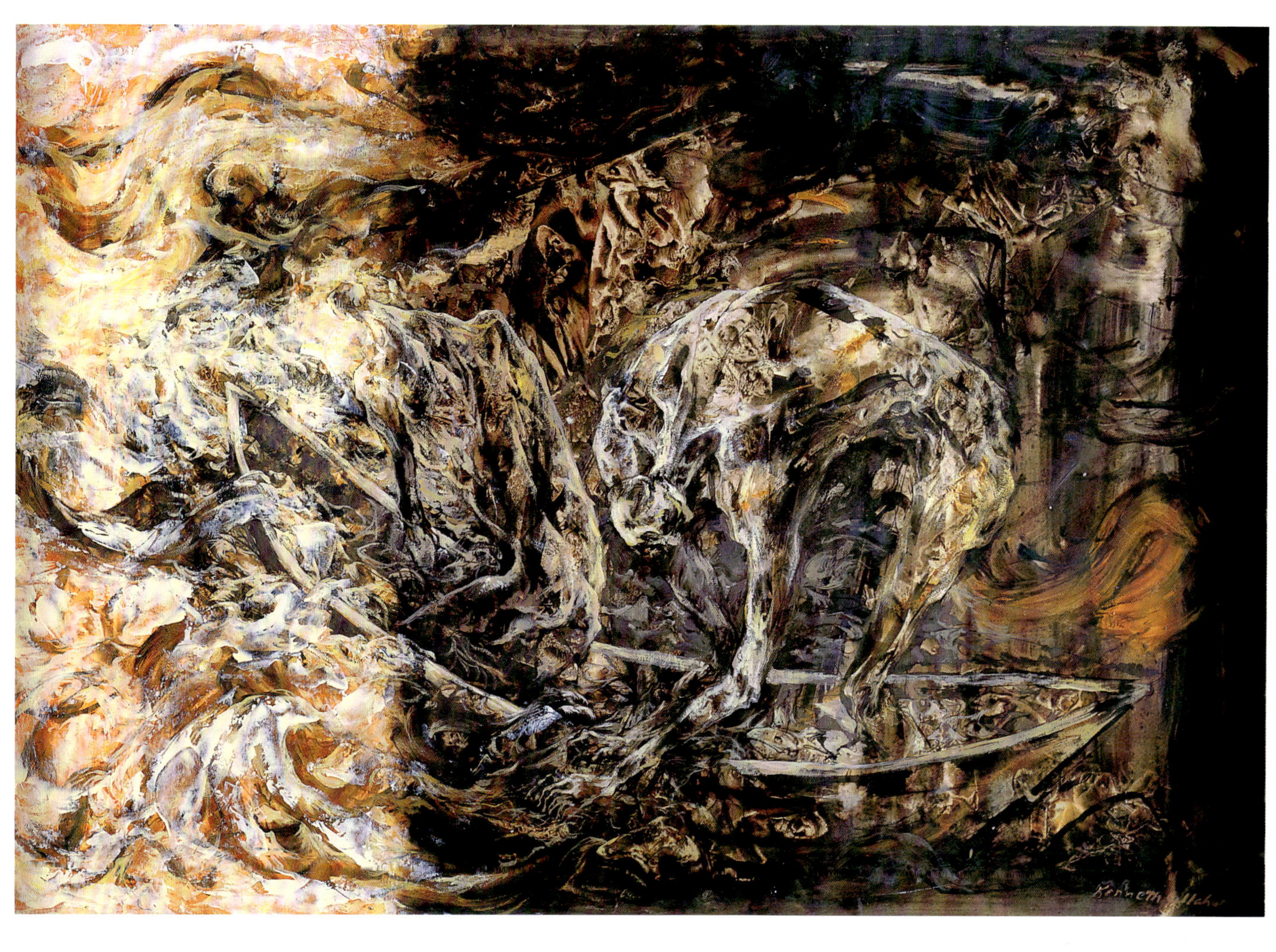

Odysseus #1, n.d.
Tempera on paper
24 × 35 inches
Courtesy, Foster/White Gallery

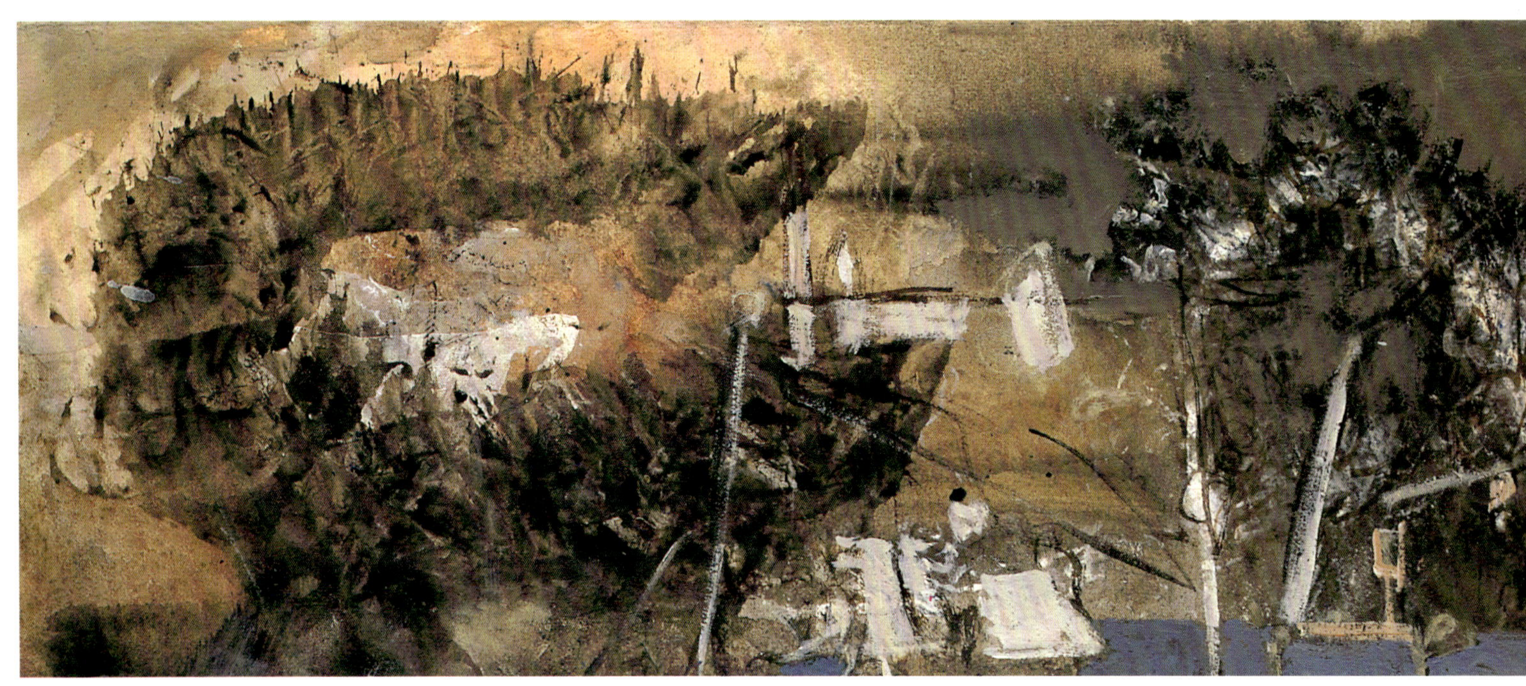

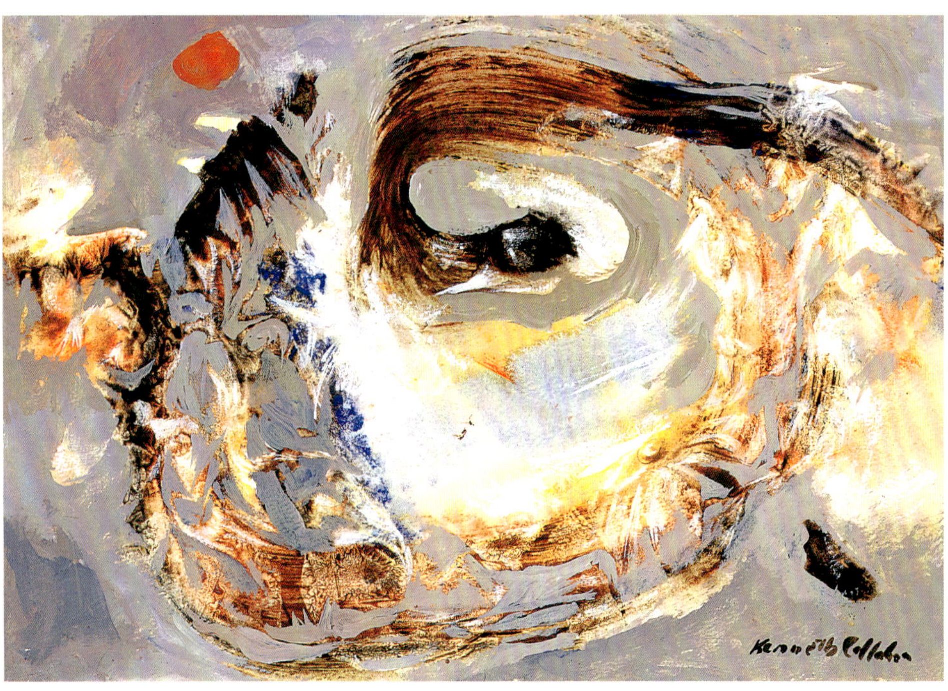

TOP:
The Floating City, 1970
Oil and tempera on board
$6\frac{1}{2} \times 30$ inches
Law Offices of Seligmann Beckerman and Flaherty

BOTTOM:
Tidepool, 1970
Tempera and oil on paper
$10\frac{1}{4} \times 15$ inches
Collection of Don and Marcia Emenhiser

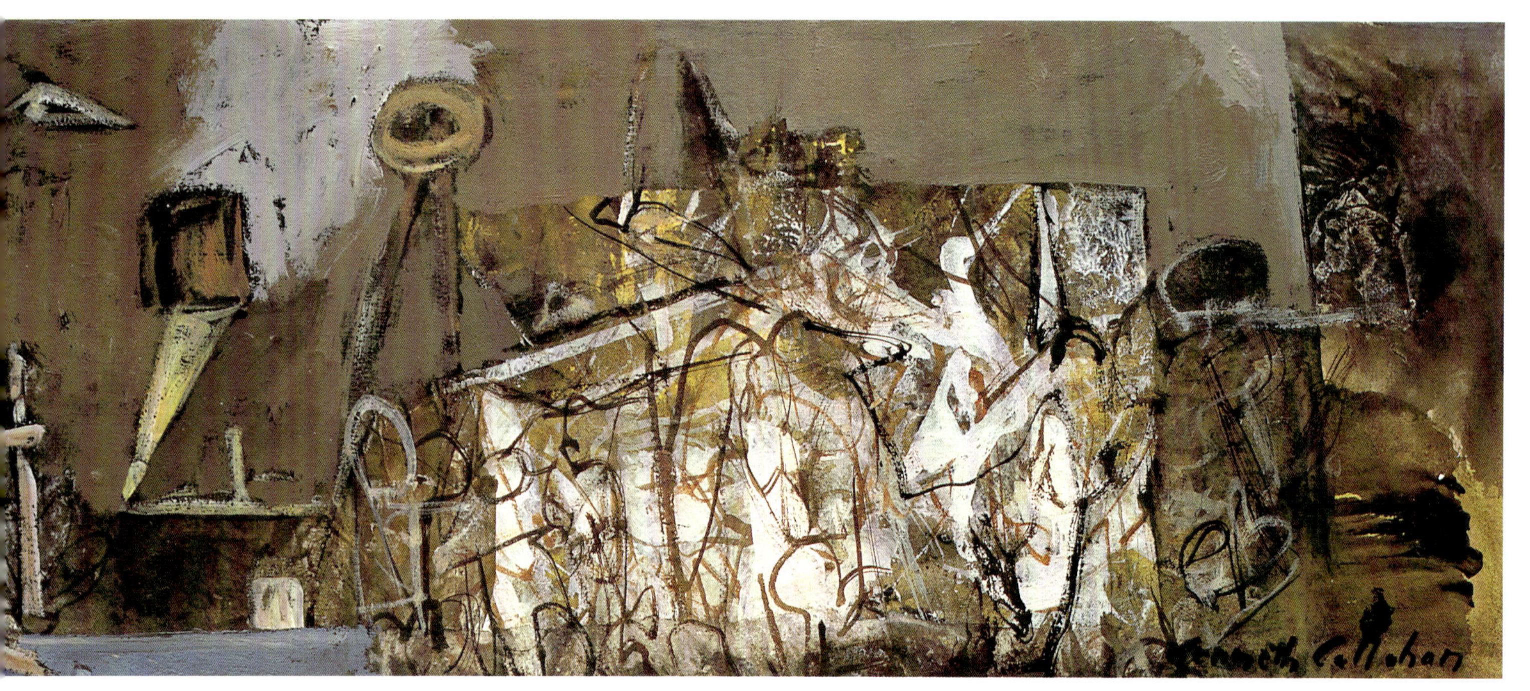

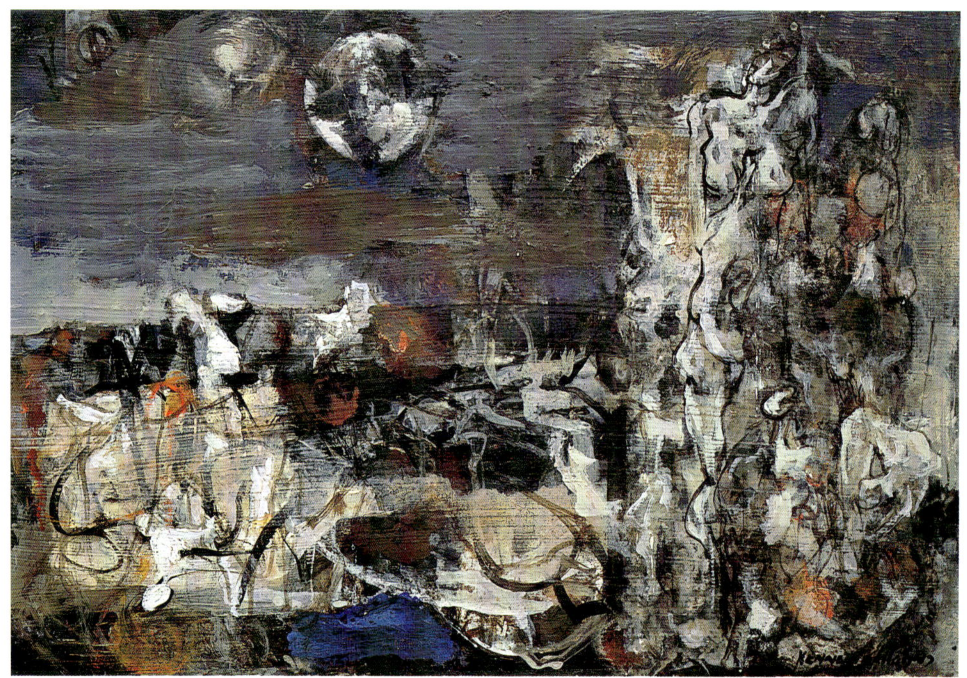

The Gathering, 1970
Tempera and oil on panel
$10 \times 14\frac{1}{2}$ inches
Collection of Erica and Robert William

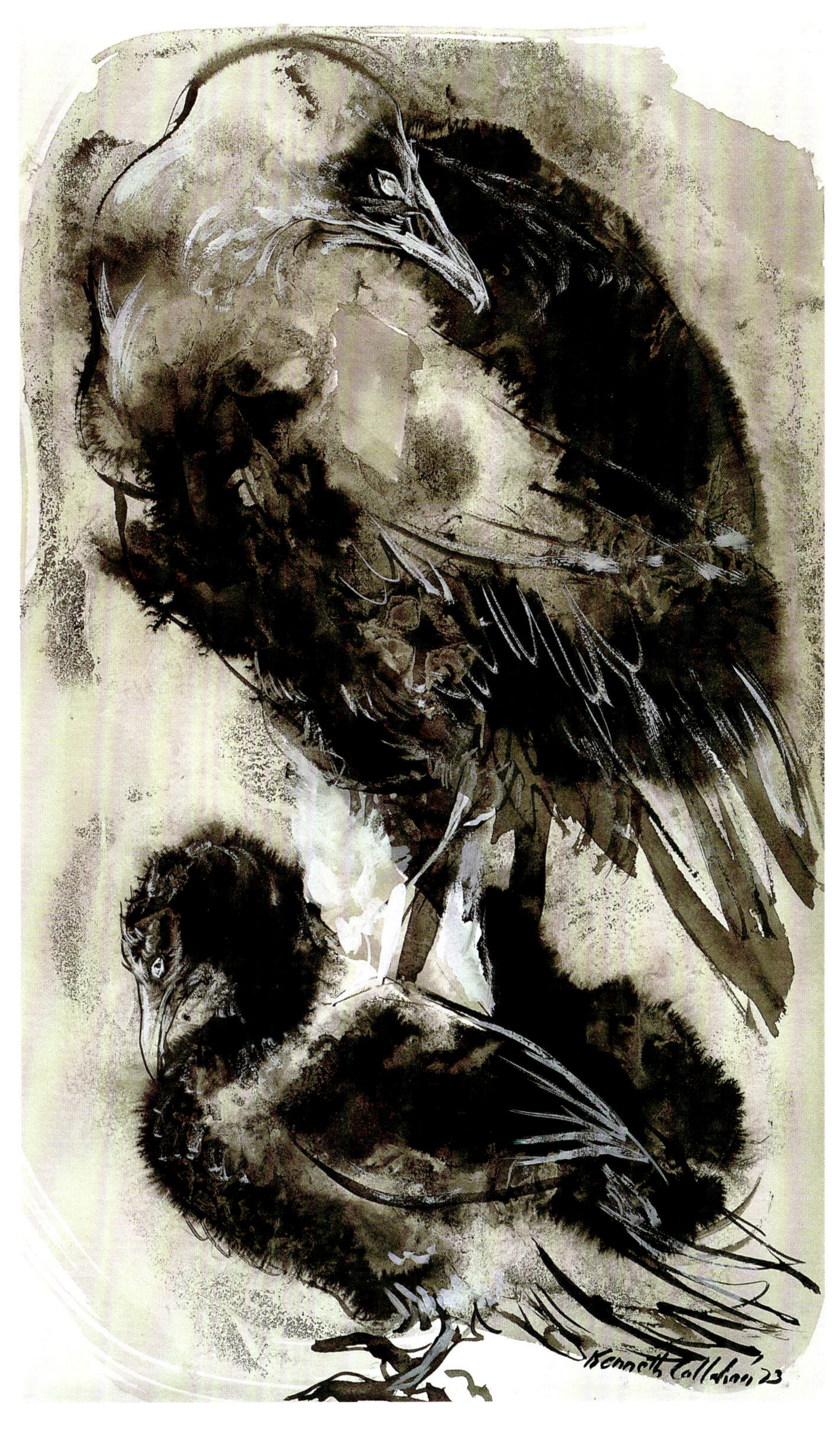

Crows, 1973
Sumi ink on paper
20 × 13 inches
Collection of Dr. and Mrs. Nicholas Berman

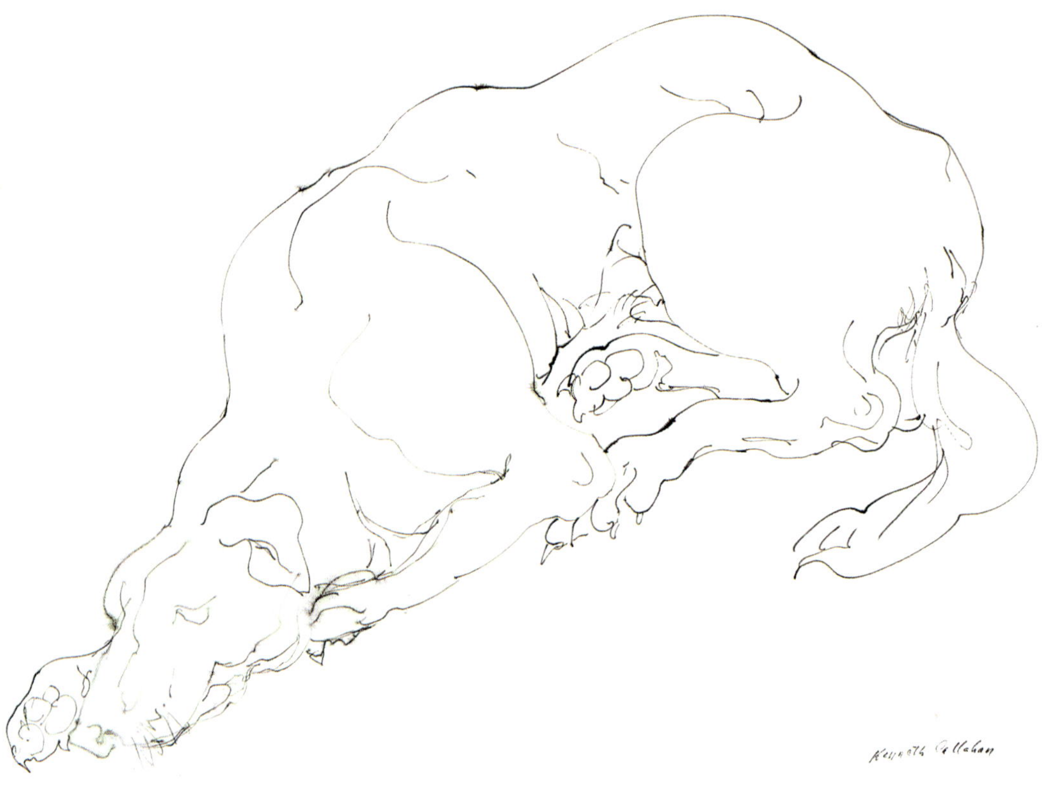

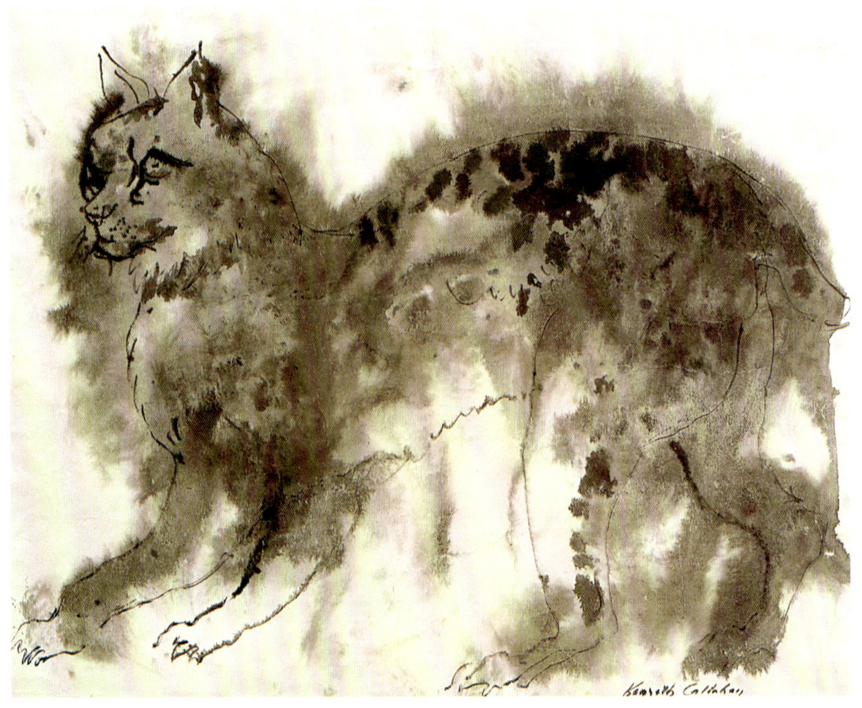

TOP:

Mexican Dog, 1970
Ink and board
$21^{3}/_{4} \times 29^{3}/_{4}$ inches
Collection of Mikell and Brian T. Callahan

BOTTOM:

Cat, n.d.
Ink on paper
$16^{1}/_{2} \times 20^{1}/_{2}$ inches
Private collection

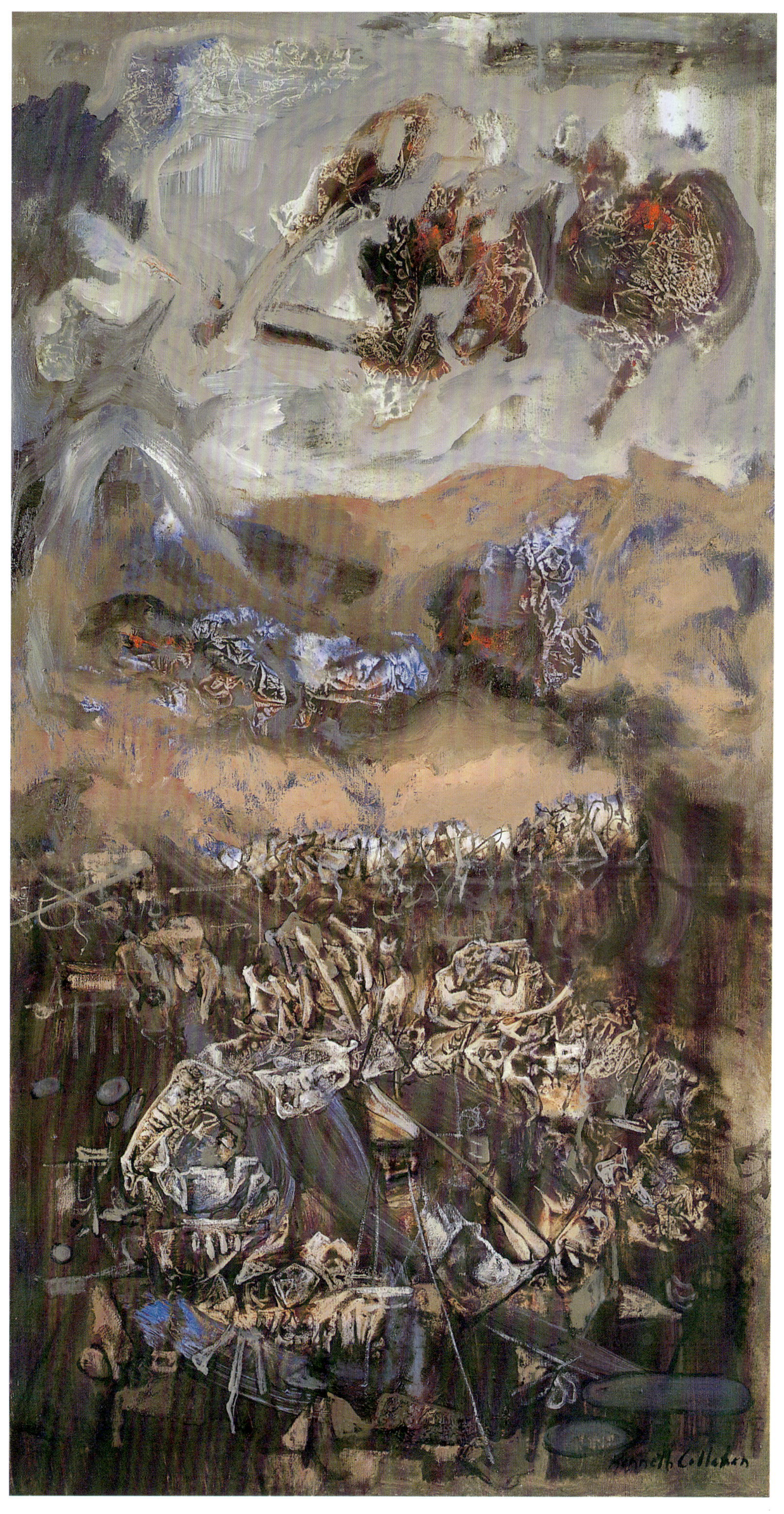
Kenneth Callahan

OPPOSITE:

The Ring, 1971
Oil on canvas
44 1/8 × 23 7/8 inches
Washington State University Museum of Art,
gift of Beth Callahan

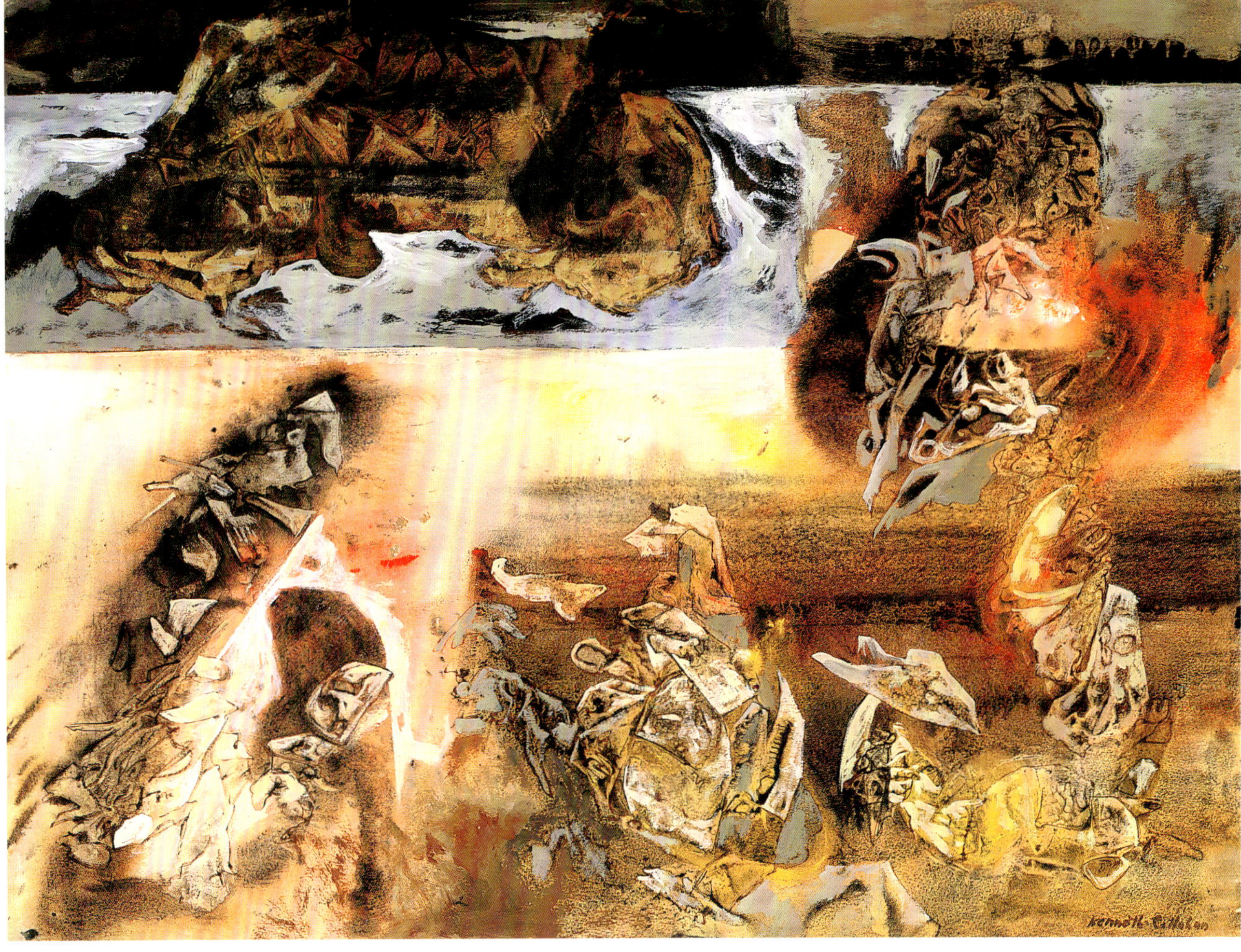

The Island, ca. 1972–73
Tempera and oil on paper on board
22 × 29 1/2 inches
Private collection

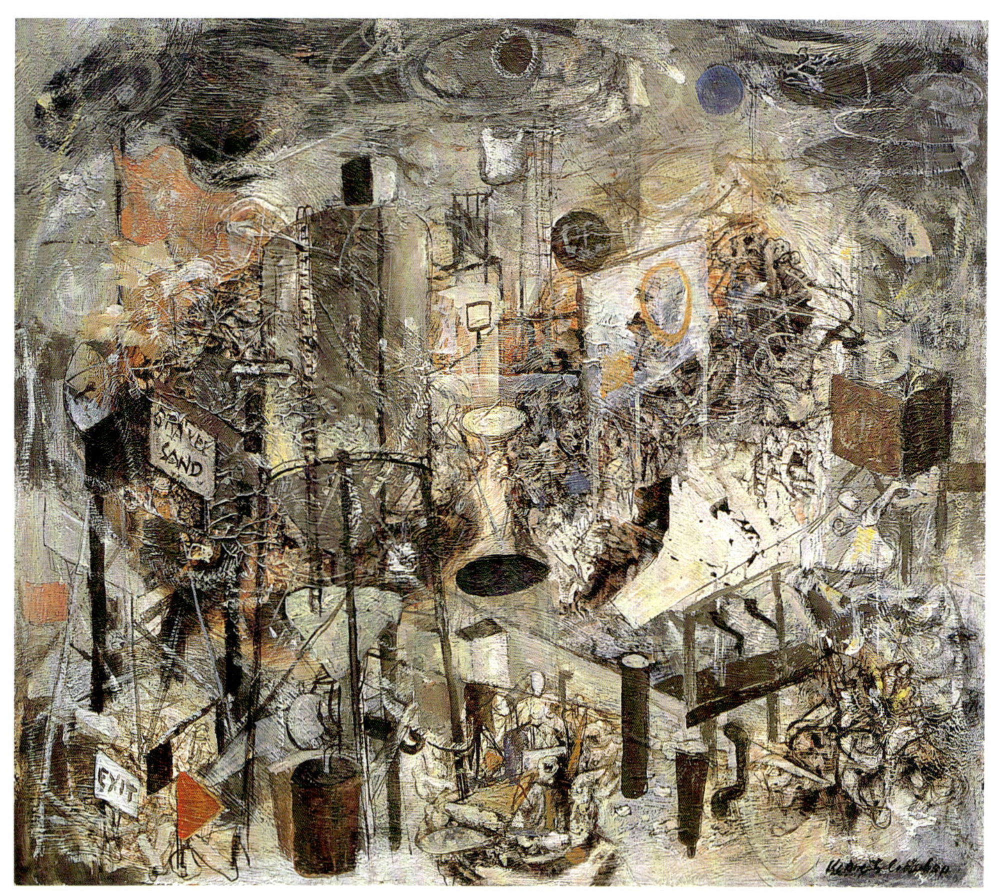

City Scene, 1973
Tempera and oil on panel
18 × 21 inches
Collection of Curtis and Paula Green

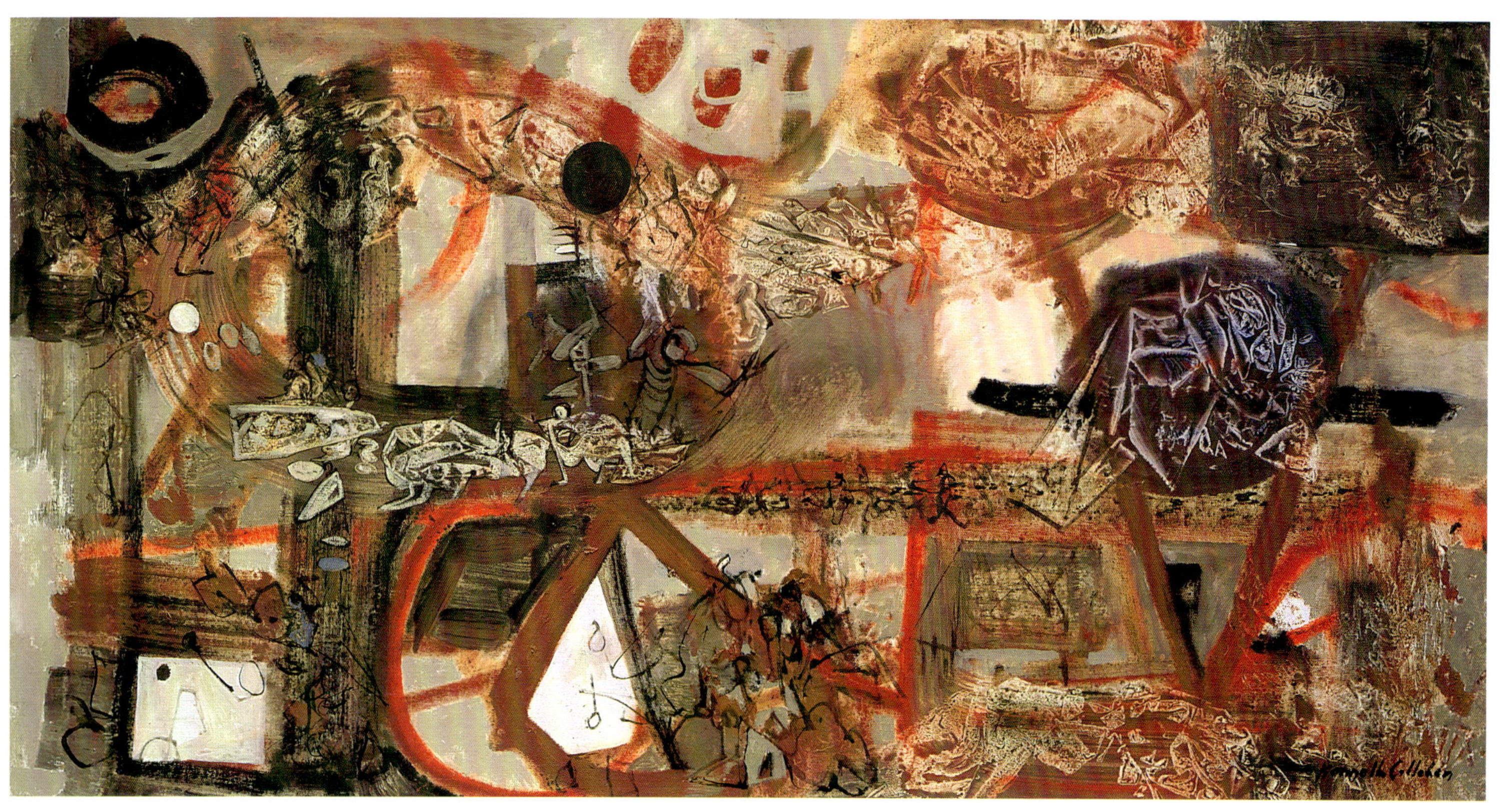

Structural Shift, 1971
Oil on canvas
26 × 51 inches
Collection of Lee and Barbara Yates

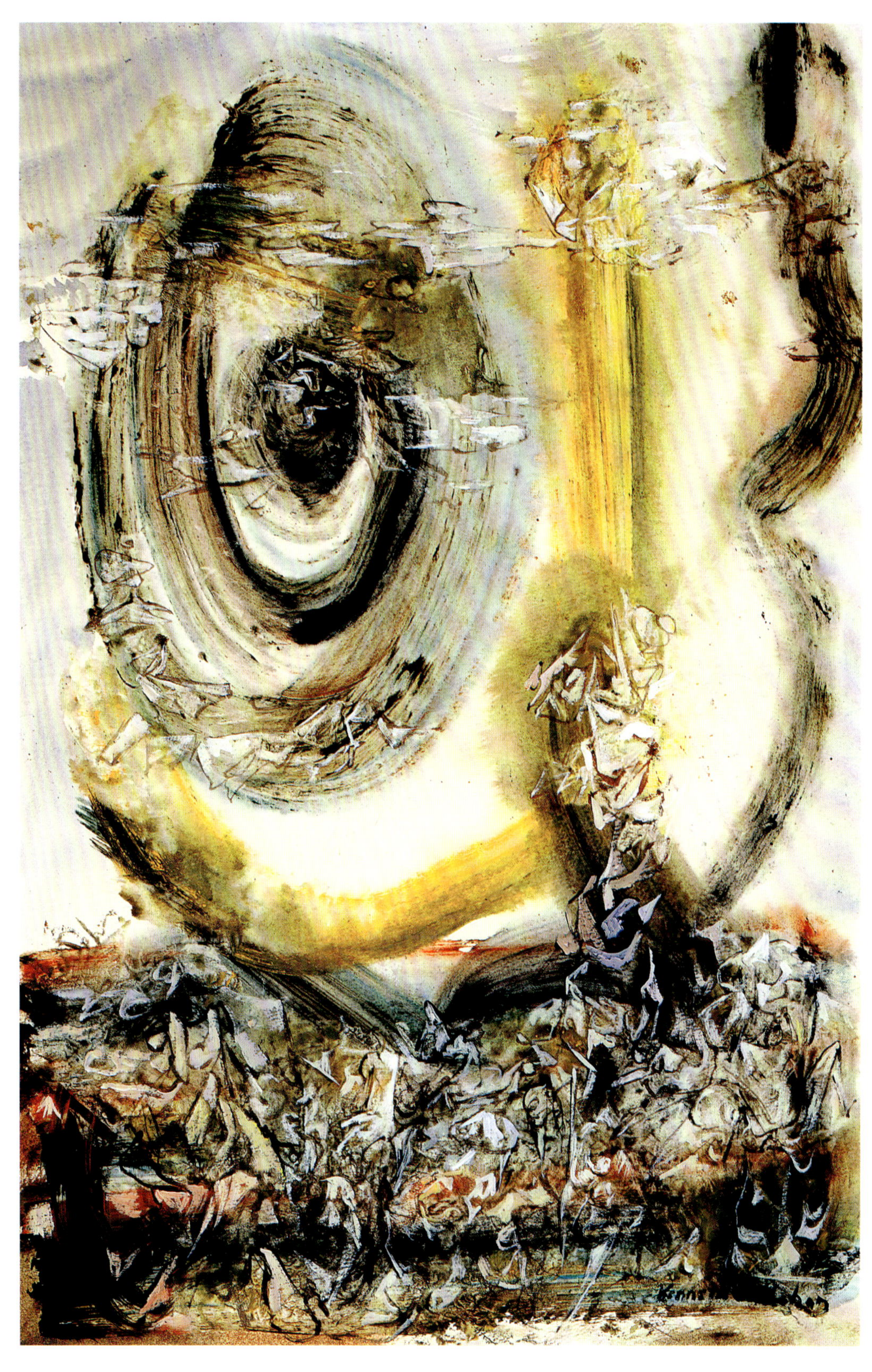

Festival, ca. 1974
Egg tempera and oil
$27\frac{1}{2} \times 20\frac{1}{4}$ inches
Collection of Don and Marcia Emenhiser

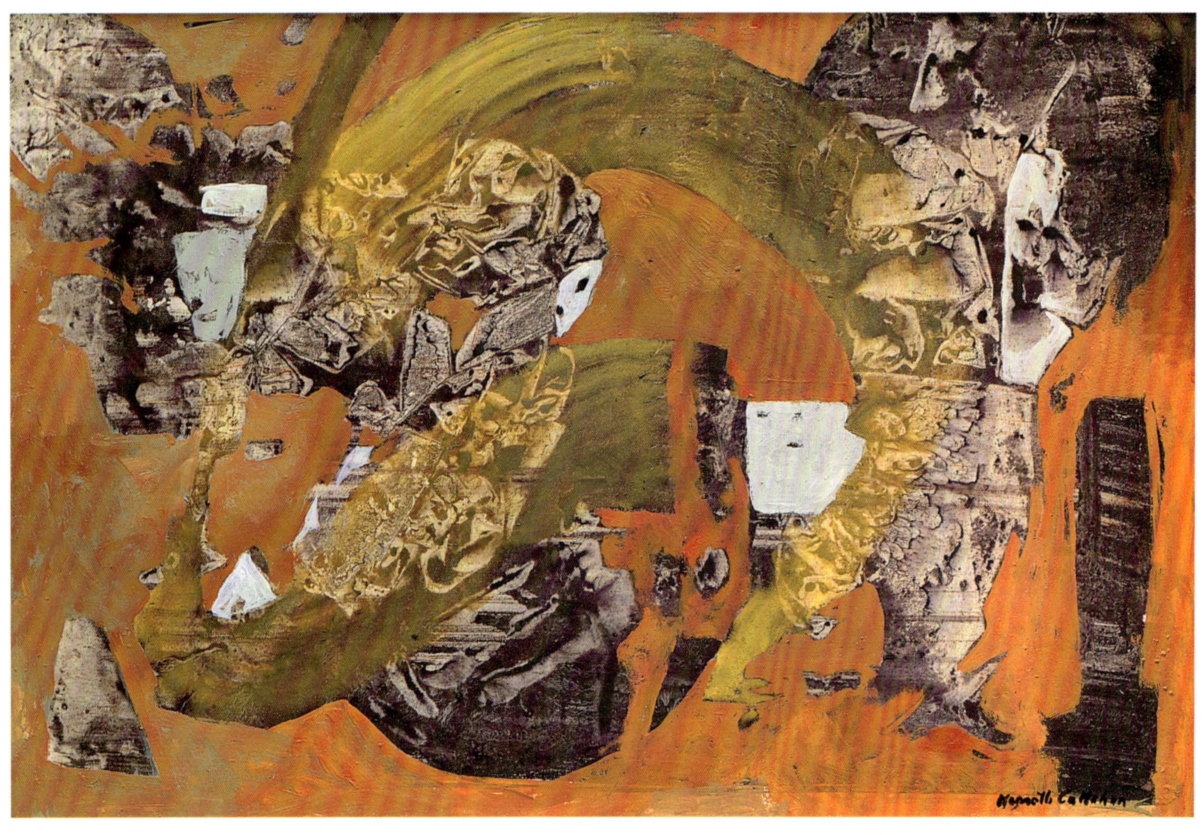

Red Wall, 1975
Tempera on paper
15 × 23 inches
Collection of Ann S. and John W. Ormsby

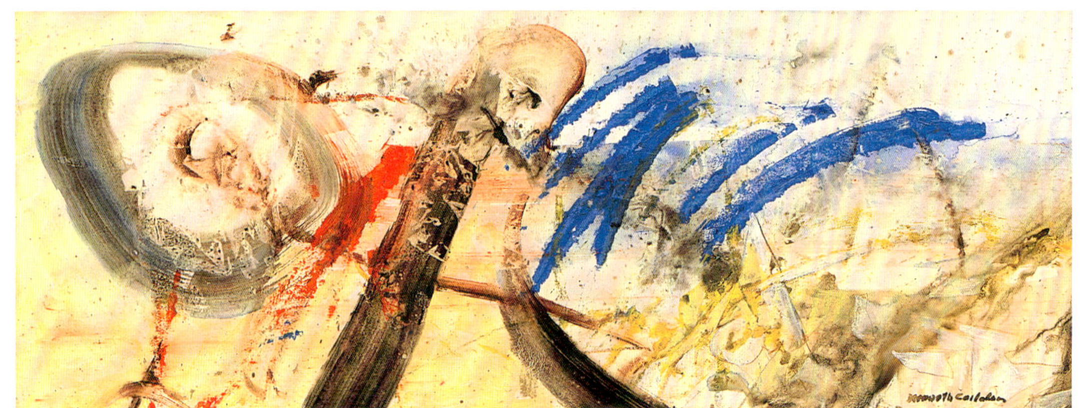

Summer Landscape, 1976
Oil and tempera on canvas
10 × 27 inches
Collection of Lee and Barbara Yates

Summer Rhythms, 1976
Oil and tempera on board
40 × 60 inches
Collection of Lee and Barbara Yates

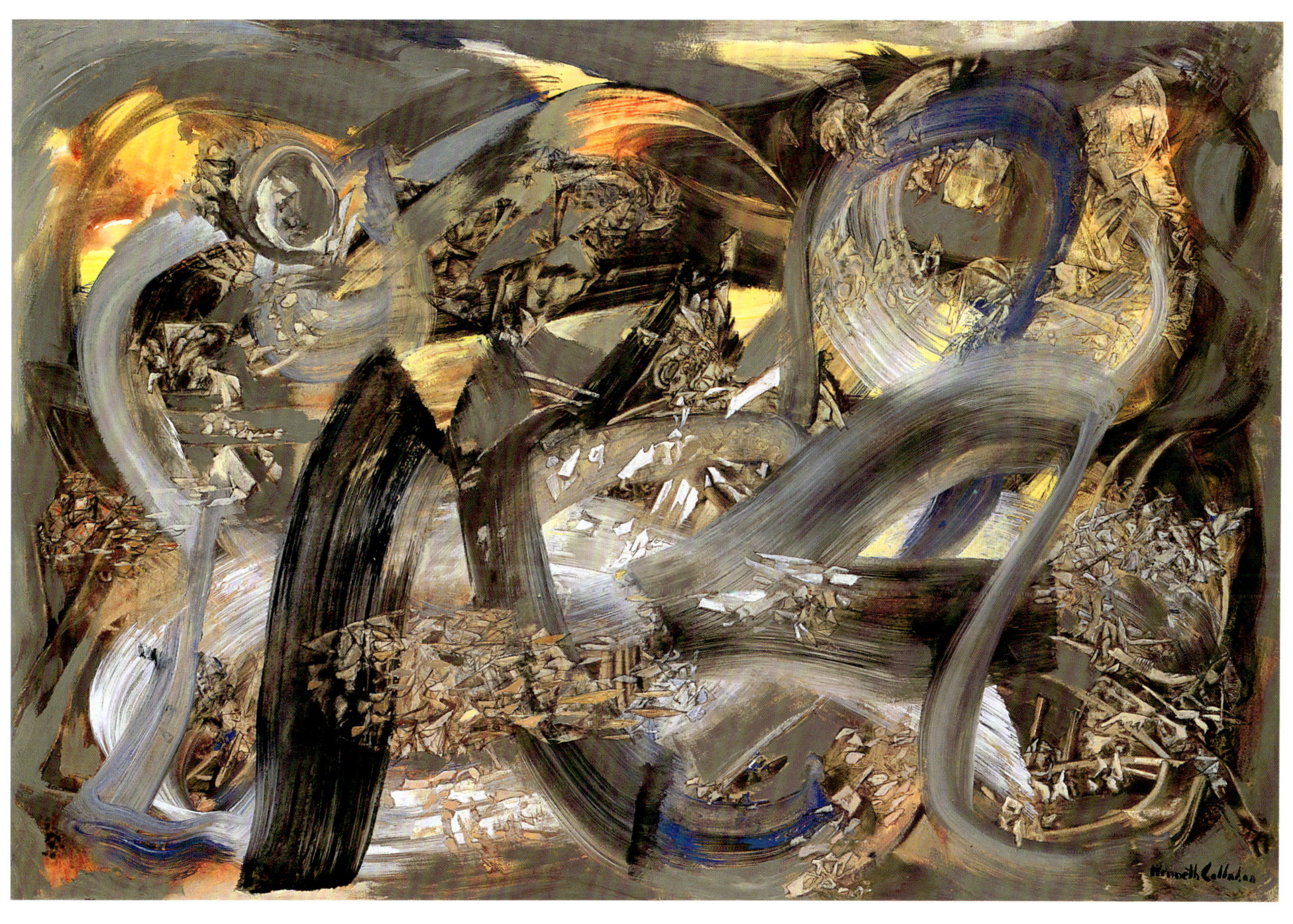

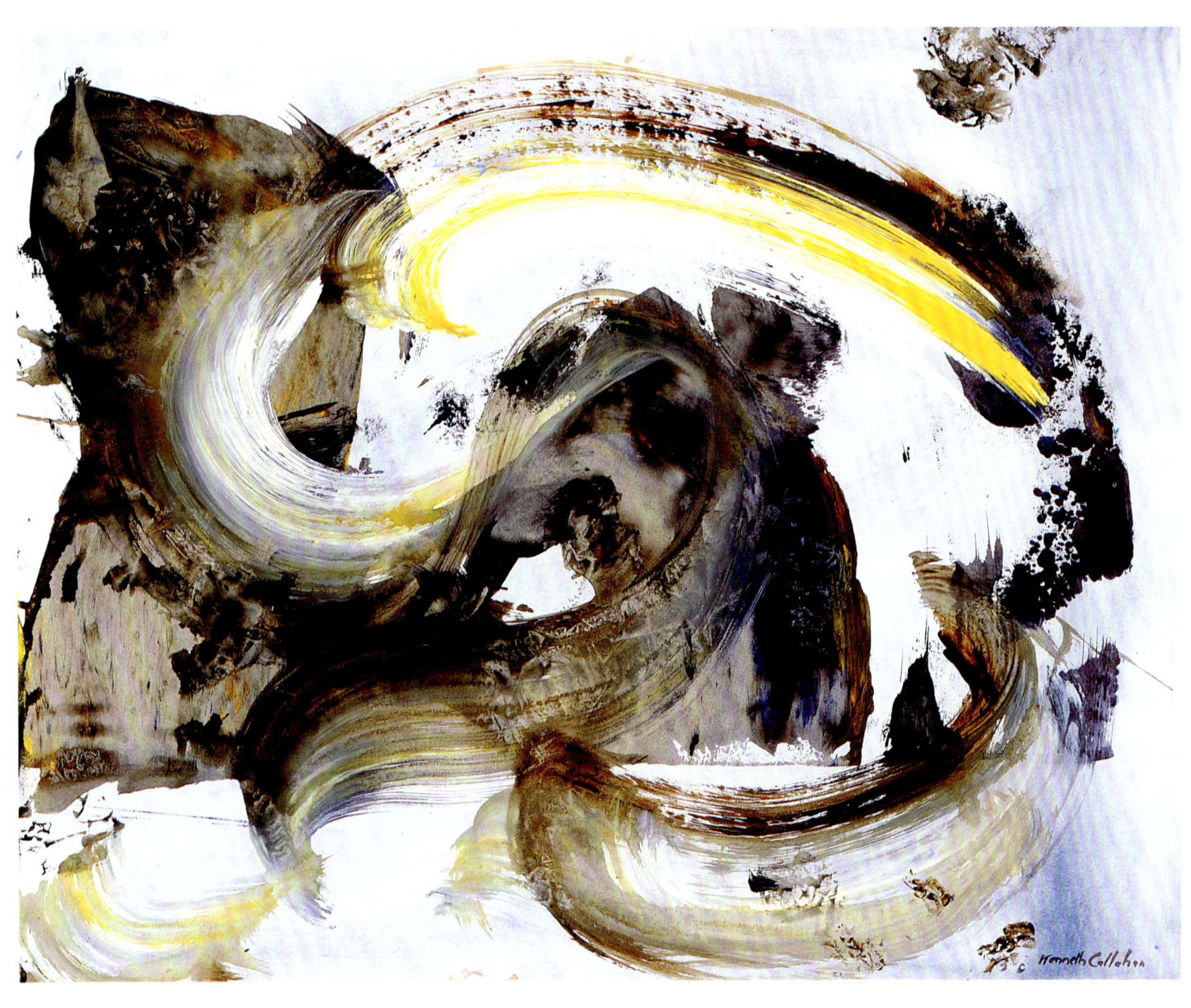

Northern Seascape, 1978
Acrylic on paper on Masonite
34 × 42 inches
Courtesy, The Laura Russo Gallery

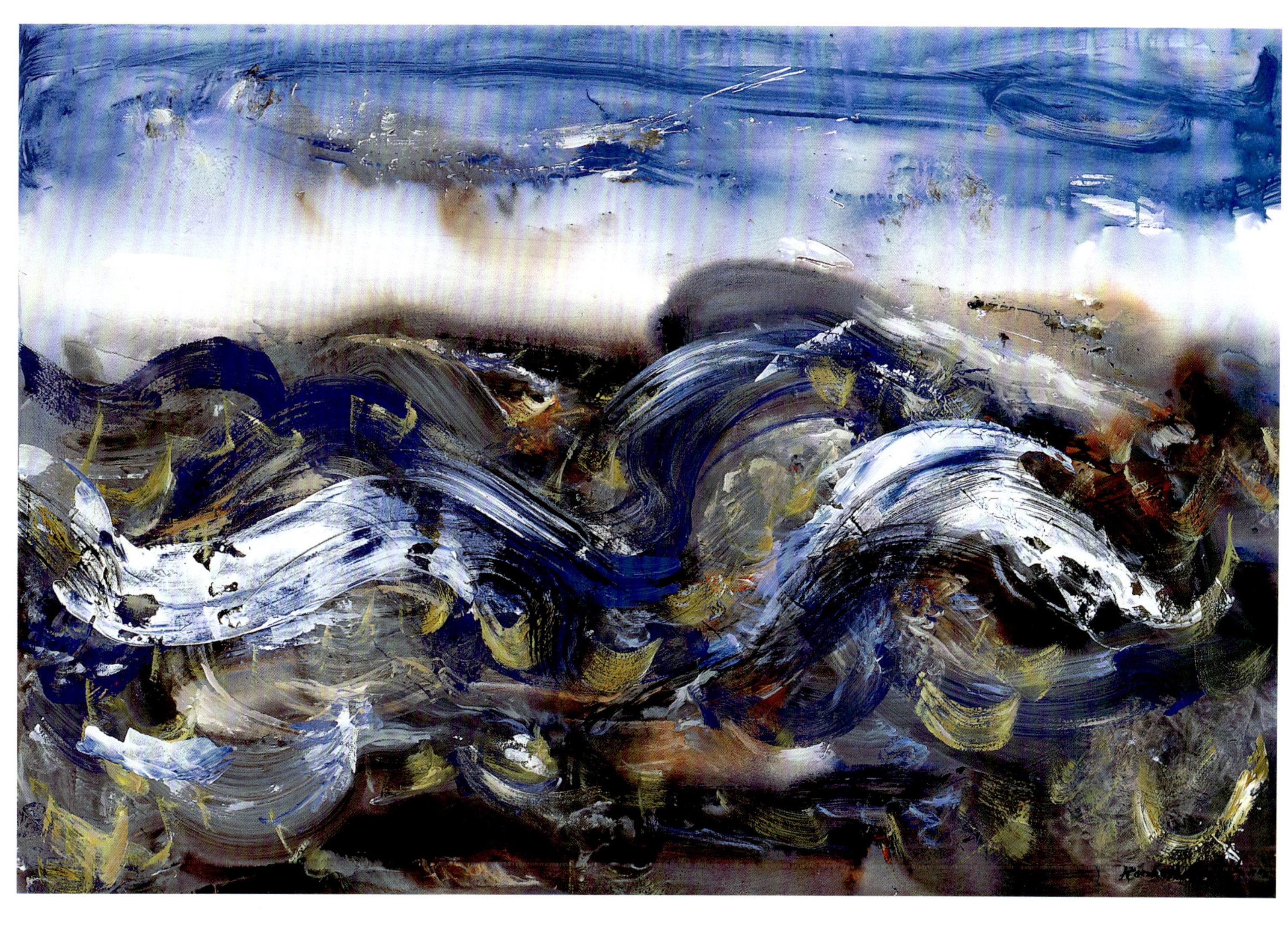

Untitled, ca. late 1970s
Acrylic on rag board
40 × 60 inches
Collection of Tom Blue

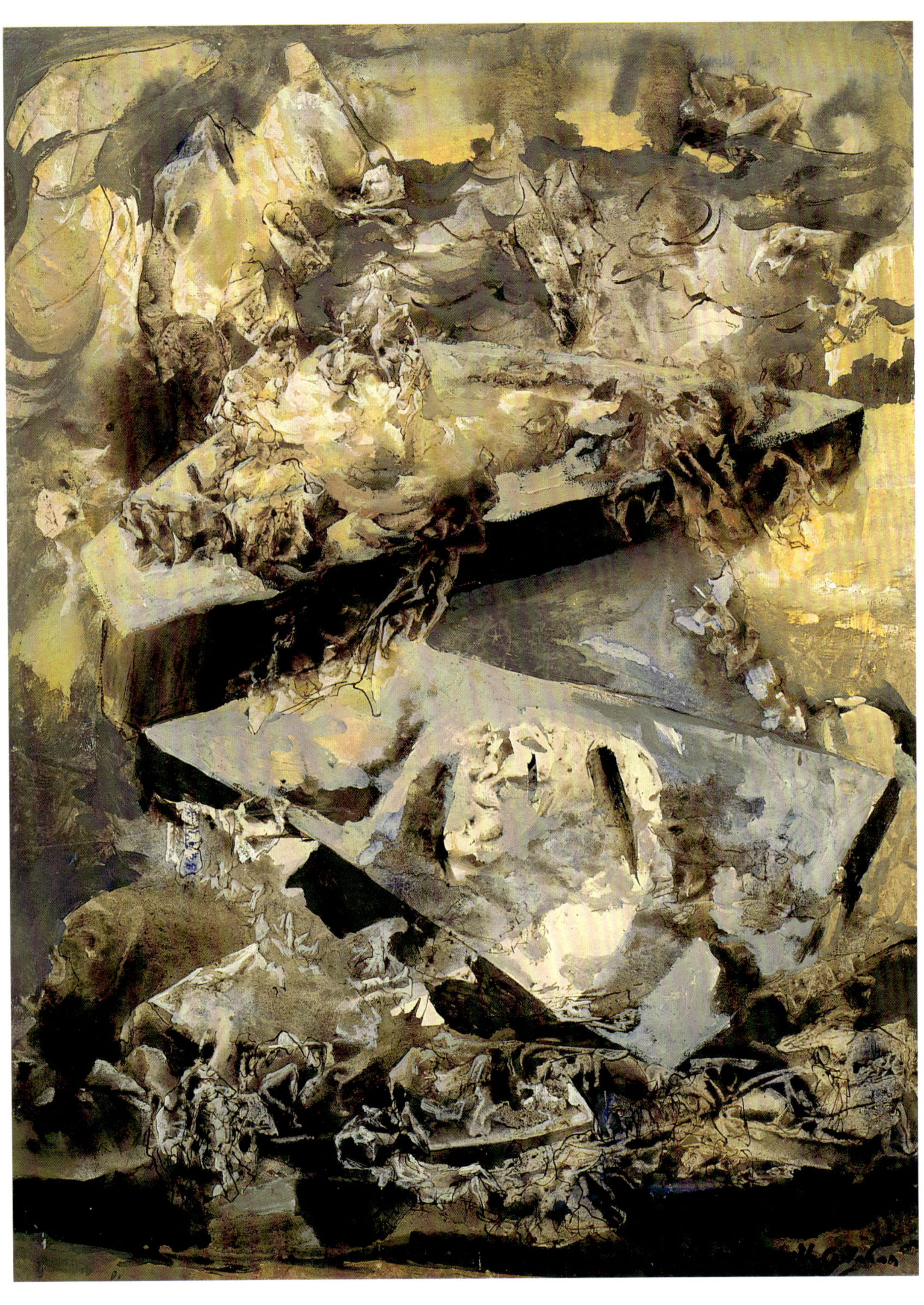

Rock Fragments, ca. late 1970s
Oil and tempera on panel
24 × 18 inches
Collection of Tom Blue

OPPOSITE:
Beach Image, ca. 1979
Acrylic or tempera on board or wood panel
38½ × 30½ inches
Collection of Richard and Deanne Rubinstein

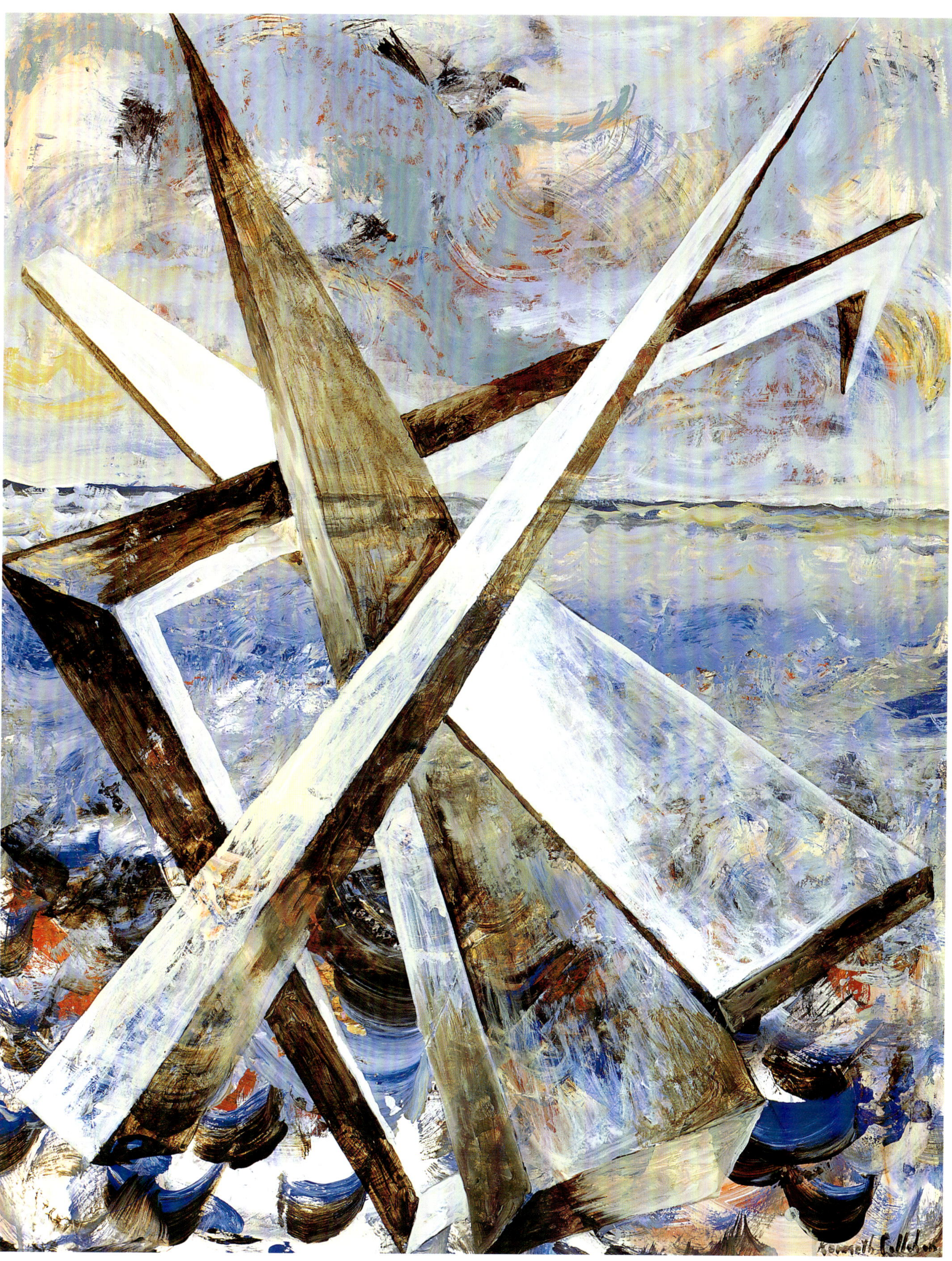

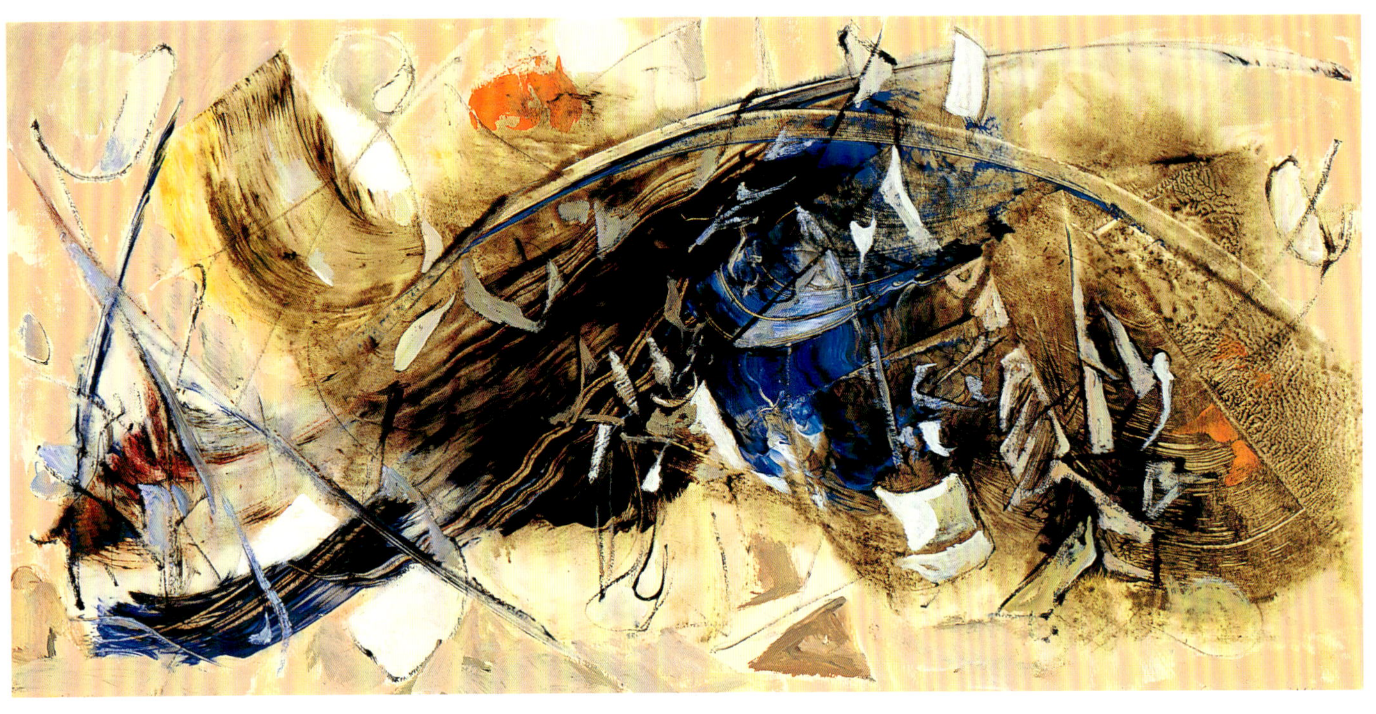

Tidal Shift, ca. 1970s–80s
Unknown medium
20 × 36½ inches
Joseph and Natalie Gisler

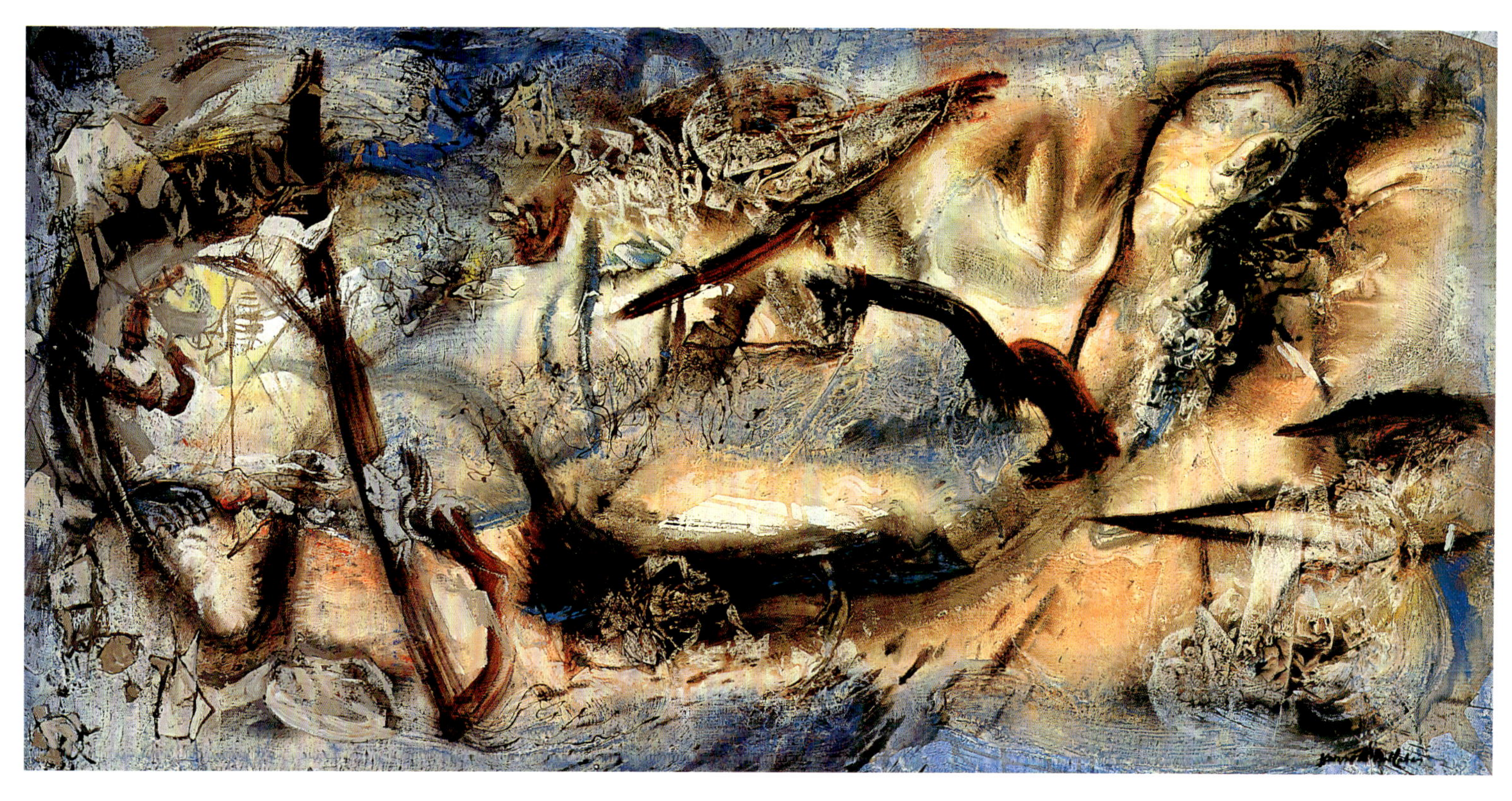

Swamp, ca. 1970s–80s
Unknown medium
24½ × 49 inches
Joseph and Natalie Gisler

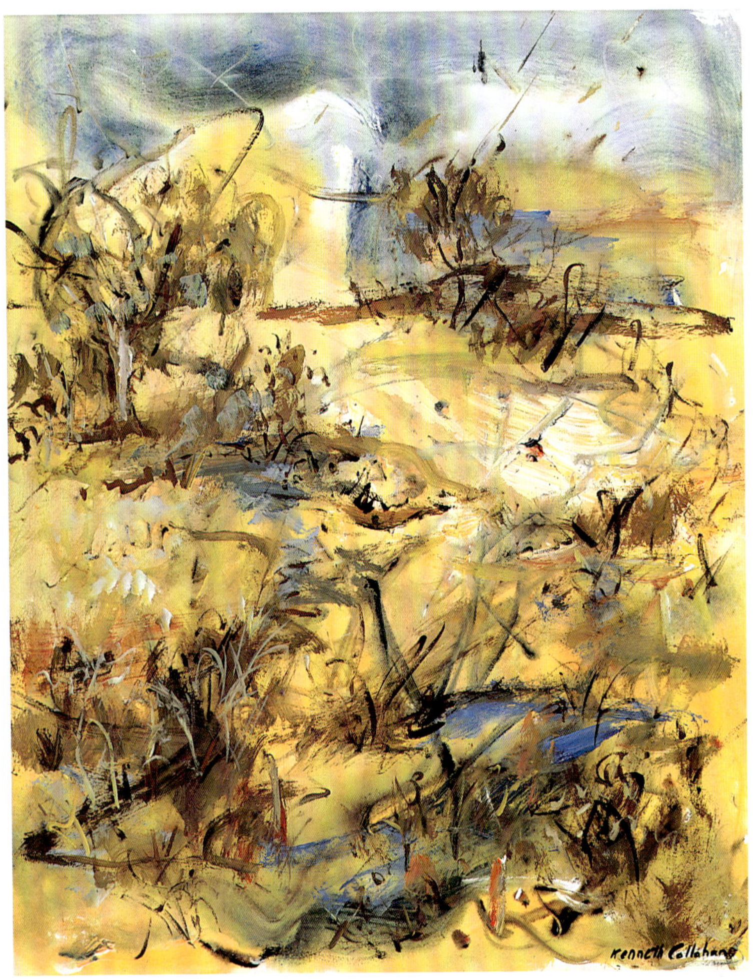

Untitled, ca. early 1980s
Acrylic on rag board
40 × 32 inches
Horizon House Collection

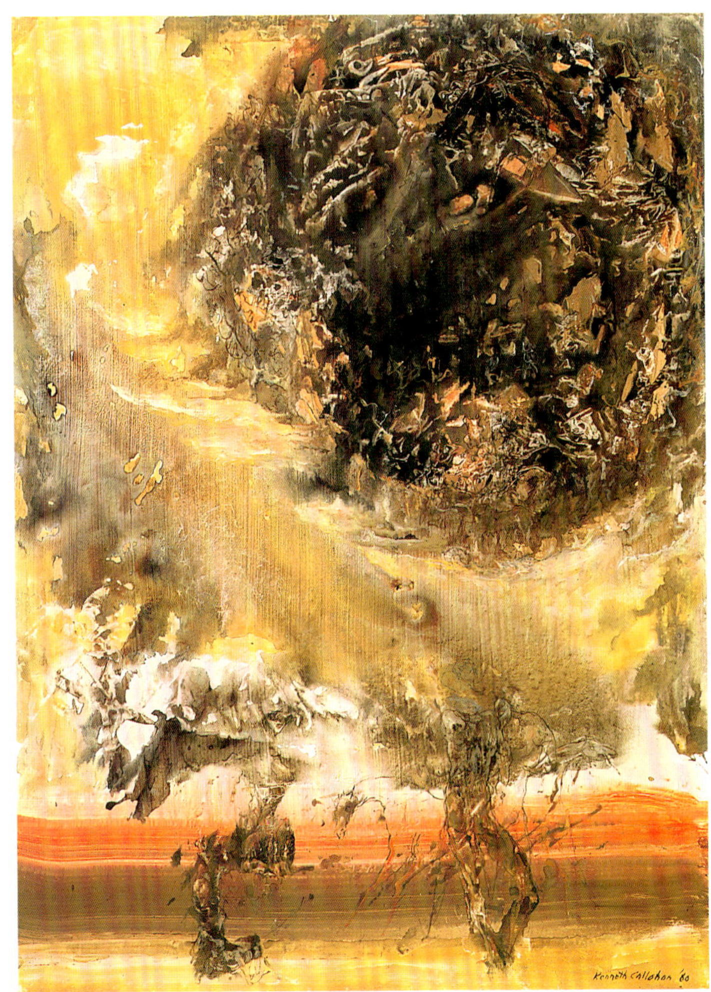

Untitled, 1980
Tempera on panel
28 × 20 inches
Private collection

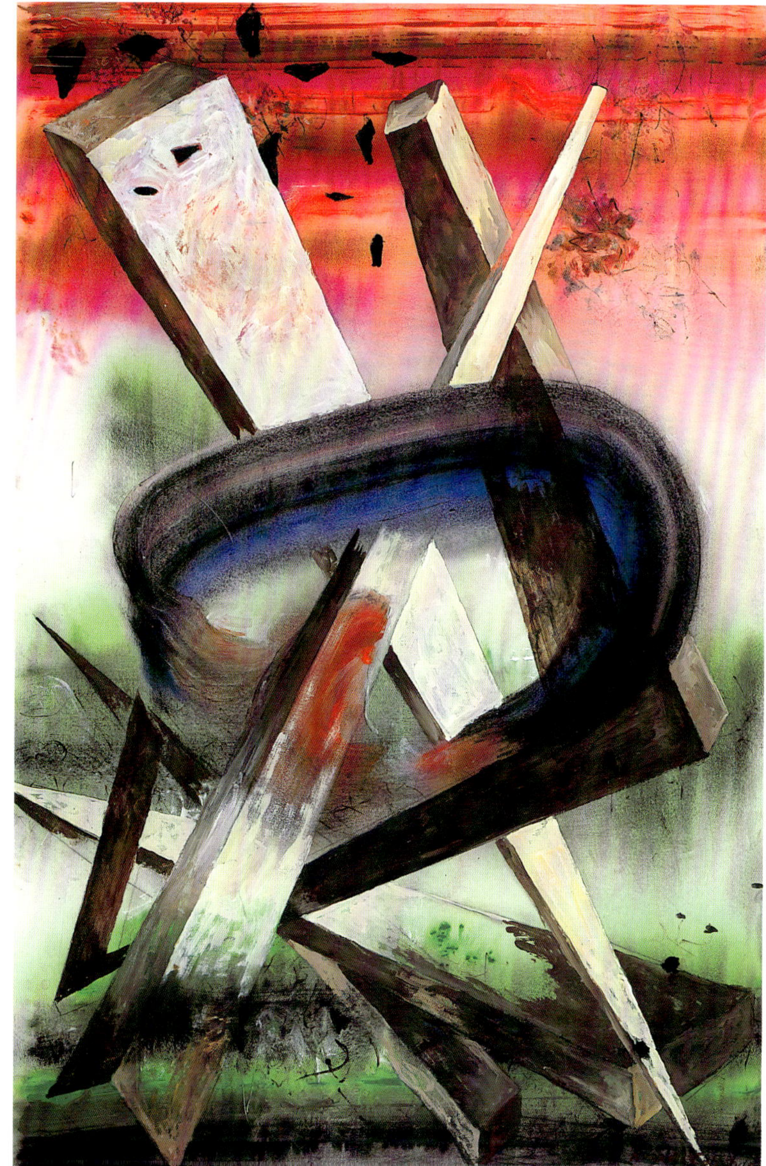

Rhythm Fragments, ca. early 1980s
Acrylic on rag board and Masonite
59 × 39¼ inches
Collection of Dr. and Mrs. E. C. Alvord, Jr.

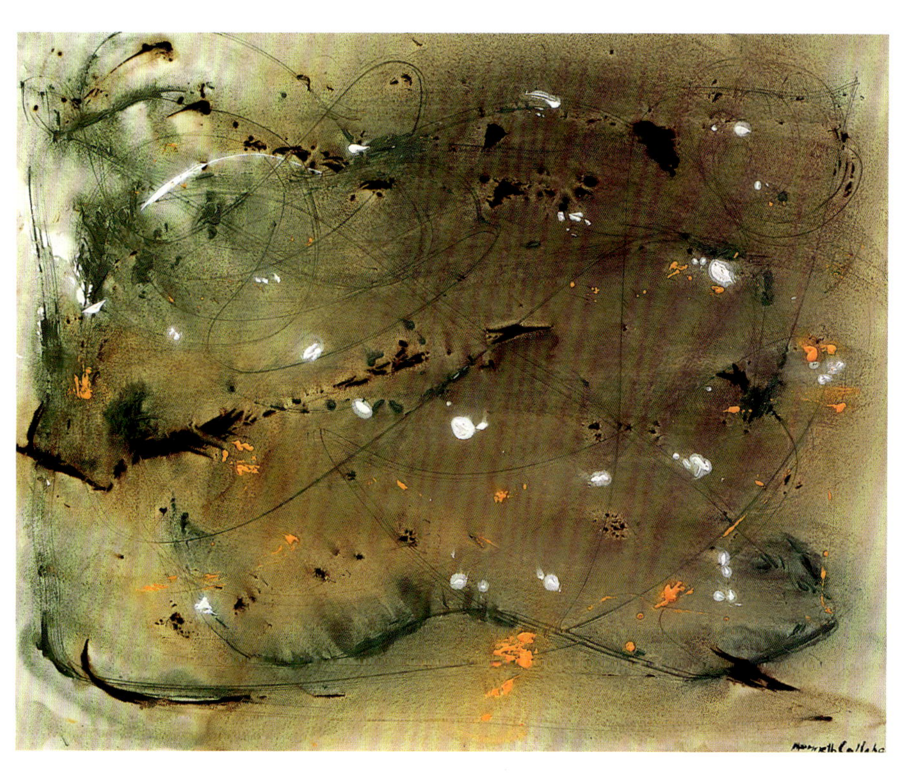

Space Fragment, 1980
Acrylic on rag board
32 × 40 inches
Private collection

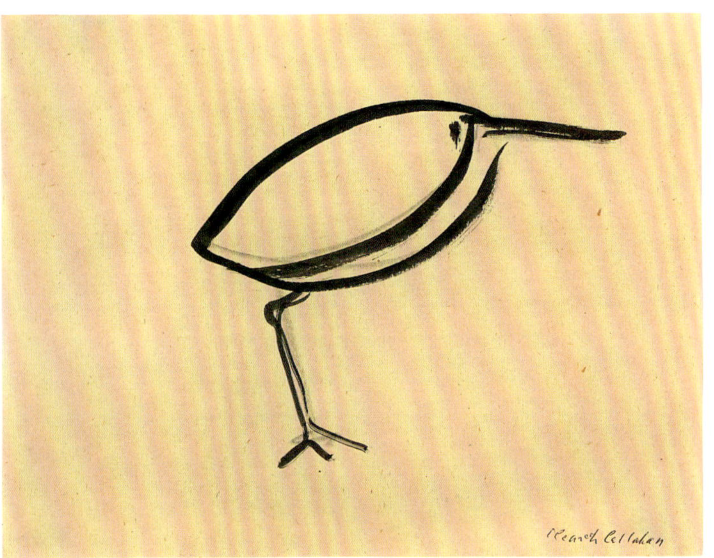

Single Bird, n.d.
Ink on paper
8 × 10½ inches
Collection of Donna Benaroya

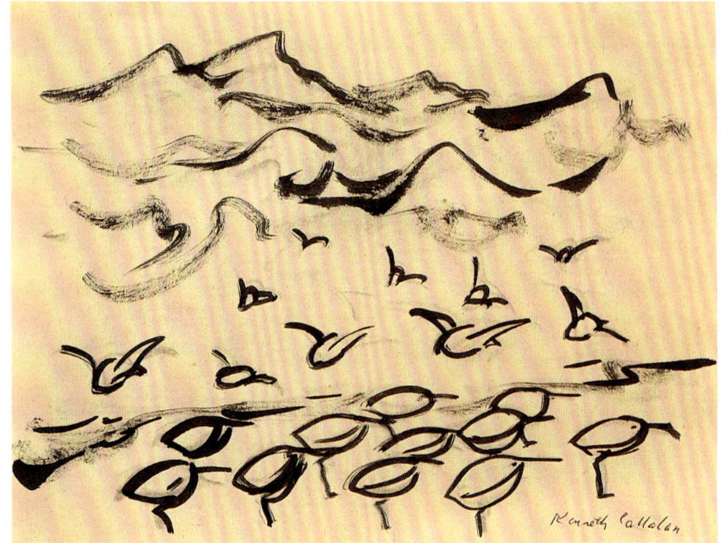

Many Birds, n.d.
Ink on paper
8 × 10½ inches
Collection of Donna Benaroya

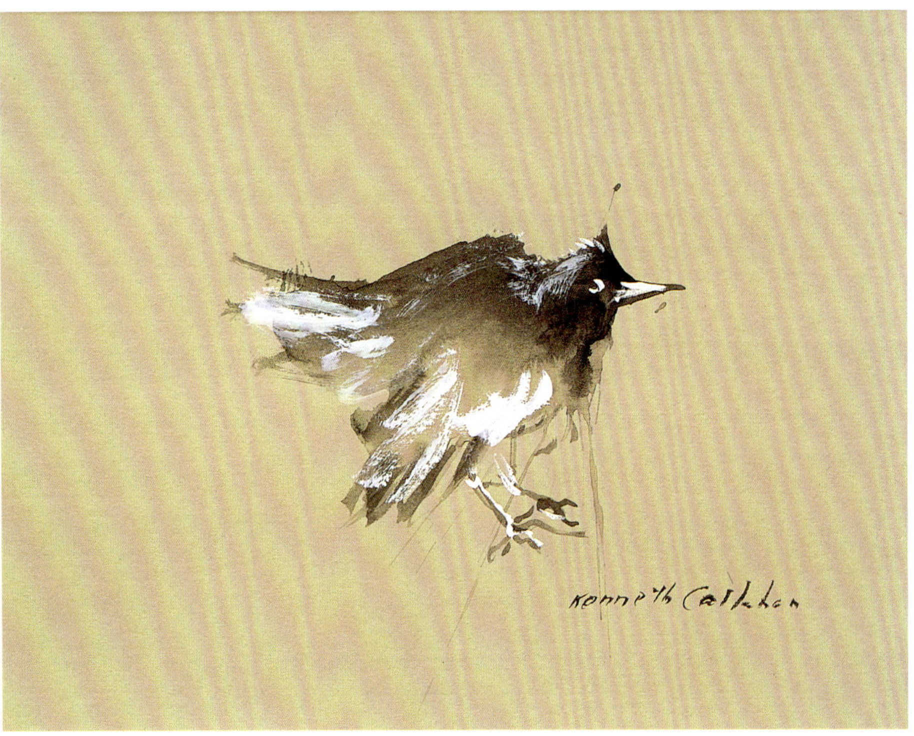

Untitled [*Small Bird*], n.d.
Ink and white pigment on paper
10 × 12¾ inches
Collection of Fred Goldberg

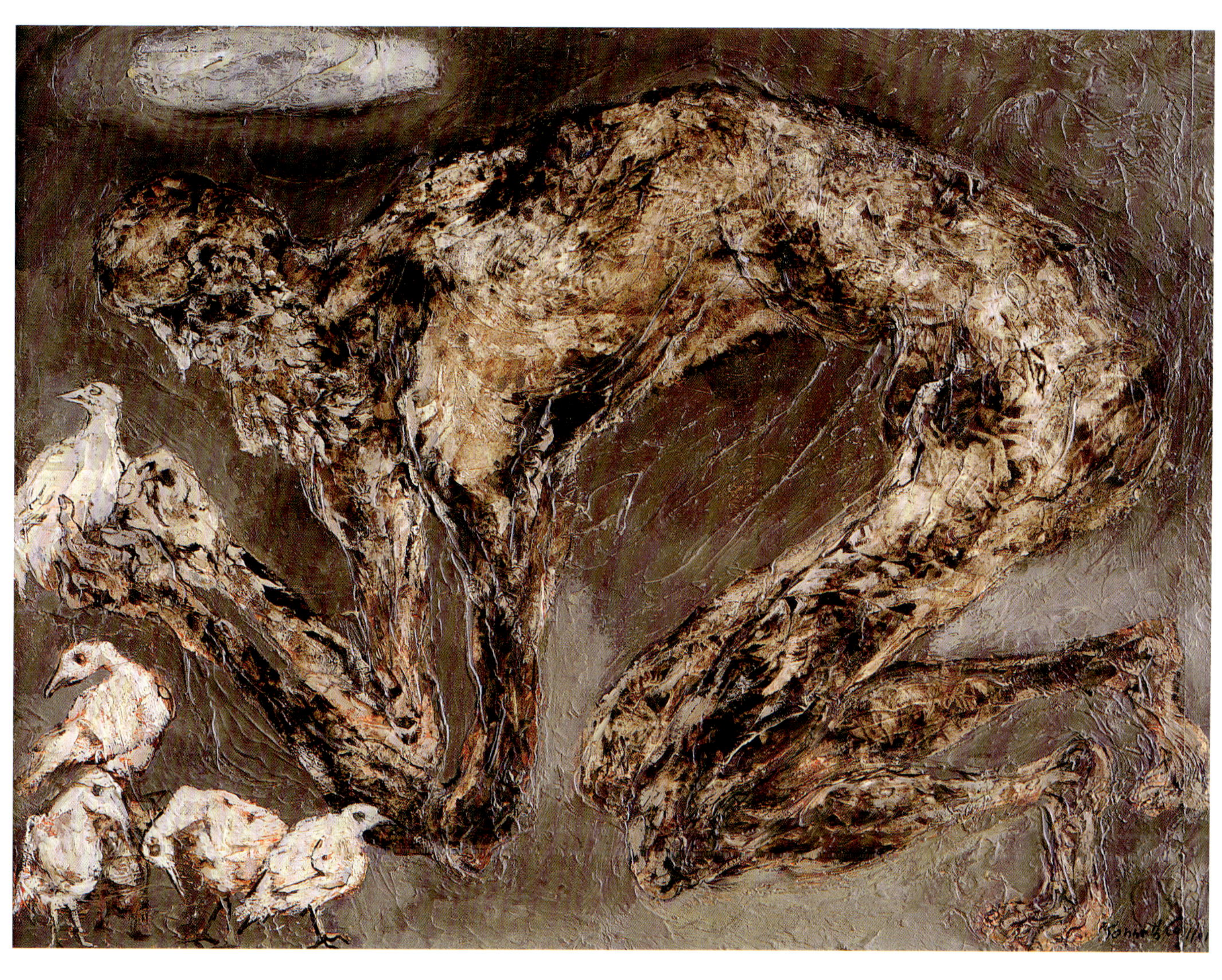

The Birds, n.d.
Oil on board
20 × 27 inches
Courtesy, Foster/White Gallery

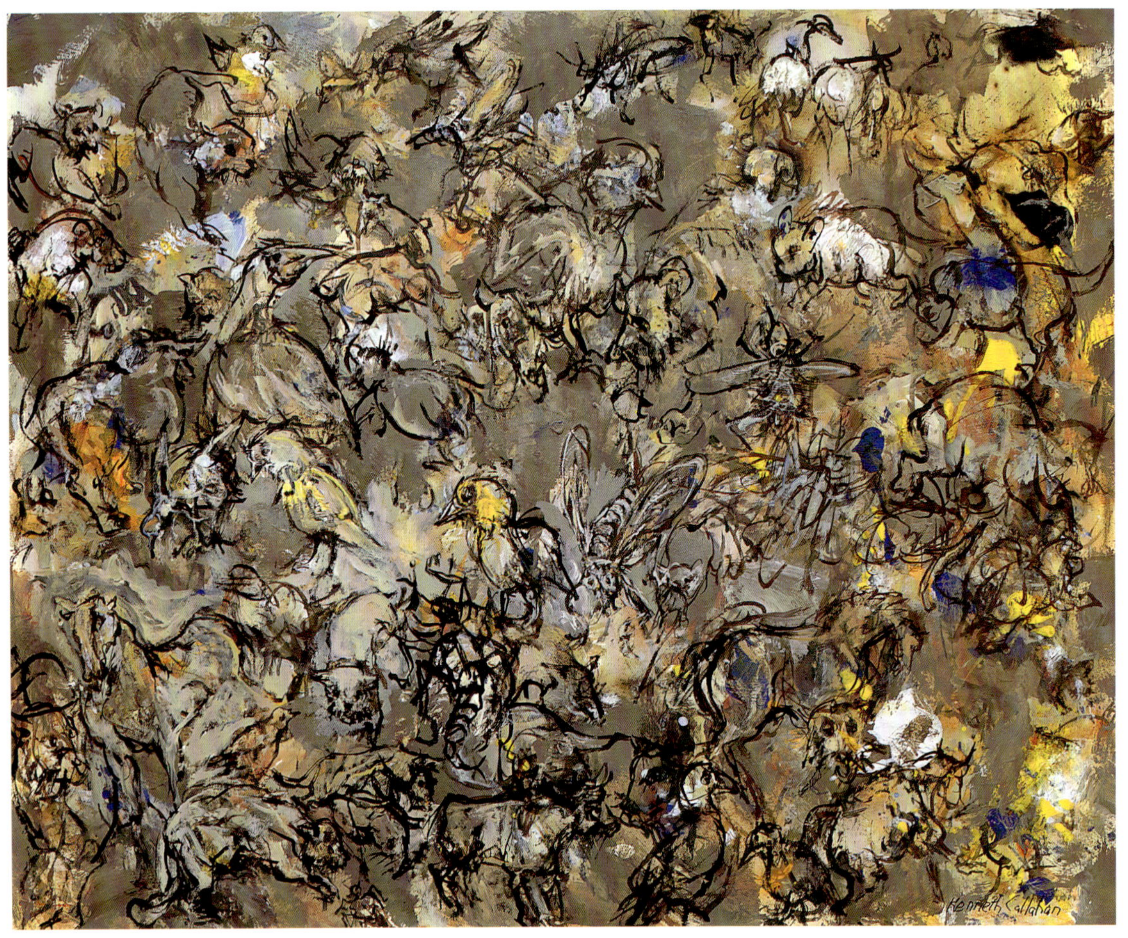

Untitled, n.d.
Tempera on board
32 × 40 inches
Collection of Pamela and Sturges Dorrance

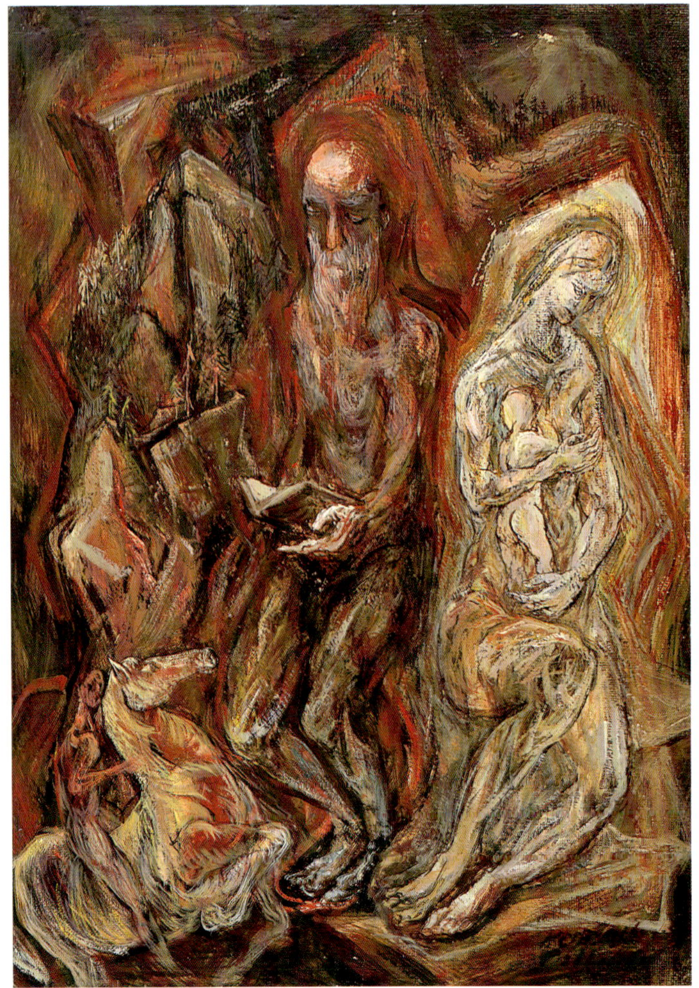

Untitled, n.d.
Oil on panel
$23\frac{3}{8} \times 17$ inches
Collection of Mr. and Mrs. Michael D. Alhadeff

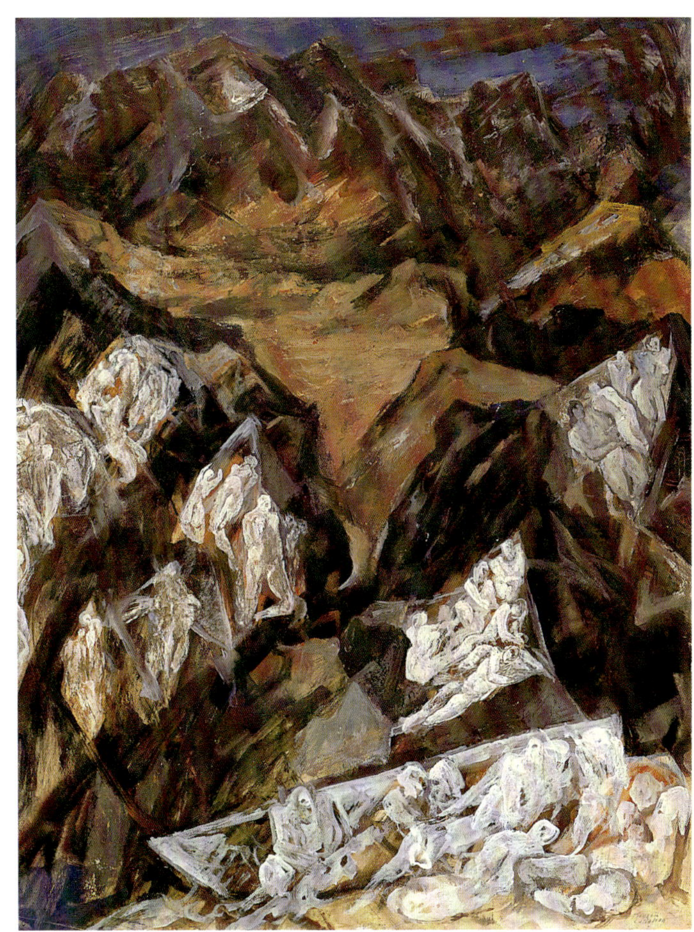

Untitled, n.d.
Tempera on board
22 × 16 inches
Collection of Fred Goldberg

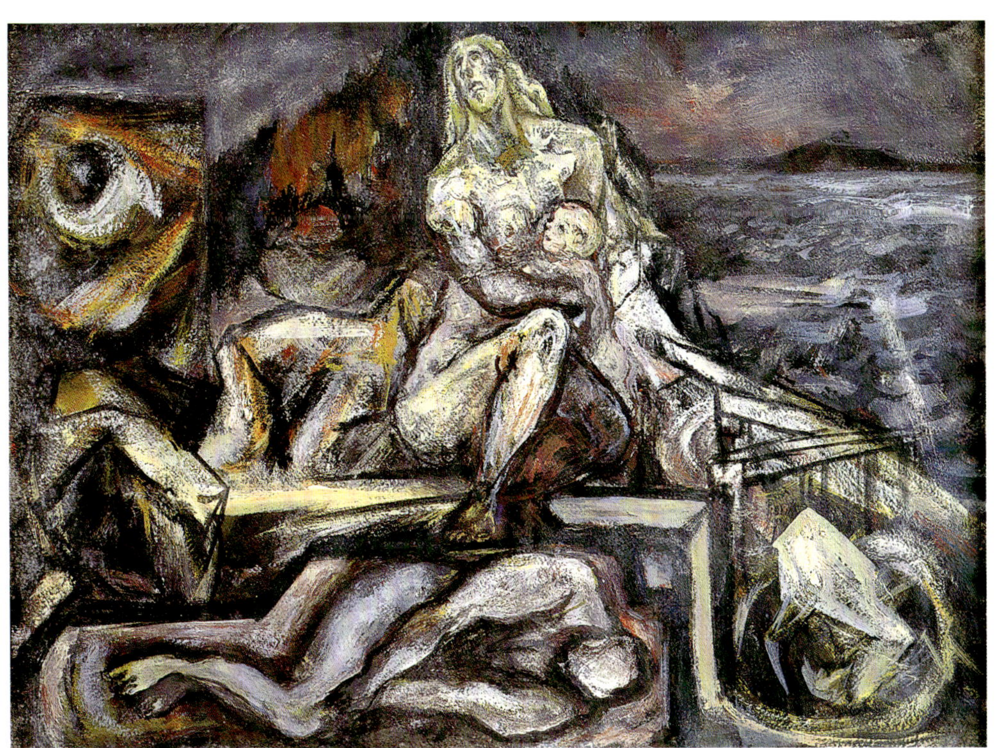

Mother and Child, n.d.
Oil on panel
24 × 33 inches
Courtesy, Foster/White Gallery

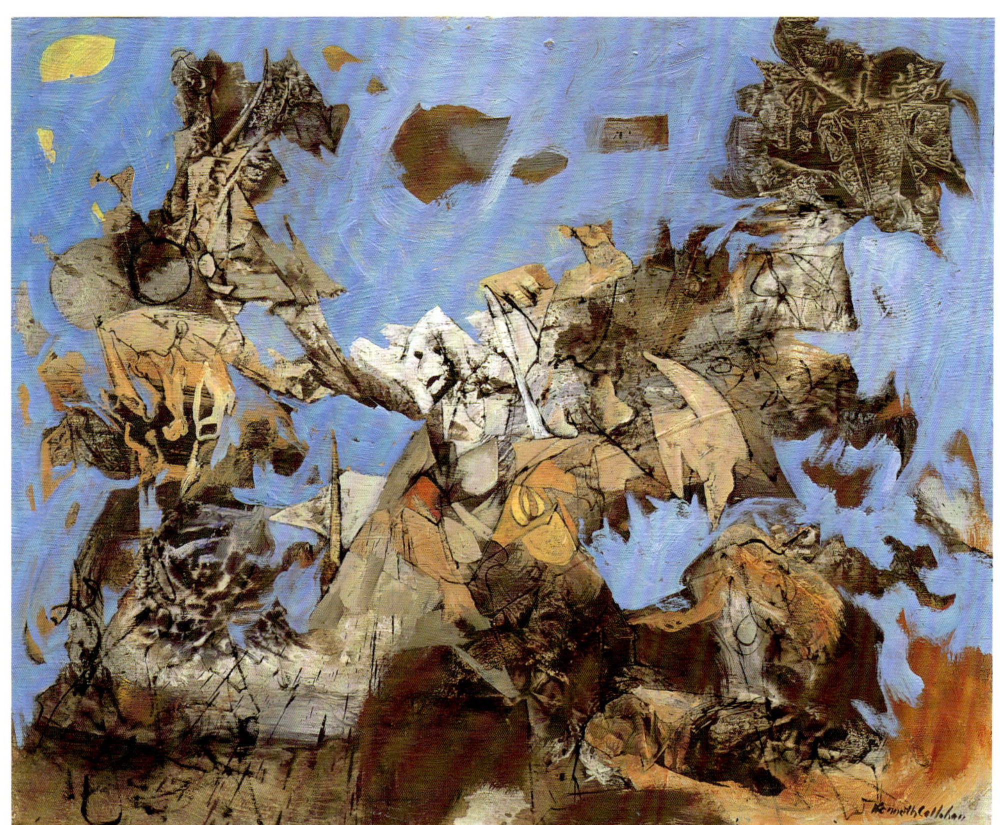

Untitled, n.d.
Oil on panel
24 × 30 inches
Collection of Ann S. and John W. Ormsby

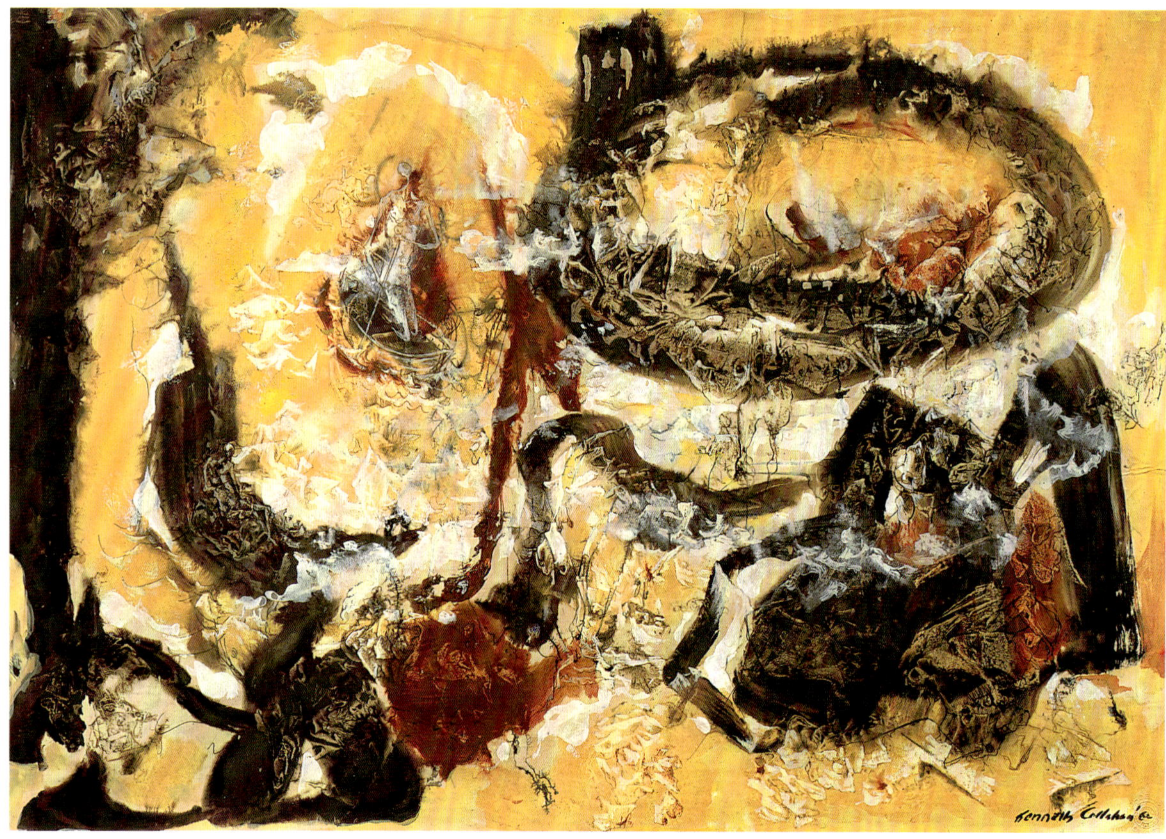

Untitled, n.d.
Oil and tempera on panel
24 × 35 inches
Collection of Mr. and Mrs. Steven L. Sherman

Untitled, n.d.
Oil and tempera on Masonite
10 × 15 inches
Collection of Mark Levine

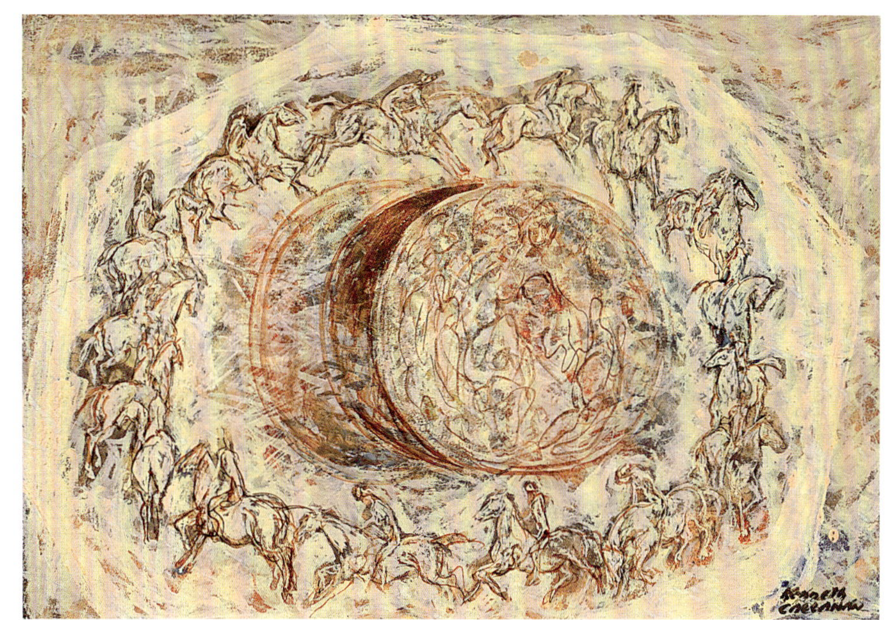

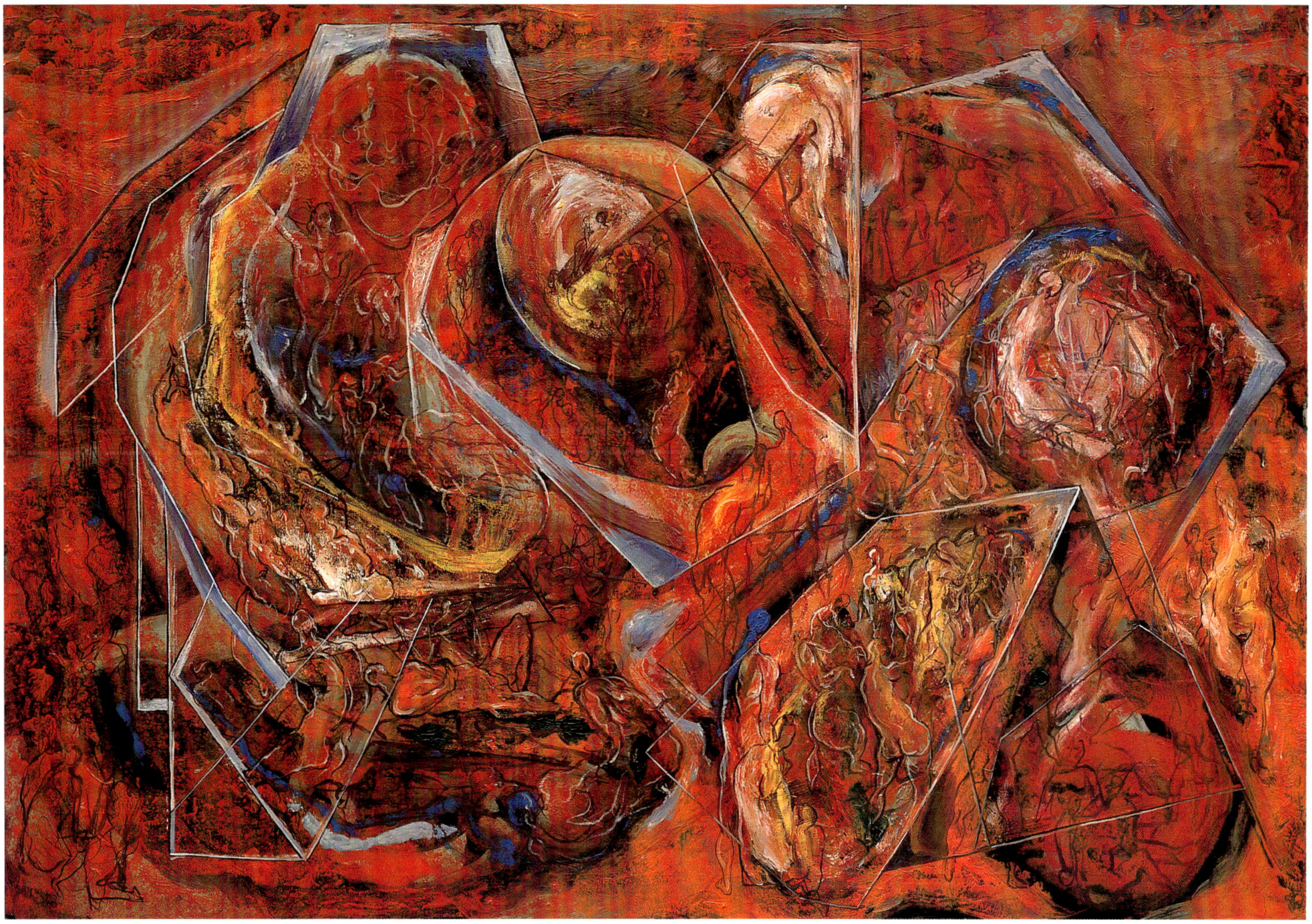

Molten World, n.d.
Tempera and oil on panel
28 × 41 inches
Collection of Mr. and Mrs. Robert Ohashi,
Seattle

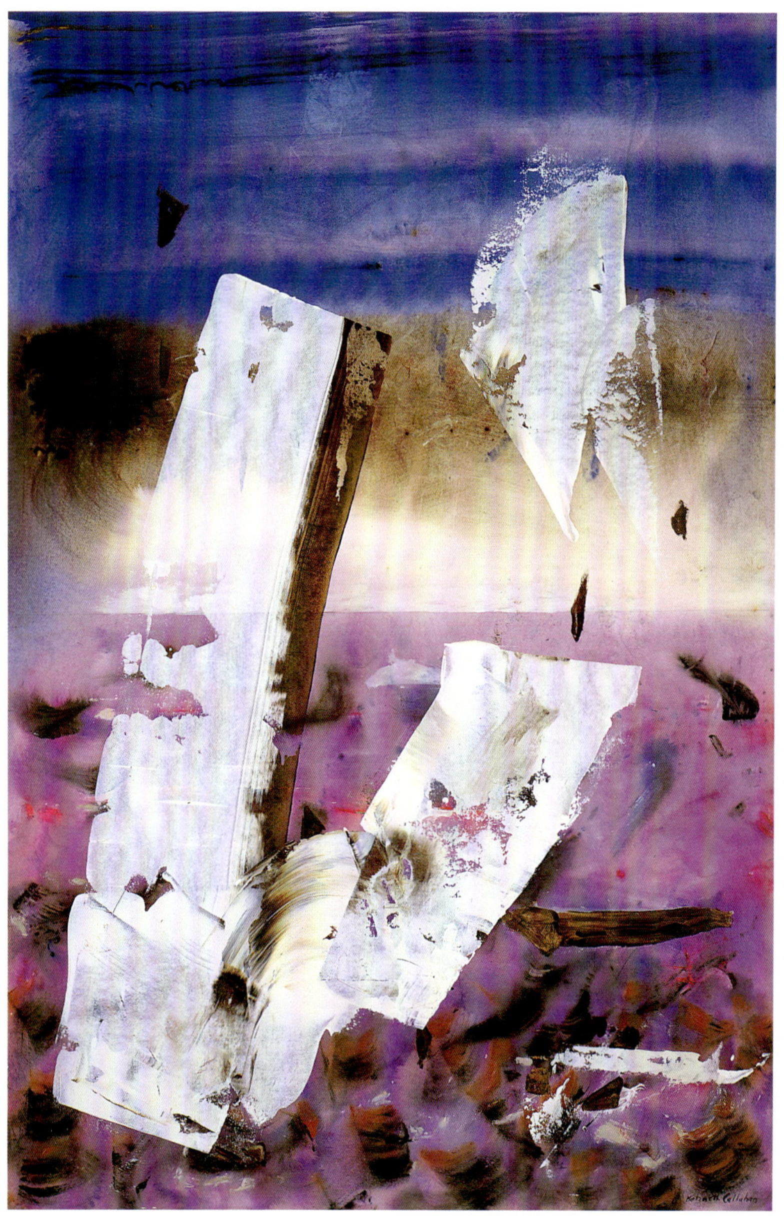

Orpheus, n.d.
Acrylic on paper on board
$59 \times 39\frac{1}{4}$ inches
Courtesy, Kraushaar Galleries, New York

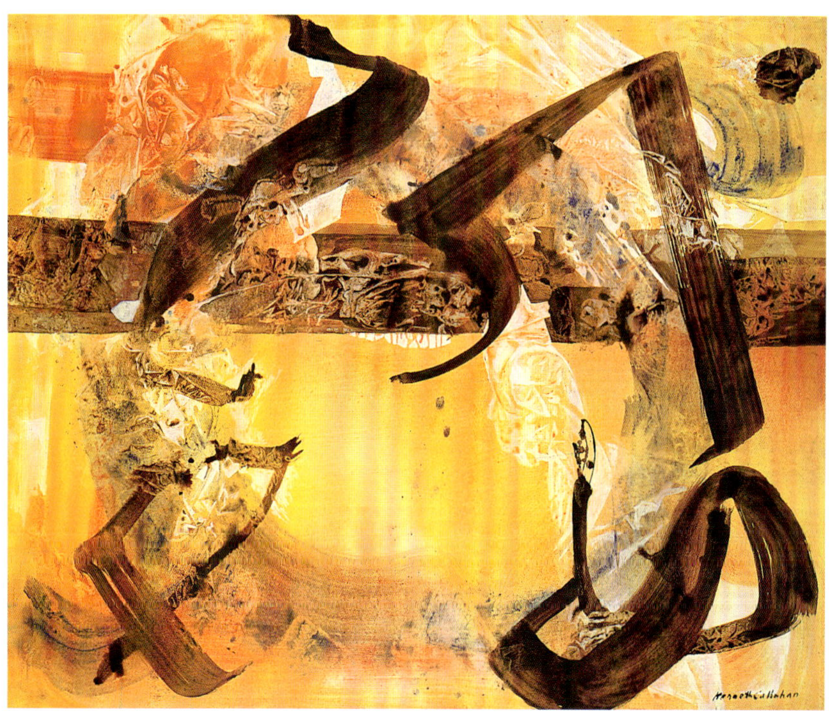

Rising Winds, n.d.
Tempera on paper
$47\frac{1}{2} \times 58$ inches
Courtesy, Kraushaar Galleries, New York

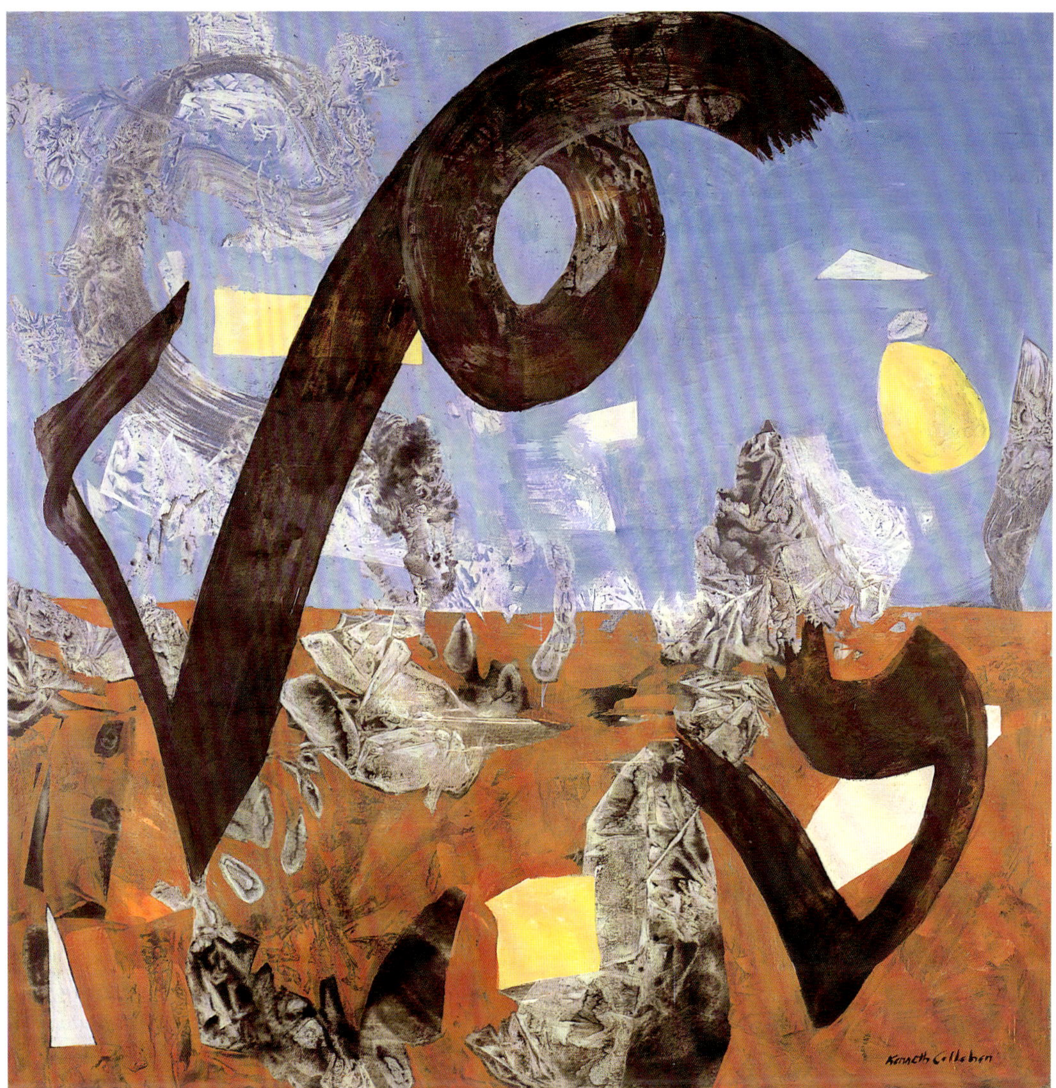

Wind Song, n.d.
Tempera on paper
57 × 58 inches
Courtesy, Kraushaar Galleries, New York

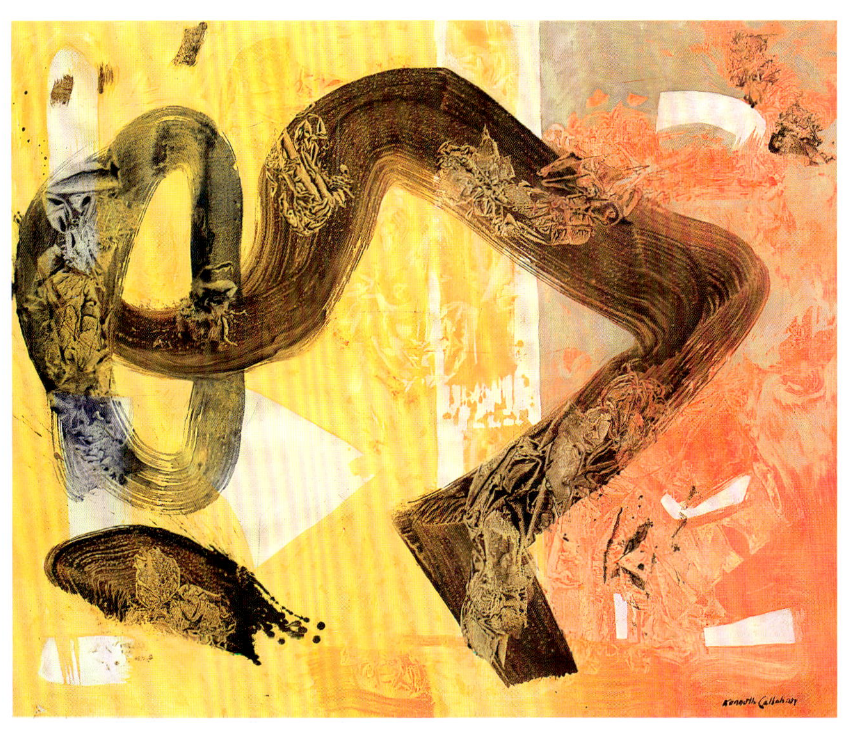

The Source, n.d.
Acrylic on paper
48 × 60 inches
Collection of Alvin and Jacqueline Goldfarb

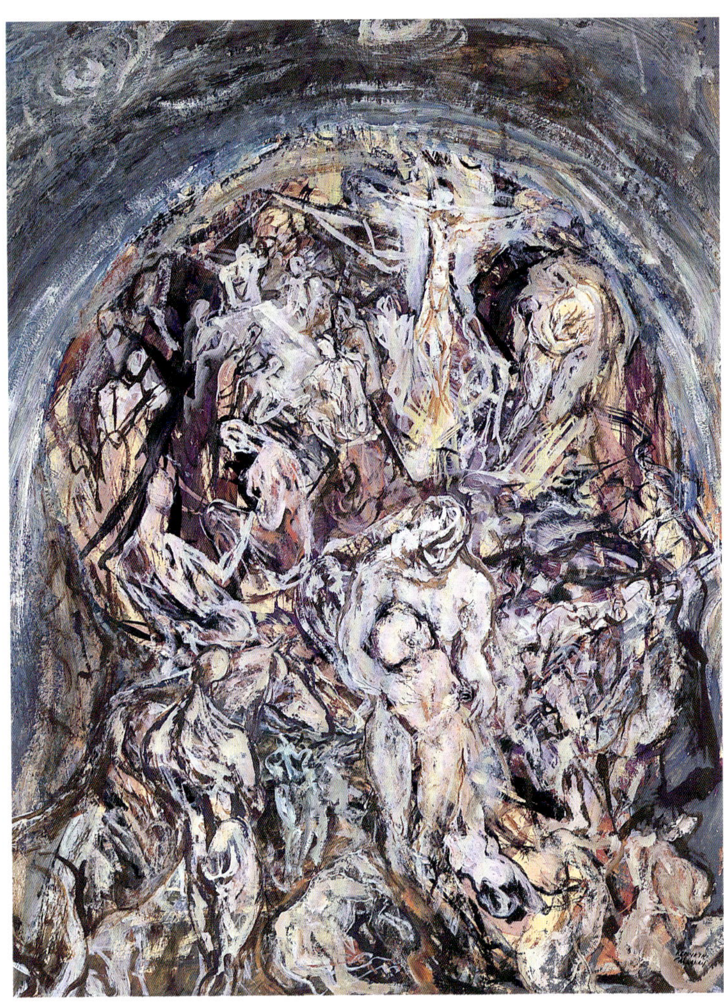

The Window, n.d.
Oil on Masonite
$21\frac{1}{2} \times 15\frac{1}{2}$ inches
Collection of Arlene and Harold Schnitzer

Performance of the Visions, n.d.
Watercolor
$17 \times 21\frac{3}{4}$ inches
Springfield Art Museum, Missouri

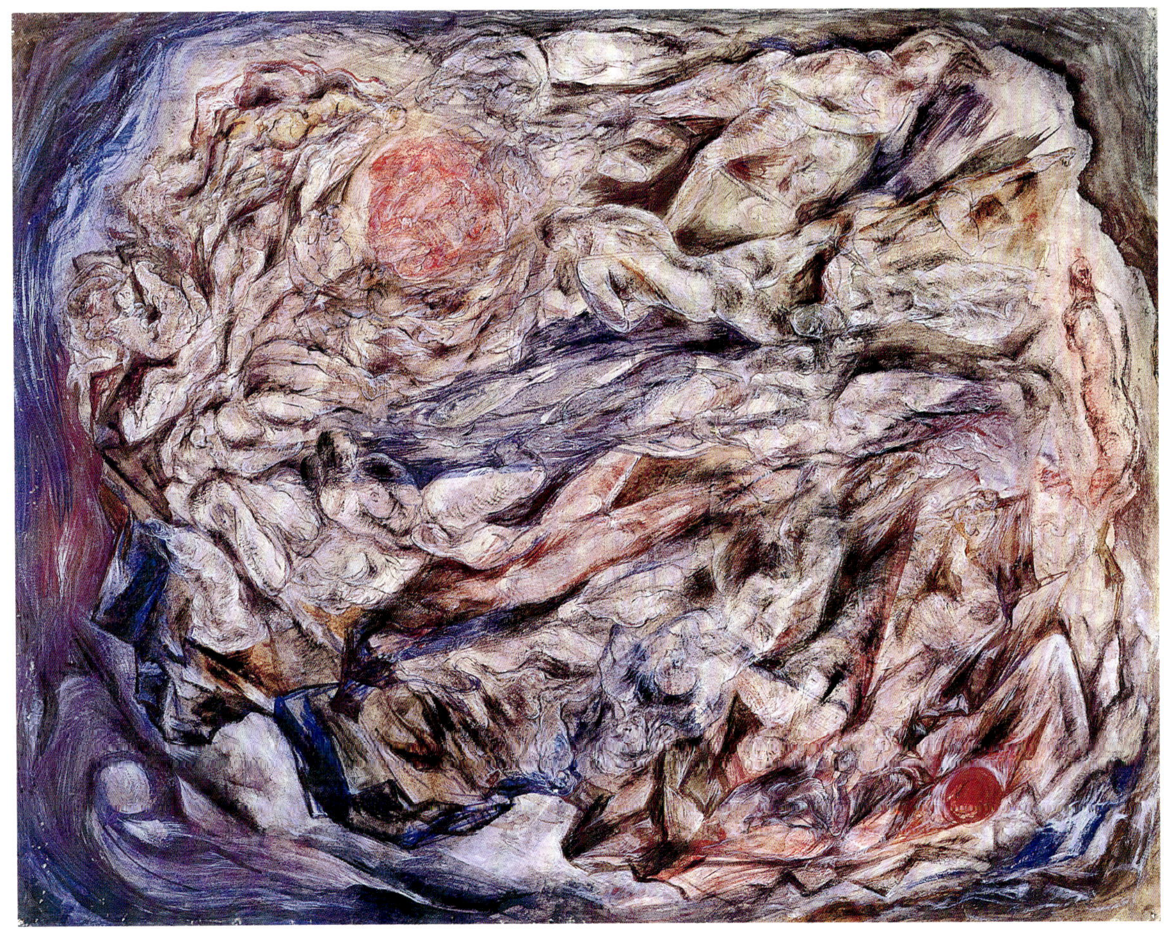

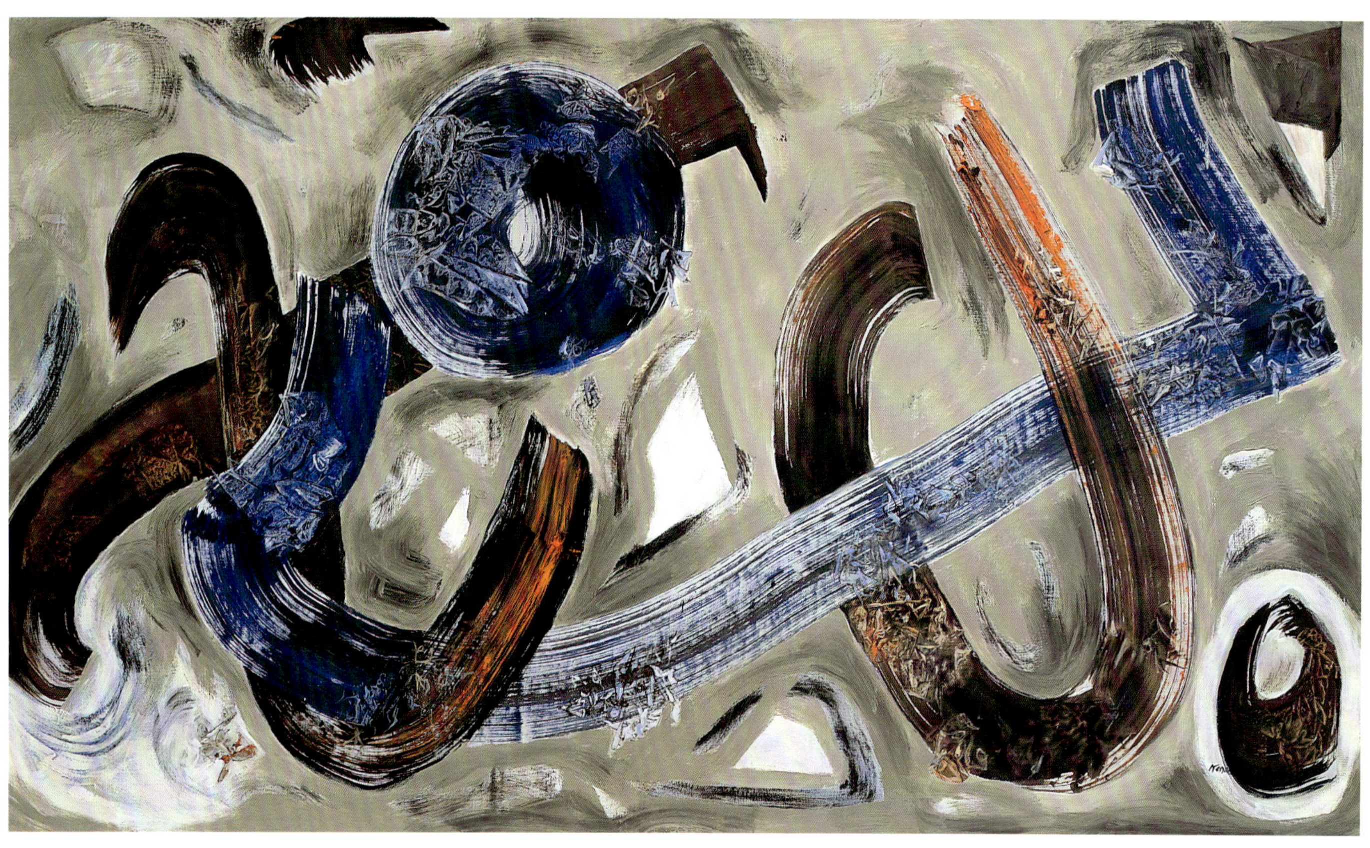

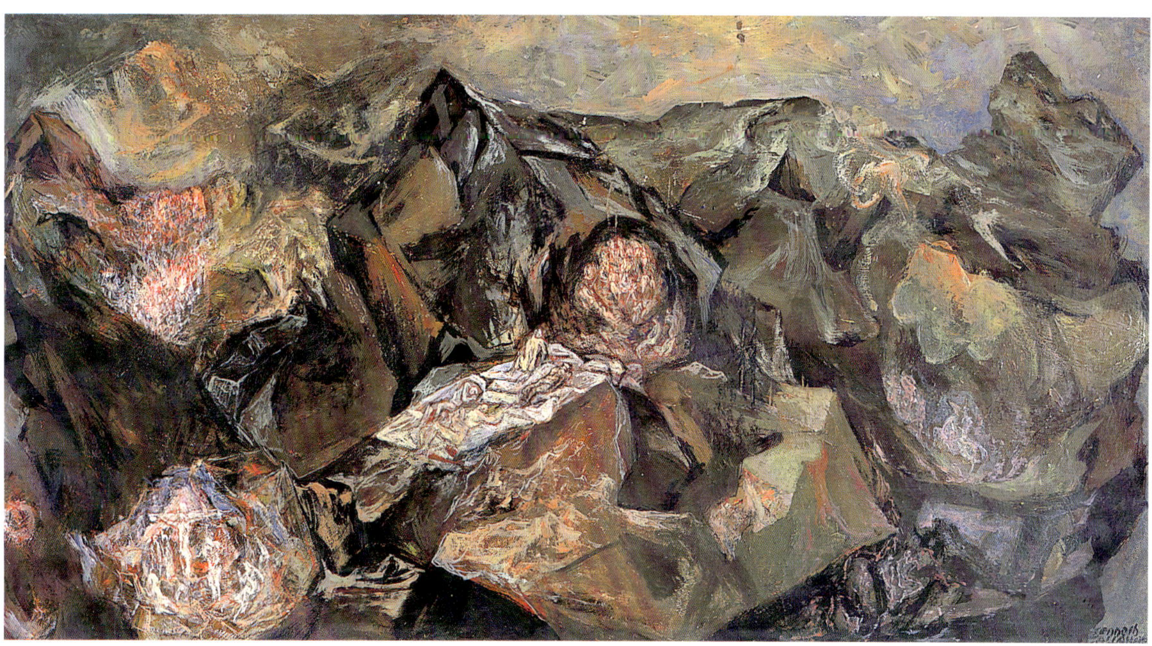

TOP:

Surf and Kelp, n.d.
Acrylic on canvas
54 × 91 inches
Washington State Convention and Trade Center, on extended loan from private collection

BOTTOM:

People Resting on Plateau, n.d.
Mixed media on board
12 × 22¾ inches
Museum of Art, Washington State University, gift of Beth Callahan

exhibitions

Solo

1926
San Francisco Towne Gallery

Schwabacher-Frey Gallery, San Francisco

1928
Seattle Art Museum

1929
Matson Navigation Company, San Francisco

1930
Art Institute, Seattle

Harry Hartman's Print Gallery, Seattle

1932
Gabulson Motor Service, Seattle

Winthrop Hotel, Tacoma

1935
Penthouse Gallery, Seattle

Seattle Art Museum

1937
Federal Housing Administration, Tacoma Armory, Tacoma, Washington

1938
Portland Art Museum, Oregon

San Francisco Museum of Art

1945
Studio Gallery, Seattle

1946
American-British Art Center, New York

Maynard Walker Gallery, New York

1947
Maynard Walker Gallery, New York

Seattle Art Museum

1948
Galerie Georges Giroux, Brussels, Belgium

1949
Kharuba Gallery, Portland, Oregon

Maynard Walker Gallery, New York

1950
Maynard Walker Gallery, New York

1952
Maynard Walker Gallery, New York

1953
Maynard Walker Gallery, New York

1954
Zoe Dusanne Gallery, Seattle

1955
Seattle Art Museum

1956
Harris Hall, University of Southern California, Los Angeles

Maynard Walker Gallery, New York

1958
Maynard Walker Gallery, New York

Woessner Gallery, Seattle

1959
Bainbridge Arts and Crafts, Bainbridge Island, Washington

Maynard Walker Gallery, New York

1961
Maynard Walker Gallery, New York

1962
The Bryant M. Hale Galleries, Los Angeles

Cheney Cowles Memorial Museum, Spokane, Washington

Santa Barbara Museum of Art, California

Seattle Art Museum

1963
Maynard Walker Gallery, New York

University of Arkansas Fine Arts Center Gallery, Fayetteville

Williams College Museum of Art, Williamstown, Massachusetts

1964
Department of Fine Arts, Lehigh University, Bethlehem, Pennsylvania

Memorial Art Gallery, University of Rochester, New York

1965
Arts II Building Gallery, Penn State University, State College, Pennsylvania

Gordon Woodside Gallery, San Francisco

Seattle Art Museum

1967
Kraushaar Galleries, New York

1968
Cheney Cowles Memorial Museum, Spokane, Washington

1969
Gordon Woodside Gallery, Seattle

1970
The Fountain Gallery, Portland, Oregon

1971
Kraushaar Galleries, New York

1973
Kenneth Callahan: Universal Voyage, Henry Art Gallery in association with the Pacific Northwest Arts Center. Traveled to Portland Art Museum, Oregon; Everson Museum of Art, Syracuse, New York

Kraushaar Galleries, New York

1974
The Fountain Gallery, Portland, Oregon

Michael R. Johnson Gallery, Seattle

1975
Foster/White Gallery, Seattle

School of Fine Arts, Eastern Washington State College, Cheney

1976
Foster/White Gallery, Seattle

Frederick & Nelson Art Gallery, Seattle

Kraushaar Galleries, New York

Longacres Race Track, Renton, Washington

1977
Foster/White Gallery, Seattle

1979
Foster/White Gallery, Seattle

Seattle Art Museum, Modern Art Pavilion at Seattle Center

1980
Foster/White Gallery, Seattle

Gallery '76, Wenatchee, Washington

Kraushaar Galleries, New York

1981
Broadway Performance Hall, Seattle Central Community College

Foster/White Gallery, Seattle

1982
Kraushaar Galleries, New York

1983
Foster/White Gallery, Seattle

The Fountain Gallery, Portland, Oregon

1985
Kraushaar Galleries, New York

Tacoma Art Museum, Washington

1986
Seattle Art Museum

1987
Museum of Art, Washington State University, Pullman

1988
Foster/White Gallery, Seattle

1989
Washington State Capital Museum, Olympia, Washington

1990
Kraushaar Galleries, New York

Laura Russo Gallery, Portland, Oregon

1992
Foster/White Gallery, Kirkland, Washington

Gunnar Nordstrom Gallery, Kirkland, Washington

1994
Laura Russo Gallery, Portland, Oregon

Museum of Northwest Art, La Conner, Washington

1995
Museum of Art, Washington State University, Pullman

1997
Foster/White Gallery, Seattle

Laura Russo Gallery, Portland, Oregon

2000
Foster/White Gallery, Seattle

Laura Russo Gallery, Portland, Oregon

2001
Kraushaar Galleries, New York

Museum of Northwest Art, La Conner, Washington

Group (Selected)

1925
Northwest Annual, Seattle; also 1956, 1965

Unknown California competition

1933
First Biennial Exhibition of Contemporary American Sculpture, Watercolors, and Prints, Whitney Museum of American Art, New York

Sixteen Cities Exhibition, Museum of Modern Art, New York

1934
Western Watercolor Exhibition, Los Angeles Art Association

1935
Paintings by Artists West of the Mississippi, First Annual Exhibition, Colorado Springs Fine Arts Center, Colorado College; also 1936, 1937, 1940, 1941, 1948, 1949

1939
Annual Exhibition of Contemporary American Sculpture, Watercolors, and Drawings, Whitney Museum of American Art, New York; also 1945, 1946, 1947, 1949, 1951, 1952, 1956, 1957, 1960

Contemporary Art, Golden Gate International Exposition, Department of Fine Arts, San Francisco

Eighth Annual Exhibition of Painting and Sculpture, Portland Art Museum, Oregon

Exhibition of Painting and Sculpture Designed for Federal Buildings, Corcoran Gallery of Art, Washington, D.C.

1940
Art, Palace of Fine Arts, Golden Gate International Exposition, San Francisco

1941
First American Drawing Annual, Albany Institute of History and Art, New York

1946
Exhibition of Oils and Tempera, Rotunda Gallery, Paris

Painting in the United States, Carnegie Museum of Art, Pittsburgh; also 1948, 1949

Paintings of the Year, Pepsi-Cola's Annual Art Competition, National Academy of Design, New York. Traveled to Pennsylvania Academy of the Fine Arts, Philadelphia; Walker Art Center, Minneapolis; Syracuse Museum of Fine Arts, New York

Watercolors and Drawings, Fifty-Seventh Annual American Exhibition, Art Institute of Chicago; also 1948

1947
Contemporary American Exhibition, Belgium and France

International Drawing Show, Addison Gallery, Andover, Massachusetts

International Watercolor Exhibition, Fourteenth Biennial, Brooklyn Museum of Art, New York

Twentieth Biennial Exhibition of Contemporary American Oil Paintings, Corcoran Gallery of Art, Washington, D.C.

1950
American Painting, 1950, Virginia Museum of Fine Arts, Richmond

American Painting of Today—1950, The Metropolitan Museum of Art, New York

John Davis Hadok Collection of American Drawings of the Twentieth Century, Williams College Museum of Art, Williamstown, Massachusetts

New Accessions USA, Colorado Springs Fine Arts Center, Colorado College

One Hundred and Forty-Fifth Annual Exhibition of Painting and Sculpture, Pennsylvania Academy of the Fine Arts, Philadelphia; also 1951, 1953, 1958, 1967, 1969

Washington Artists 1950, Western Washington Fair, Puyallup

1951
Contemporary Art in the United States, Worcester Art Museum, Massachusetts

Revolution and Tradition, Brooklyn Museum, New York

1952
Art, Oregon State College, Corvallis

Twelfth Annual Exhibition, Tacoma Art League, College of Puget Sound, Washington

1953
Candidates for Grants in Art, The National Institute of Arts and Letters, Academy Art Gallery, New York; also 1954

The Edward Root Collection, The Metropolitan Museum of Art, New York

1954
Painting in the U.S.A. 1721–1953, Los Angeles County Fair, Pomona, California

Western Painters Annual Exhibition, Oakland Art Museum

Younger American Painters, Solomon R. Guggenheim Museum, New York

1955
São Paulo Bienal, Musee de Arte Moderna, Brazil

Sixty-First Western Annual, Denver Art Museum

1956
Contemporary American Painters, 1950–1955, T. W. Stanford Art Gallery, Stanford University, California

Seattle Art Museum

Sixty-Sixth Annual Exhibition of Contemporary Art, Nebraska Art Association, University of Nebraska, Lincoln

1957
Amerika i Tidenskunst, Lyngby Rådhus, Denmark

Eight American Artists, United States Information Agency, Tour of Europe: Amerika Haus, West Berlin

Second Pacific Coast Biennial Exhibition of Paintings and Watercolors, Santa Barbara Museum, California; California Palace of the Legion of Honor, San Francisco; Seattle Art Museum; Portland Art Museum, Oregon

1958
1958 Pittsburgh Bicentennial International Exhibition of Contemporary Painting and Sculpture, Carnegie Museum of Art, Pittsburgh

1959
Contemporary American Painting and Sculpture, University of Illinois, Urbana

1961
The Art of the Northwest Coast, Sloan Galleries of American Paintings, Valparaiso University, Indiana

Emily Winthrop Miles Collection, Tour of American Museums, 1961–64

Pacific Northwest Art Annual, University of Oregon Museum of Art, Eugene

Painting from the Pacific, venues in Australia, Japan, New Zealand, United States

1962
American Art since 1950, Brandeis University Institute of Fine Arts and Institute of Contemporary Art, Boston

Art since 1950, Century 21 Exposition, Seattle

Art USA Now, The Johnson Collection, venue unknown

The Artist's Environment: West Coast, The Amon Carter Museum, Fort Worth

1963
Pacific Northwest Art: The Haseltine Collection, University of Oregon Museum of Art, Eugene

Selection of Works from the Art Collection, Sheldon Memorial Art Gallery, University of Nebraska, Lincoln

1964
Faces, Figures and Forms, Winthrop College Gallery, Rock Hill, South Carolina

1965
Art across America, Mead Corporation, Knoedler Galleries, New York, and 16 U.S. cities

Art Exhibition and Sale, Skowhegan School of Painting and Sculpture, Lenox Hill Hospital, New York; also 1967, 1969

The Drawing Society National Exhibition, American Federation of Arts, New York; also 1970

The Drawing Society Regional Exhibition, California Palace of the Legion of Honor, San Francisco

Exhibit of Contemporary American Art, Phoenix Art Museum

Inaugural Exhibit of Manfred Selig Collection of Art, State Capitol Museum, Olympia, Washington

1966
American Landscape Drawing, Collection of John Davis Hatch, Berkshire Museum, Pittsfield, Massachusetts

An Exchange Exhibition between the Sister Cities, Seattle and Kobe, Kobe Municipal Art Museum, Japan

Exhibit to Benefit Garland Junior College Alumni, Collection of Helen S. Slosberg, Brookline, Massachusetts

Governor's Invitational Exhibition, State Capitol Museum, Olympia, Washington; also 1968, 1973, 1974, 1981, 1988

Twentieth Century Painting, Washington Gallery of Modern Art, Washington D.C.

1967

Art at the Chase Manhattan Bank, New York

The Collection of Mr. and Mrs. Anthony Haswell, The Dayton Art Institute, Ohio

National Institute of Arts and Letters, New York

Permanent Art Collection by Northwest Artists, Pacific National Bank of Washington, Seattle

The Third Bucknell Annual National Drawing Exhibition, Bucknell University, Lewisburg, Pennsylvania

1968

Art of Seattle First National Bank Collection, Seattle Art Museum

Collection of Mel Kohler, Cheney Cowles Memorial Museum, Spokane

Contemporary American Artists, The National Institute of Arts and Letters, New York

East Coast–West Coast Paintings, University of Oklahoma, Museum of Art, Norman

North Light, Gordon Woodside Gallery, San Francisco

Washington State Art Mobile, Washington State Arts Commission

1969

The Distorted Image, Heckscher Museum, Huntington, New York

Green Gold Harvest, Whatcom Museum of History and Art, Bellingham, Washington

Sixth Biennial National Religious Art Exhibition, Cranbrook Academy of Art, Bloomfield Hills, Michigan

Tenth Anniversary, Chase Manhattan Bank, New York

Twenty-Third American Drawing Biennial, Norfolk Museum of Art Sciences, Virginia

1970

Midyear Show 35, The Butler Institute of American Art, Youngstown, Ohio

Sixteenth Drawing and Small Sculpture Show, Ball State University, Muncie, Indiana; also 1974

1971

Drawings USA '71, Minnesota Museum of Art, St. Paul

1972

Looking West, ACA Galleries, New York

The Thirties: Art in the Pacific Northwest, Henry Art Gallery, University of Washington, Seattle

1973

The American Artist and Western Reclamation, U.S. Department of the Interior in association with the Smithsonian Institution, Washington, D.C.

Drawing America, 1973, Albrecht Gallery Museum of Art, St. Joseph, Missouri

Gallery Group, Kraushaar Galleries, New York

Museum Treasures: Four Decades of Collecting, Seattle Art Museum

1974

Art of the Pacific Northwest, National Collection of Fine Arts, Smithsonian Institution, Washington, D.C.; Seattle Art Museum, Modern Art Pavilion at Seattle Center; Portland Art Museum, Oregon

Our Land, Our Sky, Our Water, International Exposition, Spokane, Washington

1975

Northwest Artists Today, Part I: Works on Paper, Seattle Art Museum

Northwest Painters Invitational, Museum of Art, Washington State University, Pullman

Summer '75, Foster/White Gallery, Seattle

1976

Northwest Visionaries, Institute of Contemporary Art, Boston

One Hundred and Fifty-first Annual Exhibition, National Academy of Design, New York; also 1981, 1983

Two Centuries of Art in Washington, 1776–1976, State Capitol Museum, Olympia, Washington

1977

Five Decades, Henry Art Gallery, University of Washington, Seattle

Perceptions of the Spirit, Indianapolis Museum of Art

Tribute to Zoe Dusanne, Seattle Art Museum, Modern Art Pavilion, Seattle Center

1978

Northwest Traditions, Seattle Art Museum

Olin Gallery, Whitman College, Walla Walla, Washington

Racy Art at Longacres, Seattle Art Museum Guild, Longacres Racetrack, Renton, Washington

Seattle Selects, Seattle Arts Commission

1979

Drawing, 1900–1945, Museum of Art, Washington State University, Pullman

1980

Collection of Drawings, The Fountain Gallery, Portland, Oregon

Northwest Legacy, Foster/White Gallery, Seattle

Paintings and Sculpture by Candidates for Art Awards, American Academy and Institute of Arts and Letters, New York

West Coast Artists: Art for the Vice President's House, Washington, D.C.

1981

Images of Age, Bowling Green State University, Ohio

National Museum of American Art, Washington, D.C.

Northwest Visionaries, Boston Institute of Contemporary Art

Washington State Artists, Portopia '81 Exposition, Kobe, Japan

1982

Northwest Contemporary Art, The Squibb Gallery, Princeton, New Jersey

Pacific Northwest Artists and Japan, National Museum of Art, Osaka, Japan

Spiritualism in Northwest Art, Henry Art Gallery, University of Washington, Seattle

1983

Group Show, Foster/White Gallery, Seattle

Self Portraits, Linda Farris Gallery, Seattle

1984

Art Faculty Collects, The Art Gallery, University of Maryland, College Park

Northwest Art from Corporate Collections, Seattle Parks Centennial Celebration

1985

Animals Through the Artist's Eye, Foster/White Gallery, Seattle

Images of Seattle, 1925–1985, Jackson Street Gallery, Seattle

Northwest Masters' Drawings, Foster/White Gallery, Seattle

1986

Twenty-Fifth Anniversary Exhibition, The Fountain Gallery, Portland, Oregon

Selections from the permanent collection, Seattle Art Museum

1987

Art Grazing, Bellevue Art Museum, Washington

Fur, Feather and Scales, Bellevue Art Museum, Washington

1989

Decade of Abstraction, 1979–1989, Bumbershoot Biennale, Seattle

Permanent Collection, Tacoma Art Museum, Washington

1991

Art Collectors Show: Northwest Masters, Wing Luke Asian Museum, Seattle

1992

Foster/White Gallery, Seattle

1993

Collection of Tom Blue, The Kinsey Gallery, Seattle University

1994

Northwest Classics Art Exhibit, The Rainier Club, Seattle

Northwest Masters, Foster/White Gallery, Seattle

Northwest School, Museum of Northwest Art, La Conner, Washington

1995

Jet Dreams: The '50s in the Northwest, Tacoma Art Museum, Washington

Northwest Art Shaped by the Spirit, Shaped by the Hand, Museum of Northwest Art, LaConner, Washington

Northwest 1930s, Seattle Art Museum

1999

What It Meant to Be Modern: Seattle Art at Mid-Century, Henry Art Gallery, University of Washington, Seattle

APPOINTMENTS, HONORS, AND COMMISSIONS

1933
Seattle Art Museum: staff appointment

1934
Marine Hospital, Seattle: mural, 11 panels, *Men Who Work the Ships* (now at Museum of History and Industry, Seattle)

1935
United States Post Office, Centralia, Washington: mural, industries of Lewis County

1936
United States Post Office, Anacortes, Washington: mural, *Halibut Fishermen*

1938
Artists' Council of Washington: secretary/treasurer

1942
United States Post Office, Rugby, North Dakota: mural

1944
Weyerhaeuser Timber Co., Everett, Washington: mural, 16 panels, logging, Paul Bunyan

1954
John Simon Guggenheim Memorial Foundation: fellowship, travel and study in Europe

Seattle University: visiting artist

University of Southern California: visiting artist, through 1956

Women's University Club, Seattle: painting class

1955
Jackson Lodge, Grand Teton National Park, Jackson Hole, Wyoming: mural

Seattle Arts Commission: member

United Nations Building, New York: mural competition, submitted sketches (other competing artitists: Jacob Lawrence, Stuart Davis, Fred Conway, Mitchell Johnson)

1959
Skowhegan School of Painting and Sculpture, Maine: artist in residence

Tamarind Lithography: board member, through 1969

1960
Washington Room, Washington State Library, Olympia: mural, 4 panels: *Primitive Life, Historical Period, Rise of Industry, Twentieth Century*

1962
Seattle Civic Theatre, Seattle: mural

Spokane Art Center, Washington State University: master painting class

1963
Skowhegan School of Painting and Sculpture, Maine: artist in residence

1964
Haven Hall, Syracuse University, New York: mural, *Cycle*

Memorial Art Gallery, University of Rochester, New York: artist in residence

1965
Penn State University, State College, Pennsylvania: visiting artist

1966
Boston University: visiting artist

Skowhegan School of Painting and Sculpture, Maine: artist in residence

1968
Ford Foundation: member

Fort Wright College, Spokane, Washington: visiting art critic

Kalamazoo Art Center, Michigan: work with casting reliefs in bronze

National Institute of Arts and Letters: grant

State of Washington, Governor's Invitational Exhibition of Washington Artists: Award of Special Commendation

1969
Lower Columbia Arts and Crafts Festival, Lower Columbia College, Longview, Washington: guest artist

1970
United States Department of the Interior, Bureau of Reclamation: helicopter trip down the Colorado with Richard Diebenkorn

Washington Mutual Savings Bank, Seattle: mural

Washington State Arts Commission: member (until 1973)

1972
American Academy of Arts and Letters: Purchase Award for *Prepared Table* (given to New Orleans Museum of Art)

KOMO-TV: documentary profile, *Callahan: The Artist*, written and directed by Nancy Burgin; program won three Emmy Awards

Seattle Art Museum: Board of Trustees, until 1976

Seattle Repertory Theatre: visual conception of 10th anniversary production of *MacBeth*

Seattle Symphony Orchestra: honored for contributions to the arts

Washington State Bicentennial Medal Design Competition: judge

1975
Board of Governors, The Studio School, Spokane, Washington: member

National Academy of Design: associate

National Society of Literature and the Arts: member

1976
Broadway High School Alumni Association (Class of 1924): Hall of Fame Award

1977
National Academy of Design: acamedician

1983
Seattle Opera: poster image for *The Ring Festival*

State of Washington: Governor's Arts Award

1985
Broadway High School Alumni Association: Distinguished Alumnus Award

BIBLIOGRAPHY

Books

Acton, David. *Master Drawings from the Worcester Art Museum.* New York: Hudson Hills Press in association with Worcester Art Museum, 1998.

Baier, Lesley K. *The Katharine Ordway Collection.* New Haven, Conn.: Yale University Art Gallery, 1983.

Baur, John I. H. *Revolution and Tradition in Modern American Art.* New York: F. A. Praeger, 1967.

Bowen, Betty. *Tobey's 80: A Retrospective.* Seattle: Seattle Art Museum and University of Washington Press, 1970.

Callahan, Kenneth. *Kenneth Callahan, a Portfolio of Prints.* Seattle: Seattle Art Museum, 1979.

Cheney, Martha Smathers Candler. *Modern Art in America.* New York: McGraw-Hill, 1939.

Cheney, Sheldon. *Expressionism in Art.* New York: Liveright, 1934.

———. *A Primer of Modern Art.* New York: Liveright, 1966.

———. *The Story of Modern Art.* New York: Viking Press, 1941.

Cowles, Charles, and Sarah Clark. *Northwest Traditions.* Exh. cat. Seattle: Seattle Art Museum, 1978.

Cumming, William. *Sketchbook: A Memoir of the 1930s and the Northwest School.* Seattle: University of Washington Press, 1984.

Davenport, William Wyatt, and the editors of *Sunset. Art Treasures in the West.* Menlo Park, Calif.: Lane Magazine & Book Co., 1966.

Davidson, Marshall B., and the editors of *American Heritage. The American Heritage History of the Artists' America.* New York: American Heritage, 1973.

Eliot, Alexander. *Three Hundred Years of American Painting.* New York: Time, 1957.

Farah, Ted. *Art Collecting for Pleasure and Profit.* New York: Cornerstone Library, 1964.

Fuller, Richard. *A Gift to the City.* Seattle: Seattle Art Museum, 1993.

Gardner, Albert Ten Eyck, comp. *History of Watercolor Painting in America.* New York: Van Nostrand Reinhold, 1966.

Geldzahler, Henry. *American Painting in the Twentieth Century.* New York: Metropolitan Museum of Art, 1965.

Guenther, Bruce. *50 Northwest Artists: A Critical Selection of Painters and Sculptors Working in the Pacific Northwest.* San Francisco: Chronicle Books, 1983.

Johnson, Michael R., ed. *Kenneth Callahan: Universal Voyage.* Exh. cat. Seattle: University of Washington Press in association with Henry Art Gallery, 1973.

Kingsbury, Martha. *Art of the Thirties: The Pacific Northwest.* Seattle: University of Washington Press in association with Henry Art Gallery, 1972.

———. *Celebrating Washington's Art: An Essay on 100 Years of Art in Washington.* Olympia, Wash.: Washington Centennial Commission, 1989.

———. In *Art of the Pacific Northwest from the 1930s to the Present.* Washington D.C.: Smithsonian Institution Press, 1974.

Kirk, Ruth, and Carmela Alexander. *Exploring Washington's Past: A Road Guide to History.* Seattle: University of Washington Press, 1995.

Martin, Jean L., Martha A. Greer, and Helen L. McCown, eds. and comps. *The Sheldon Memorial Art Gallery Cookbook.* Lincoln, Neb.: Nebraska Art Association, 1978.

Mead Corporation. *Art across America: An Exhibition of Fifty Contemporary American Paintings and Wall-Hung Constructions.* Exh. cat. Dayton, Ohio: Mead Corporation, 1965.

Miles, Emily Winthrop. *An Exhibition of Paintings and Drawings by Kenneth Callahan.* New York: Ram Press, 1960.

Museum of Art, Rhode Island School of Design. *The Neuberger Collection: An American Collection: Paintings, Drawings, and Sculpture.* Exh. cat. Providence, R.I.: Museum of Art, Rhode Island School of Design, 1968.

O'Connor, Francis V., ed. *The New Deal Art Projects: An Anthology of Memoirs.* Washington, D.C.: Smithsonian Institution Press, 1972.

Nordness, Lee, ed. *Art: USA: Now.* Vol. 1. New York: Viking Press, 1963.

Piper, Raymond Frank, and Lila K. Piper. *Cosmic Art.* New York: Hawthorn Books, 1975.

Pousette-Dart, Nathaniel, ed. *American Painting Today.* New York: Hastings House, 1956.

Richardson, Edgar Preston. *Painting in America: The Story of 450 Years.* New York: Thomas Y. Crowell, 1956.

———. *A Short History of Painting in America: The Story of 450 Years.* New York: Thomas Y. Crowell, 1963.

Rupp, James M. *Art in Seattle's Public Places: An Illustrated Guide.* Seattle: University of Washington Press, 1992.

Samuel P. Harn Museum of Art. *Biennial Report: Samuel P. Harn Museum of Art, 1991–1993.* Gainesville, Fla.: University of Florida, 1994.

Shamash, Diane, and Steven Huss, eds. *A Field Guide to Seattle's Public Art: With Self-Guided Tours, Essays, Maps, Project Profiles, and a Comprehensive Directory.* Seattle: Seattle Arts Commission, 1991.

Some Work of the "Group of Twelve." Seattle: Dogwood Press, 1937.

Spaeth, Eloise. *American Art Museums and Galleries.* New York: Harper & Brothers, 1960.

Tacoma Art Museum. *A Tribute to Kenneth Callahan on the Occasion of His Eightieth Birthday.* Exh. cat. Tacoma, Wash.: Tacoma Art Museum, 1985.

Tippet, Maria. *Emily Clark: A Biography.* Toronto, Ontario: Penguin Books, 1982.

University of Illinois. *Contemporary Painting and Sculpture.* Urbana, Ill.: University of Illinois, 1959.

Warren, James R. *King County and Its Queen City, Seattle.* Woodland Hills, Calif.: Windsor Publications, 1981.

Magazines

Baillargeon, Patricia. "Kenneth Callahan, Artist by the Sea." *Search* 10, no. 8 (1976): 170.

Berkson, Bill. "Report from Seattle: In the Studios." *Art in America* 74, no. 5 (1986): 28–29.

Callahan, Kenneth. "The First 700 Miles." *The Treasure Chest for California Boys and Girls,* August 1926.

———. "Kenneth Callahan," *Northwest Art News and Views,* March/April 1970, 36.

———. "Mystic Painters of the Northwest," *Life,* 28 September 1953, 87.

———. "Pacific Northwest," *ArtNews,* July 1946, 22.

———. "Ruminations." *Puget Soundings,* May 1965.

"A Conversation with Kenneth Callahan." *Cascades* 6 (spring 1965): 24–27.

Cumming, William. "Look Back in Laughter." *Puget Soundings,* January 1965.

Faber, Jim. "Baja on My Mind." *Seattle* 7, no. 8 (November 1970): 58–60, 63.

Glowen, Ron. "Seattle." *Contemporanea,* November 1990, 20–21.

Gray, Maxine Cushing. "The Arts of the Pacific Northwest." *The Argus Annual* 68, no. 49 (1961): 52.

"Highlights This Week." *Seattle Guide* 25 January–2 February, 1985, 40.

Hull, Roger. "The Lure of Pacific Northwest Art." *American Art Review* 11, no. 1 (1999): 168–77.

Keed, Judith Kaye. "Kenneth Callahan: Northwest Mystic." *Art Digest* 20, no. 10 (1946): 11.

"Kenneth Callahan." *Magazine of Art* 41, no. 4 (1948): 143.

"Kenneth Callahan." *Northwest Art* 1, no. 2 (March/April 1970): 36–39.

Lamont, Dan. "Portraits: A Northwest Album." *Pacific Northwest* 16, no. 9 (November 1982): 55–69.

Martin, Harry. "Harmony in Seattle." *Architectural Digest* 36, no. 1 (1979): 120–27.

"Northwest Artists Work, Fight and Paint." *Art Digest* 18, no. 3 (1943): 22.

Rexroth, Kenneth. "Two Masters of the U.S. Northwest: Mark Tobey of Seattle, Washington." *ArtNews* 50, no. 3 (1951): 17–19.

——. "Two Masters of the U.S. Northwest: C. S. Price of Portland, Oregon." *ArtNews* 50, no. 3 (1951): 20–21.

Robbins, Tom. "Local Painters Re-Appraised." *Seattle* 2, no. 20 (November 1965): 6–8.

Scigliano, Eric. "Callahan Show a Rich If Incomplete Panorama," *Argus*, 4 January 1980, 6.

Spector, Robert. "A State Is Born!" *Washington* 2, no.4 (January/February 1986) 102–3.

"Tapas." *Seattle Homes and Lifestyles*, March/April 1998, 58.

"Washington Seen through the Artist's Eye." *Washington State* 4 (summer 1976): 8–11.

Webb, Michael. "Cool Oasis in the Desert." *Architectural Digest* 48, no. 5 (1991): 138–45.

Other

Kendall, Sue Ann. "Northwest Oral History Project: Kenneth Callahan, NWOHP No. 3." Archives of American Art, Smithsonian Institution. 27 October, 21 November, 19 December 1983.

Kendall, Sue Ann, et al. "Interview with Kenneth Callahan." Videocassette, 4 vols. Seattle Public Library, 1984.

Reese, J. H. "Conversation with an Artist: Kenneth Callahan." Tully, New York, n.d.

PHOTO CREDITS

© Addison Gallery of American Art, Phillips Academy. All rights reserved: 61 top

Bill Bachhuber: 41 bottom, 44, 45 bottom, 46, 54 bottom, 56, 63 top, 65, 74, 80 top, 84, 89, 90, 94, 98 bottom, 103, 105, 108, 111

E. Irving Blomstrann: 93 top

Brooklyn Museum of Art: 50

David Browne: 17 top, 48

Marsha Burns: 9

Brian T. Callahan: 23

Columbia Museum of Art: 12–13, 66 top

Corcoran Gallery of Art: 87

Paul Cordes, New York: 24 top left

© 1998 The Detroit Institute of Arts: 78 top

Jim Frank: 92

Richard Gehrke: 53 bottom, 71 bottom, 85

Howard Giske, Museum of History and Industry, Seattle: 34, 35

Boomer Jerritt, Photographer, Comox, B.C., Canada: 2–3, 47 top, 60 bottom, 64, 101 top

John Lamka: 77 top, 122, 123 top

Paul Lee: 33, 102, 125 bottom

Stuart Lynn: 95

Paul Macapia: 18, 36, 37, 39

Robert Mates © Solomon R. Guggenheim Foundation, New York: 78 bottom

Scott McClaine: 78 middle

Joseph McDonald: 42 top, 124 top

Allen McMakin: 112, 113

© 2000 The Metropolitan Museum of Art: 30–31, 49

Minneapolis Institute of Art: 67

B.L. Mosher: 79

Munson-Williams-Proctor Museum of Art: 51

Johsel Namkung: 25 bottom left

Richard Nicol: 47 bottom, 52, 88

Nora Eccles Harrison Museum of Art: 76

Pennsylvania Academy of the Fine Arts: 59

The Phillips Collection: 55

Portland Art Museum: 32 bottom, 77 bottom

Saint Louis Art Museum: 42 bottom

Roger Schreiber: 53 top, 82, 97, 117, 119 bottom

Springfield Art Museum: 124 bottom

Lee Stalsworth: 75

Joseph Szaszafi: 93 bottom

Ken Wagner: front cover, 6, 14, 15, 16, 19, 26 top, 27 top, 32 top, 38, 40, 41 top, 43, 45 top, 54 top, 57, 58, 60 top, 61 bottom, 62, 63 bottom, 66 bottom, 69, 70, 71 top, 72, 73, 80 bottom, 81, 83, 86, 91, 96, 98–99 top, 99 bottom, 100, 101 bottom, 104, 106, 107, 109, 110, 114, 115, 116, 118, 119 top, 120, 121, 123 bottom, 125 top

Wichita Art Museum: 68